Blacks, Unions, and the EEOC

Blacks, Unions, and the EEOC:
A Study of Administrative Futility

Benjamin W. Wolkinson
Michagan State University

Lexington Books
D.C. Heath and Company
Lexington, Massachusetts
Toronto   London

Library of Congress Cataloging in Publication Data

Wolkinson, Benjamin W
   Blacks, Unions, and the EEOC.

   Bibliography: p. 167
   1. Trade-unions — United States — Negro membership. 2. United States. Equal Employment Opportunity Commission. I. Title.
HD6490.R2W64   331.88   73-7646
ISBN 0-669-86686-5

Second printing June 1975.

Published simultaneously in Canada.

Printed in the United States of America.

International Standard Book Number: 0-669-86686-5

Library of Congress Catalog Card Number: 73-7646

To my Mother and Father

Contents

List of Figures

List of Tables

Preface

In February 1970 I was hired by Andrew Muse, Chief of Conciliations, Equal Employment Opportunity Commission, to examine the effectiveness of the Commission's conciliation process. Until that time, no systematic study of the Commission's conciliation process based on actual case files had ever been initiated. Indeed, independent investigation of the Commission's remedial efforts was frustrated by the confidentiality requirements of Title VII which prohibited public examination of conciliation records. Thus my employment at the EEOC was an essential prerequisite for the study's performance.

Because of my interest in the employment problems blacks have faced as a result of union discrimination, I decided to focus upon the Commission's success or failure in remedying racially discriminatory union practices. Lack of time and assistance precluded an expansion of the study to evaluate the EEOC's effectiveness in remedying other types of employment discrimination. To other scholars remains the necessary task of analyzing the results of the conciliation process where employers have discriminated on the basis of racial and sex considerations. Where, however, union discrimination was intertwined with or supported discriminatory employer practices, I have analyzed the Commission's settlement attempts with both unions and employers. Joint union-employer discrimination was most prevalent in seniority cases where collective-bargaining agreements had institutionalized seniority arrangements restricting blacks to inferior job classifications.

This study presents some unique problems of documentation as most of the material is based upon confidential government records and memoranda. Additionally, many who were interviewed gave information on the condition that their anonymity be respected. Consequently, most of the sources used cannot be checked by the disinterested reader. At the same time I have identified nearly every record and memorandum used by its case number and date, and therefore government personnel are in a position to examine the sources used. Should these records be made available to the public at some future date, others will be able to do so as well.

In order to avoid misunderstanding, this study does not pretend to examine the degree to which unions discriminate on the basis of race or have engaged in affirmative action. I have concentrated solely on the negative end of union racial policies, analyzing what has happened when blacks have filed meritorious charges with the EEOC against unions for discriminating against them. How successful the EEOC was in this type of situation is the major problem under review. From this investigation we can gain a critical perspective of the viability of the conciliation process as a means of producing compliance with civil-rights legislation.

Special thanks are owed Andrew Muse who authorized this study and who supported the author's research endeavors, and Charles Wilson, Muse's successor as Chief of Conciliations, under whose direction, research for this study was completed. This work itself was written while I was employed as Assistant Professor of Industrial Relations, Michigan State University, and I wish to thank Jack Stieber, Director of the School of Labor and Industrial Relations and Einar Hardin, the school's Chairman of Academic Studies for providing me with the research and financial assistance necessary for its completion. At the EEOC, the author received significant assistance from the following individuals: Richard Grossman, Roland Bessette, Everett Ware, Theodore Bukowski, and Sheryl Gendelman.

In the course of the study, over 100 union officials and charging parties were interviewed. They provided invaluable information concerning the conciliation process. Harry Brickman, former Chief, Operations Analysis Section, National Labor Relations Board, and Professors Michael Borus and Albert Blum of Michigan State University, and Professors Frederic Freilicher, Alice Cook, and Kurt Hanslowe of Cornell University read drafts of the manuscript and offered many helpful comments and suggestions. The typing of the manuscript was done by my secretary, Kathy Knippenberg, a woman of great conscientiousness, skill, and integrity, To Harry Brickman, I owe a very heavy debt of thanks. It is he who first stimulated and encouraged my interest in analyzing the effectiveness of federal labor laws which too often are left unevaluated, the subject matter instead of courtroom briefs and the scholastic discussion of law journals. His support of the author's first research efforts and his continual willingness to be of assistance will always be appreciated.

The editor and publisher of the Industrial Relations Research Association Series have kindly permitted me to reproduce some of the material originally published in the following article: "The Effectiveness of the EEOC Policy in the Construction Industry," Proceedings of the Twenty-Fifth Annual Winter Meeting, December 1972.

Finally, the author wishes to acknowledge the assistance and indispensible companionship of his wife, Este, who typed the preliminary drafts of the manuscript and who, over the years, has helped the author maintain his equilibrium by her love, encouragement, and understanding.

The help of these individuals was vital and without it, this study could not have been completed. Naturally, the author assumes full responsibility for any errors that exist, opinions expressed, and conclusions drawn in the study.

Foreword

When the Equal Employment Opportunities Commission (EEOC), established under Title VII of the Civil Rights Act of 1964, was denied enforcement powers, it was widely predicted that it would be seriously handicapped in its efforts to eliminate discriminatory employment practices. Professor Benjamin Wolkinson has now documented the accuracy of this prediction with respect to one area of the Act, racial discrimination by labor unions.

Professor Wolkinson has studied 75 cases involving four distinct types of racial discrimination by unions: 1) exclusion of Negroes from membership and apprenticeship training programs in craft unions; 2) discriminatory seniority arrangements; 3) segregated locals; and 4) failure of unions to accord Negroes "fair representation" in processing grievances. His overall conclusion is that the EEOC was successful, through its conciliation processes, in remedying union discrimination in only a small proportion of these cases. Even in cases where the EEOC succeeded in negotiating agreements with the offending unions, Wolkinson found that the settlements often provided inadequate relief to the workers involved or were not adhered to by the unions. The major cause of the EEOC's poor record in these cases, according to Wolkinson, was the absence of enforcement power which lowered the risk run by unions in refusing to accept EEOC proposed settlements as compared with the relatively high economic and political costs of agreeing to remedy the losses suffered by blacks who had been discriminated against. This conclusion is equally applicable to the much greater task facing the EEOC in dealing with discrimination by employers.

In the course of discussing cases of union discrimination, Professor Wolkinson presents a highly illuminating and perceptive analysis of the underlying economic, social and political bases for union racial discrimination, the effects of discrimination on both white and black workers and their local unions, the background of discriminatory provisions in collective bargaining agreements and the difficulty of devising remedies which will effectively compensate those who have suffered from discrimination and also prevent discriminatory behavior in the future. He also examines the role of the international unions, the AFL-CIO Civil Rights Division, and the National Association for the Advancement of Colored People in helping or hindering the EEOC in carrying out its mission. Finally, Professor Wolkinson provides a critical evaluation and recommendations to improve the conciliation process as he has seen it practiced in the EEOC. These are all significant byproducts of the broader objectives of the study.

In 1972, the United States Congress amended the 1964 Civil Rights Act to grant the EEOC enforcement power, though not the authority to issue cease and desist orders against employers and/or unions found to have practiced unlawful discrimination. It remains to be seen whether EEOC conciliation efforts will be more successful when backed up with enforcement power than during the earlier period when such power was lacking.

In recent years there has been considerable criticism of laws enacted with the objective of effecting social change, on the ground that experience under such measures is rarely evaluated. Professor Wolkinson's study is an excellent example of research which can contribute toward evaluating social policy and suggesting appropriate changes. The EEOC is to be commended for cooperating with Professor Wolkinson to make this study possible. The School of Labor and Industrial Relations is glad to have been of assistance in helping Professor Wolkinson complete this important study.

> **Jack Stieber, Director**
> **School of Labor and Industrial**
>   **Relations**
> **Michigan State University**

Blacks, Unions, and the EEOC

1

The Conciliation Process of the Equal Employment Opportunity Commission

Introduction

After nearly two decades of frustrated efforts, Congress in July 1964 passed an omnibus civil rights statute prohibiting discrimination in education, voting, and employment. Title VII of the Civil Rights Act of 1964 (act) enumerated an entire category of unlawful discriminatory employment practices, whether engaged in by employers, labor unions, joint apprenticeship committees, or employment agencies. Regarding labor unions specifically, it was unlawful:

1. To exclude or to expel from its membership or otherwise to discriminate against any individual because of his race, color, religion, sex, or national origin
2. To limit, segregate, or classify its membership or to classify or fail to refuse for employment any individual, in any way which would deprive or tend to deprive any individual of employment opportunities, or would limit such employment opportunities or otherwise adversely affect his status an an employee or as an applicant for employment, because of such individual's race, color, religion, sex, or national origin
3. To cause or attempt to cause an employer to discriminate against an individual in violation of this section[1]

This act represented the federal government's renewed commitment to ban union discrimination, a commitment unfulfilled since the demise of the second Federal Employment Practice Committee in June of 1946. In the absence of federal action, blacks had been excluded from certain unions, segregated in others, and frequently denied equal representation within the bargaining unit.[2] The thrust of Title VII, then, was to eliminate the color line that existed not only in industry but in portions of the American labor movement as well.

To administer Title VII of the Civil Rights Act of 1964, a five-member Commission was established.[3] This Commission was charged with the responsibility of investigating and eliminating employment discrimination. The central question examined in this study is whether or not the Commission through its conciliation process was successful in remedying labor-union discrimination. Before examining how the study attempts to answer this question, it will be useful to describe the nature and structure of the Commission's compliance process.

The Commission had two main compliance functions: investigation and conciliation. The Commission was authorized to investigate charges of unlawful

1

employment practices against employment agencies, employers, and labor organizations for discriminating on the basis of an individual's race, color, religion, or sex. The charges were normally initiated by individual discriminatees; however, the statute authorized an individual commissioner to file charges if he had reason to believe that the act had been violated.[4] Through fiscal year 1969, the EEOC has investigated 20,119 charges of discrimination.[5]

The filing of a charge was followed by investigations which were carried out by field-office personnel. Commencing with the Atlanta office in February 1966, the Commission has established thirteen regional and area offices whose initial responsibility was to investigate charges of discrimination.[6] These investigations were based upon interviews with the parties concerned and examination of relevant documents. In cases involving an employer as respondent, the investigator would have examined the company's hiring and payroll records, analyzed the collective bargaining agreement for any discriminatory impact it had on minority workers, and conducted an on-site inspection of the plant. With a labor union, the investigator would have inspected the local's membership, apprenticeship, and hiring-hall records and examined the union's qualifications for referral, membership, and apprenticeship. The act enabled the Commission to obtain a court order to compel a respondent to supply the Commission's investigators with all records relevant to the charge(s) under investigation.[7] Once a charge was investigated, the field office submitted a final report to the Commission in Washington, D.C. The Commission reviewed the report and then rendered its decision as to whether or not it found "reasonable cause to believe that the charge is true."[8]

The writing of decisions was performed by the Decisions and Interpretations Division. Initially the commissioners themselves wrote the decisions. The field-office reports were referred on a rotation basis to individual commissioners who drafted the decision. This process was too time-consuming as each commissioner was aided by only one or two assistants. As a result, during fiscal year 1967, the Commission established the Decision and Interpretations Division. The creation of the new division operated to increase the Commission's output from approximately twelve decisions per week in 1967 to twenty-five decisions per week in 1969.[9] Through fiscal year 1969 the Commission decided 4,793 cases, of which 2,492 (52 percent) were "reasonable cause" decisions.[10]

With this short review of the investigative and decision-writing stages completed, we can now examine the conciliation stage, the focal point of the study. Organizationally, the conciliation process was administered by the Division of Conciliations. Initially, all conciliations were handled by Commission personnel from the headquarters office in Washington, D.C. Beginning in the spring of 1967, field-office personnel were authorized to engage in settlement efforts, although the headquarters office retained considerable review authority over all conciliation actions. Through fiscal year 1968, the Commission completed conciliation efforts in 882 cases.[11]

The conciliation effort itself was set into motion by the issuance of a "reasonable cause" decision. Under the 1964 Civil Rights Act, once such a decision was rendered, the Commission was empowered to attempt to eliminate the unlawful employment practice through "informal methods of conference, conciliation, and persuasion."[12] The conciliator commenced settlement efforts by sending letters to the charging parties, respondents (those charged with discrimination), and interested persons or organizations indicating to them that a "reasonable cause" finding had been made and that the Commission intended to contact them to initiate settlement efforts. Interested persons and organizations referred to such groups as the National Association for the Advancement of Colored People (NAACP) and the Urban League, which may have been assisting charging parties, and the parent internationals of local unions against which charges were filed.

In the settlement efforts, the conciliator had two primary objectives: to secure a written agreement which both provided relief to the charging party and affected class members and which eliminated the discriminatory employment practices generating the complaint.[13] Clearly, these two objectives, while interrelated, are not coextensive. For example, affording union membership to a black worker who was refused admission does not prevent the local union from rejecting other black applicants by applying membership standards that are openly discriminatory. In effect, in many cases a single charging party may represent a class of aggrieved workers who have not necessarily filed charges. Consequently, the conciliator must secure an agreement which will bring relief to the charging party and all similarly situated individuals while simultaneously eradicating union or employer policies which generate the discriminatory situation.

In presenting conciliation proposals to a respondent, the conciliator took the position that his proposals were not final but rather were tentative and designed to provide a basis for discussion.[14] Most conciliation efforts somewhat resembled collective bargaining negotiations wherein proposals and counter-proposals are exchanged and reviewed. At the same time, the conciliator, like any employer or union in collective bargaining, had certain minimum objectives he would sacrifice. For him, the conciliation agreement had to contain minimum standards of relief to remedy the complainant's charge and to eradicate discriminatory conditions. The refusal of the respondents to sign an agreement incorporating these minimum standards of relief would have resulted normally in a termination of the settlement negotiations and a notification to the charging party of his right to sue.[15]

The parallel between collective-bargaining negotiations and the conciliation effort can be carried one step further. In both, a failure to reach an agreement could have resulted in the imposition of sanctions on the parties. In collective bargaining a strike or lockout could occur. In the civil rights dispute, the respondent could have been sued in Federal court, either by the charging party or the Justice Department in a public suit. Upon the Commission's failure to resolve the complaint, it was authorized to notify the discriminatee of this and that he had thirty days from receipt of the Commission's notice to commence a court suit if he so desired.[16] Alternatively, the Commission could refer the case to the attorney general of the United States with the recommendation that he utilize his authority to institute a suit charging that a "pattern or practice" of discrimination exists.[17] From the Commission's perspective, its intervention generally terminated with the conclusion of its settlement efforts.[18]

The potential private or public suit was the main leverage the conciliator could use to promote a settlement. While meeting with respondents, the conciliator's objective was to secure the company's or union's compliance with the act to avoid the possibility of a law suit. The conciliator could back up his position by pointing out that in a successful conciliation agreement, the charging party would waive his right to sue while the Commission would waive its right to refer the case to the Justice Department.[19] Significantly, under the act the Commission itself had no enforcement authority; it could neither issue a cease and desist order nor compel a respondent to take affirmative action to remedy the discriminatory complaint. In effect, the Commission effort was reduced to a policy of moral suasion, or inducing respondents that their best interest lay in compliance.

The compliance process was thus characterized by a series of steps initiated to resolve complaints of job discrimination. These included the filing of a charge, its investigation, conclusions regarding its merits, conciliation where discrimination was uncovered, and finally the possibility of a suit in federal court by the complainant or Justice Department. Basically, this compliance process is presently utilized by the Commission with, however, one major difference. In March 1972 Congress amended the 1964 act to endow the Commission with enforcement authority.[20] The Commission is now empowered to sue respondents who reject settlement. In this study, we are primarily concerned with the Commission's ability to remedy union discrimination during the period it lacked enforcement authority. In short, this study examines the viability of the conciliation process as a means of administering a law designed to produce basic social changes.

Since the act's inception, commentators have questioned the ability of the Commission to secure effective settlement agreements absent any enforcement powers.[21] Can one expect an employer or labor organization voluntarily to modify or eliminate employment practices which have become institutionalized by collective-bargaining agreements? Changes in plant or union practices are not only costly in terms of dollars but may also generate employee resentment leading to friction and strikes. Consequently, employers and unions may naturally resist change except if it is forcibly imposed upon them by governmental authority. Then, too, it is doubtful that potential private or public suits are a sufficient inducement to signing a conciliation agreement. As a practical matter, a complainant may look upon the Commission's failure to conciliate as the end of the road in his efforts to gain redress. Many may lack the resources or knowledge to hire an attorney to commence court proceedings.

Professor Sovern raised the issue in the following manner: "Consider for a moment how an employer [or union] intent on preserving his discriminatory practices might react to a visit from the EEOC. If he is polite but firm, it must eventually go away. At that point the employer [union] may be sued by the person harmed, but the odds are against it, and if he does sue, one can always settle with him instead of the Commission."[22]

Sovern did raise the hope that vigorous enforcement of Title VII by the attorney general might induce respondents to conciliate.[23] In a similar manner, the intervention of organizations like the NAACP Legal Defense Fund, in support of private litigants, advising them and in some cases supplying them with counsel, might make the right to sue a reality. Consequently, the threat of litigation may be sufficient to induce settlement.[24]

Nature of the Study: Scope of the Problem

This study attempts to determine the success or failure of the Commission's conciliation process established under the Civil Rights Act of 1964 in eliminating and rectifying union discrimination. The basic question to be answered is: Given the power to conciliate but not to compel, was the Commission able to secure these ends?

This study involves a series of stages. First an effort is made to identify various patterns of discriminatory union practices engaged in by labor unions during the mid-1960s. Underlying this examination are seventy-five Commission case files which record the Commission's efforts to settle charges of union discrimination between July 1, 1965 and June 30, 1968 (fiscal years 1966 through 1968). Four distinct patterns of racially discriminatory union practices emerge. They include: (1) craft union exclusion of blacks from membership, apprenticeship training programs, and referral, (2) discriminatory seniority arrangements, (3) segregated locals, and (4) failure to represent fairly individaul black members of the bargaining unit.[25] These case files give us a picture of the techniques the local unions and some employers have utilized to discriminate and the effects of such acts on the employment of minority workers.

The second stage of the study examines the remedies that the EEOC has developed to redress racially discriminatory union practices. Clearly, only if the remedies incorporated within the settlement agreement truly eliminate the discriminatory practices can the conciliation process become a vehicle for achieving union compliance; this fact underlies the significance of this survey. To determine the Commission's remedial policy, we again rely on the conciliation case files which frequently contain the conciliator's settlement proposal. This information is supplemented by the files of the headquarters' Conciliation Division for the period under study (fiscal years 1966 through 1968). Often, the official memoranda of the Conciliation Division detail the development of internal Commission guidelines for remedying the various types of union discrimination. We shall observe that for each of the various categories of discrimination, the Commission has developed a specific remedial policy.

Information on the Commission's remedial policies sets the framework for the analysis of the effectiveness of the conciliation process. While the Commission's remedial policies were not free of deficiencies, the author's analysis revealed they were of sufficient magnitude and effect that if implemented the discriminatory practice would have been eliminated while some relief would have been extended to the charging party and other discriminatees. Consequently, the degree to which the Commission was able to execute settlement agreements containing its standard remedies provides a preliminary basis for evaluating the relative success or failure of the Commission's remedial efforts.

Thus the execution of agreements by the Commission operates as a useful point of departure for the analyses. For each category of union discrimination the cases are divided into two groups: (1) cases where an agreement was executed, and (2) cases where no agreement was obtained. In each settlement case, the conciliation agreement is examined to determine whether or not it contained the standard remedies the Commission considered essential to eradicate the effects of the particular type of discrimination.

The next step in the analysis involves an examination of the respondents' compliance with the terms of the settlement agreement. While evaluation of the settlement agreement itself gives us an indication of the relief offered, it is prospective relief only. The agreement does not tell us whether in fact the parties have ceased discriminatory action following the closing of the case. Therefore studies were initiated to determine plant conditions and union practices following the closing of the case. These follow-up studies were based on one or more of the following sources: (1) follow-up interviews (where possible) with the charging parties for their assessment of plant conditions and union practices following the closing of the case, (2) examination of employer information reports (EEO-1) and labor-union apprentice programs and union reports (EEO-2 and EEO-3), which are filed periodically with the EEOC and which give a continuing breakdown of union membership and referral and employment classifications in the plant by race and sex, and (3) examination of employer printouts of the work force which provide a breakdown of departments and job classifications by the race, wage, and seniority of each worker.

These sources provide a clear picture of the nature of union and employer compliance with the settlement agreements, as well as some understanding of the impact of the Commission's settlement agreements on the employment status of the charging parties and affected class members.

Finally we are concerned with those cases where a signed settlement agreement was not obtained and which were closed as unsuccessful efforts, with a thirty-day right to sue notice being sent to the charging parties. In these cases the conciliation records were examined to determine whether or not the respondents had agreed to make any concessions with regard to the charge of discrimination. Thus it was recognized at the outset that a respondent may agree to make certain changes, yet refuse to make key concessions demanded by the conciliator. As a result, the conciliator would refuse to enter into an agreement which would operate to immunize the respondent against suit action. The concessions that the local union were willing to make were compared with the remedial elements sought by the Commission. As in the agreement cases, follow-up studies were initiated to determine the consequences of the respondent's failure to accept the Commission's settlement proposals upon the employment status of affected minority class members.

The analysis of the Commission's settlement efforts showed that it was generally unable to remedy racially discriminatory union practices. This finding generated a series of additional questions which the study seeks to resolve: (1) What factors contribute to the Commission's inability to obtain local union compliance? (2) To what extent do other institutions within the labor community intervene in the conciliation effort and what roles do they assume? (3) Given the relative failure of the Commission's settlement efforts, what alternative sources of relief are available to discriminatees?

Complete answers to these questions were not possible because of the general refusal of union officials to be interviewed and inaccessibility to local, international, and AFL-CIO case files. Nevertheless, the conciliation records contain a wealth of information on these issues, and this source has been supplemented by interviews with charging parties, conciliators, and state government officials. The information gained from these sources helps provide a clearer picture of the forces controlling the actions of unions, employers, and charging parties and influencing their decisions to avoid or participate in, accept or reject Commission settlement efforts.

Initially, an effort was made to examine all conciliations involving charges of union discrimination that were closed during the three fiscal years 1966 through 1968. During this period, approximately ninety-two union discrimination cases were conciliated. Of these, seventy-five were identified and located, and constitute the sample upon which this study is based.

This sample may slightly overemphasize the Commission's inability to execute settlement agreements. Thus, of the ninety-two cases identified, twenty-nine culminated in an agreement, an agreement rate of 31 percent. Of the seventy-five cases actually located and examined, agreements were obtained in only eighteen, an agreement rate of 24 percent. This bias is of minor significance because as this study shows, it is not an agreement per se that determines or demonstrates union compliance, but the remedial provisions contained in the agreement and the nature of the local union's subsequent compliance.

All seventy-five cases involve complaints that were found meritorious. In seventy-four cases, conciliation effort followed the issuance of an official Commission decision that the union had discriminated. In one, no decision was ever rendered, and the settlement effort was initiated following a preliminary determination by the regional office that discrimination had occurred.[26]

The seventy-five cases encompassed four major categories of discriminatory union practices: fourteen involved the exclusionary practices of craft unions regarding membership admission, apprenticeship, and referral; twenty-seven concerned discriminatory seniority arrangements; twenty concerned existence of segregated locals, and twenty involved union discrimination against individual black employees.[27] While the number of cases within each category is small, the cases taken as a whole do provide a clear picture of the Commission's ability to remedy racially discriminatory union practices.

2

Patterns of Union Discrimination

If unions could be arranged along a continuous spectrum according to their racial practices, there would be at one end those unions which completely exclude blacks from their organizations, while at the other end would be those unions which pursue perfectly equalitarian policies.[1] In fact, most labor unions lie between these two extremes; there still are unions, however, which can be found in the extreme negative end of the spectrum. This second chapter examines the different patterns of discrimination that present-day unions have practiced. The discriminatory union practices described here have formed the basis of unfair employment practice charges that have been brought before the EEOC between 1965 and 1968. In these cases the Commission ruled that there was probable cause to believe that the charges were true. How the EEOC developed policies to remedy union discrimination and the effectiveness of those policies will be discussed in other chapters. Here we shall examine the "negative end" of the union racial continuum — those union practices which range from complete exclusion of blacks to union failure to represent fairly individual black members of the bargaining unit.

Complete Union Exclusion of Blacks

Historically, there were many unions which excluded blacks. In the past, such exclusion was in accordance with the policy of the international which, through formal race restrictions in its constitution or rituals, barred black admission. Between 1930 and 1966 such formal exclusion was gradually eliminated as a result of pressures mobilized by civil rights organizations and state and federal governments.[2] At present, no international union constitution contains a provision providing for discriminatory treatment of blacks. Nevertheless, de facto practices of exclusion have persisted.

In its first three years of administering the 1964 Civil Rights Act, the EEOC was faced with cases of complete exclusion of blacks. These cases involved: (1) the rejection of blacks from membership, (2) the exclusion of blacks from apprenticeship training programs, and (3) the failure to refer black job applicants.

Of the seventy-five cases examined in this study, fourteen involved informal union practices of exclusion. As will be discussed later in detail, these unions are all craft unions which exercise a strong control over the labor supply in their trades. They are able to limit black job opportunities by excluding black workers

9

from membership and enforcing informal closed-shop conditions. In the closed shop, all employees seeking a job must belong to the union; hence, by rejecting blacks from membership, the unions bar them from the unionized sector of the trade.

The following sections examine the various discriminatory practices that these unions have implemented to exclude blacks from admission into membership, apprenticeship training programs, and from referral. To help us understand the factors enabling these unions to discriminate, it will be useful to scrutinize the industrial relations framework of the industries in which they operate as well as the constitutional procedures they have established to govern employee activity in their respective trades. Our examination commences with the building trade unions, as twelve of the fourteen cases of exclusion involved local unions in the building-trades industry.

Building-Trades Discrimination: Exclusion of Blacks from Membership

In eight cases, building-craft unions barred qualified black workers from admission. The techniques used ranged from the most blatant to the very subtle. In several cases, black journeymen applying for admission failed in repeated efforts to obtain application forms; business agents were unavailable when black applicants repeatedly showed up at the union office to fill out the necessary forms. A variant of this involved transmitting to black applicants multiple forms to be filled out without explaining the proper procedures to be followed in completing them, as was usually done with white applicants. This technique operated to discourage the black applicant from completing the necessary forms, while it afforded the local union business agent with the convenient "proof" that the union had few, if any, blacks because they failed to apply for membership.

In general, the membership procedures of the building trades lend themselves to discriminatory policies. Most building-trades unions admit members through a "fraternal" system which provides that applicants are accepted or rejected by a vote of the members of the local union. In addition, they require, through their international constitutions, that a candidate be sponsored by two or more members.[3] It is self-evident that where new applicants must be "endorsed" by white persons who are already members, it would be easy for a local to limit membership to friends and relatives, and bar blacks who, though thoroughly qualified, are unable to obtain the necessary sponsorship. In a case involving one local, black journeymen were unable to obtain the necessary endorsement of two union journeymen and were, for that reason, denied membership. In another, a licensed black electrician was denied admission when the local's membership voted to reject his application.

Another instrument used by these unions to bar black journeymen has been the discriminatory administration of examinations testing an applicant's qualifications. Many building-trades unions will require that a journeyman applicant pass an examination to qualify for admission.[4] Thus, for example, the international constitution of the Iron Workers specifies that each local must establish a local examining committee to test the qualifications of each applicant.[5] Significantly, the local unions are vested with enormous discretionary authority in administering qualifying examinations. Tests may be written, oral, or performance-oriented, and may consist of a combination of all three elements. This discretion lends itself to abuse. It is possible, for example, for a local union to vary its test depending on the race of the applicants, both as to their difficulty and the importance attributed to them.[6] More overt discriminatory techniques include not informing minorities when the tests are scheduled and grading blacks and whites disparately; blacks may receive fewer points than whites for essentially the same answers.

Such practices occurred in the eight membership cases. One local's examination, given only to blacks, contained a significant number of questions, the answers to which required specialized information that electricians on the job would not normally possess or need. The Commission found that the test was purposely designed to achieve a high "flunk-out" rate for blacks and thereby deter them from further attempts to become members. In two cases, examinations were graded disparately, as a passing grade for whites was a failing grade for blacks. Another local attempted to discourage black applicants by scheduling their exams on dates which did not exist (for example, February 30, June 31, and so forth).

The following case graphically describes the use of the qualifying examination as an exclusionary device:

In 1966 Lewis made three attempts to join Local 86. On the first occasion he was given a June 1966 date for his examination. Lewis took time off from work and travelled approximately 175 miles to come to Seattle for the examination. However, he was not examined because he did not bring a withdrawal card to show that he no longer belonged to another union. Lewis appeared again in July of 1966. He gave the Board his City of Seattle Welder's Certificate and other welder's certificate papers, his withdrawal card from another union and a letter of recommendation from his superintendent. He was then asked how well he could tie knots. Lewis replied that he was not very good at tying knots. He was then informed that he could not become a member of the union unless he knew how to tie knots. Thereafter, Lewis learned to tie knots and in September 1966 returned a third time to Seattle from his job site some 175 miles outside of the city. At that time he was given a knot tying test. He was able to tie the first seven knots. He was then asked to tie a knot that he had never heard of before and when he told the Examining Committee that he did not know how to tie the knot, he was informed that he had failed the examination and could not become a member.[7]

It is easy to perceive how, through a combination of various practices, the building-trades unions frustrated admission of black journeymen. Where blacks persisted and succeeded in filing proper applications, they still would face the need to pass a journeyman's examination. Even if that hurdle were overcome, there was no assurance that they could obtain the necessary sponsorship by individual members or approval by the membership. The effectiveness of such discrimination was near-total. In all eight cases, blacks constituted less than one-half of 1 percent of the local union's total membership.

Exclusion of Blacks from Building-Trades Unions' Apprenticeship Programs

Admission requirements for entry into apprenticeship programs vary with locals of the different international unions. Generally, however, a local will require that an applicant meet certain standards involving age, education, and aptitude. Typically, an applicant must be between the ages of eighteen and thirty, a high school graduate, and be able to pass a qualifying examination which may be both oral and written.[8]

In practice, the local unions and employers form joint apprenticeship committees which supervise the administration of the apprenticeship programs. These joint committees, which normally exist by virtue of a collective-bargaining agreement, set up the terms of the apprenticeships, the wage scales, and the ratio of apprentices to journeymen. The latter dictates the number of apprentices that will be permitted to enter the trade at any given time.

While the apprenticeship admission and training requirements may vary among locals, joint apprenticeship committees established often share two characteristics. First, the committee is normally composed of an equal number of management and union personnel. Second, notwithstanding this numerical arrangement, the day-to-day operation of the apprenticeship committee is handled by a apprentice coordinator who traditionally is a union member. Thus it is the apprentice coordinator who will meet with the applicants and provide them with information concerning the local's apprenticeship program. As a result, he is in a position to either block or promote the admission of black applicants.

In eight of the twelve building-craft union cases blacks were excluded from the apprenticeship programs. In all eight cases, less than 1 percent of all enrolled apprentices were black. In most of these cases, the local did not have a single black apprentice. While those local unions involved claimed to have objective criteria for admission — age, high school diploma, passage of aptitude examination — they frequently disregarded their own objective standards, or applied them in a subjective and arbitrary manner. In two cases, the joint apprenticeship committee ostensibly gave weight to an applicant's education, past working experience, and test performance. In practice, the main requirement for entry involved one's blood lines, as nearly all those admitted as apprentices were relatives of union members. In one case, the collective-bargaining agreement provided specifically for the admission of only the relatives of union members and contractors.

The illegality of the unions' apprenticeship admission policies based primarily on nepotic considerations is not clearly understandable to union members and officers. The skilled trades have traditionally held that work and experience on a job constitute a kind of property right, deserving the same protection and consideration as other forms of property. The Webbs noted this feeling among British craft unionists who considered "that the trade by which we live is our property bought by years of servitude, which gives us a vested right, and that we have the sole and exclusive claim on it."[9]

The craft unionist views his job as a possession and maintains the right to select the future possessor. Morally, he sees nothing wrong in an artisan handling down his skill to his son and gaining for him admission into the union. This view is firmly expressed in the following letter to the *New York Times:*

Some men leave their sons money, some large investments, some business connections and some a profession. I have none of these to bequeath to my sons. I have only one worthwhile thing to give: my trade. I hope to follow a centuries-old tradition and sponsor my sons for apprenticeship.

For this simple father's wish it is said that I discriminate against Negroes. Don't all of us discriminate? Which of us when it comes to a choice will not choose a son over all others?

I believe that an apprenticeship in my union is no more a public trust, to be shared by all, than a millionaire's money is a public trust. Why should the government, be it local, state or Federal, have any more right to decide how I dispose of my heritage than it does how the corner grocer disposes of his?[10]

A final argument is that the union's policy of nepotism is not designed to discriminate against blacks since it is imposed on all workers — black and white — who do not share familial ties with union members.

This position is untenable from both a social and legal viewpoint. First, the unions' barriers resulting from nepotic selection fall mainly on black workers. Having historically been denied admission into building-craft unions, blacks are permanently barred from gaining entrance into the trade. Nepotism is unlawful since it gives preference in employment opportunities to a class of employees all or most of whom are white; the comparably small class of nonwhites have few, if any, relatives or friends in the union. Second, it is wrong to argue that the federal, state, or local governments have no legitimate interest in guaranteeing the black entrance into particular trades. The building craft unions rely to a considerable extent on public works which are financed with taxpayers' money, while denying a portion of these taxpayers the right to jobs created in part by their tax contributions.[11] Moreover, the law does not absolutely prohibit the assignment of apprenticeship openings to members' relatives: it merely holds that they shall not be the exclusive recipients of such benefits where this results in racial discrimination. Conceivably, once such discrimination is ended and blacks have secured a fair share of building trades union memberships, a reversion to the "relatives only" approach to apprenticeship will no longer conflict with the Civil Rights Act.

To exclude blacks as apprentices, the unions pursued the same tactics they employed in frustrating the admission of black journeymen. Applicants would not be given applications or would be sent to the wrong official for an interview. By exploiting the subjective and nonreviewable nature of the oral interview, the local union is able to disqualify black candidates. In some locals, the personal interview comprises 50 percent of the candidate's score and allegedly is used to determine aptitude, appearance, ambition, physical potential, personality, and attitude. Typically, no record will be preserved illustrating the general type of questions asked and the applicants' responses. As a result, the oral interview can be easily manipulated to exclude blacks who successfully passed the written examination. Frequently, the Commission has found that had only the written test scores counted, blacks would have been admitted, and that whites with inferior test scores had oral scores which had been arbitrarily raised to allow for their entrance into the program.

Union practices of exclusion were reinforced by limiting information concerning the apprenticeship programs to relatives and friends of those in the trade. Minority organizations were not informed of impending examinations or classes. As a result, when blacks did apply they found themselves frequently at the bottom of long waiting lists filled by white applicants who had been informed of apprenticeship openings by relatives or friends in the trade.

The exclusion of blacks from apprenticeship programs has serious economic consequences for the black workers seeking entry into the building trade. The apprentice is generally a young man who combines on-the-job training under the supervision of skilled craftsmen with classroom instruction. While not the sole means of learning the trade, the training of apprentices is a significant basis for meeting the demand for skilled craftsmen in the construction industry.[12] Denied the opportunity of learning the trade, the black worker's chances of gaining employment as a skilled craftsman are significantly reduced.

Exclusion of Blacks from Union Hiring Halls

The key to the building-trades unions' ability completely to exclude black workers from the unionized part of the industry is their control over the labor supply. While maintaining some key personnel, most contractors have constantly fluctuating demands for workers; the level of demand of a given contractor depends on his volume of business. A contractor's reliance on the union for his labor increases when he expands outside the area of his normal operations. Then he must depend on journeymen from another local if he has entered another geographical jurisdiction. The city locals of the building-craft unions interconnect and often have reciprocal arrangements whereby each local sends its surplus workers to those locals which are experiencing a shortage of men temporarily. In this way, the contractor can fulfill his labor needs.[13]

One of the local union's major instruments for regulating the supply of workers is its hiring hall. Here, union members are registered and assigned to various employers on demand. In some instances, the local union operates an exclusive job referral system; this exists where the employer is required by contract to obtain his entire labor force from the union.[14] In some cases, even absent such a provision, the union in practice supplies the contractor with all the workers. Building-trades unions also operate under nonexclusive referral systems where the union does not refer all men that the company hires. In many localities, the contractor may hire a portion of his workers on his own and acquire the balance of his labor force from the local union.

For example, a master labor agreement between the Southern California General Contractors and the Carpenters enables the contractor to hire up to 25 percent of his employees, with the remainder to be supplied by the local unions.[15] Where an exclusive or nonexclusive referral system exists, the local union influences significantly the composition of the contractor's labor force.

The use of the hiring hall has been denied to blacks through a variety of means. For white applicants, the local union business agent will explain referral procedures and the opportunities available for employment. On the other hand, blacks seeking referral are provided either no information or misinformation regarding the procedures to be followed in getting one's name placed on the out-of-work list. Typically, blacks are not told that they are eligible for referral on the basis of the referral procedures established by local unions' collective-bargaining agreements and bylaws. In several referral cases, the local unions failed to give black applicants the proper application form for referral and did not dispatch them to jobs because of deficient applications. In one case, a black applicant for referral was told to show up at the hiring hall at 7:00 A.M. over a period of several months; yet, he was never referred. To discourage black applicants, local union business agents may indicate that there is "no work" or "things are pretty slow," when in fact the local unions could only meet the demand for workers by calling in union members from sister locals and by providing white nonunion workers with temporary work permits.

Another practice utilized to bar blacks from referral is to establish fictitious requirements which serve as exclusionary devices. At times, black workers were not referred on the grounds they were employed elsewhere or were members of other local unions. For example, black members of the Laborers' Union were barred from transferring to a craft local; at the same time, the craft union permitted other whites to transfer from the Laborers' Union and did not accept only those out of work.

Supporting these exclusionary devices are structural characteristics built into the local unions' referral systems that operate to limit the referral opportunities of blacks who are allowed to register for work. Many craft locals in the building industry will, for purposes of referral, divide their members and referral applicants into several priority groups. The criteria the unions have established to identify the referral category to which an applicant is assigned, and thereby to determine whether or not he has priority over others in being referred, will consist of one or more of the following factors: experience in the trade, membership in the union, past record of working for union contractors.

In four referral cases, the local unions were found to utilize such criteria. Local 46 of the IBEW was a good example.[16] Under its collective-bargaining agreement, applicants were placed in one of four referral groups. Those placed in Group 1 were referred first while those in Group 4 were sent out last. To get into Group 1, an applicant had to have four or more years of experience in the trade; he must have passed a journeyman's examination; he also must have worked at least one year under a union contractor. These criteria subject blacks to requirements they cannot meet because of the local union's previous practices of racial exclusion. Thus, having been denied membership, blacks had no opportunity to work for a union contractor. Where the craft is thoroughly organized, absence of membership status can result in their virtual exclusion from the trade. These work referral practices thus operate to place blacks at the bottom of the referral register with an opportunity for referral only after all whites have obtained employment. In the five referral cases, less than 1 percent of the workers referred were blacks.

Craft Union Discrimination in the Printing Industry

The printing industry parallels the construction sector in the union's ability to control and regulate the industry's labor supply. Prior to the Taft-Hartley Act, most organized firms were closed shops, with the result that union membership became a prerequisite for employment.[17] Following congressional prohibition of the closed shop in 1947, organized firms have been converted to union shops. The employer's reliance on the union for his supply of workers, however, has not diminished. There is little "off the street" hiring of workers. Journeymen vacancies are filled by resorting to the union's hiring hall, commonly known as the "out of work room." Here, unemployed journeymen obtain information regarding job openings.

The main source of journeymen printers remains the apprentice trainees. In some instances, apprentices are trained on the job. Traditionally, apprentices have been selected by the employer from the group of unskilled workers who perform utility work. At the same time, the employer's selection must be approved by the union. Generally, the union and the employer will form a joint apprenticeship committee to screen and approve apprentice applicants. In becoming an apprentice, the worker will join the union which has jurisdiction over the skilled job. Since union membership as a practical matter is a prerequisite on the job, an individual's failure to obtain union admission would block his opportunity for promotion.

The printing crafts' strong control over apprenticeship selection can lead to the exclusion of blacks. In both cases involving printing crafts, the employers' selection of black workers as apprentices were blocked by the unions' refusal to admit those selected to membership. In these cases, the unions' procedures for admitting members contributed to their discriminatory policies. In one, the local's bylaws provided that an applicant for membership would be rejected if more than five negative votes were cast. In the other, a two-thirds vote of acceptance was required. As with the building trades, the strong interrelationship between union membership and job opportunity can promote the exclusion of black workers.

Discriminatory Seniority Arrangements

In the initial discussion we have been concerned with unions which have totally excluded blacks from membership and rigidly limited their job opportunities. The common denominator in these cases is that they involve craft unions which exercise a strong control over the labor supply. By enforcing closed-shop conditions, unions have made membership a prerequisite for employment. In the construction and printing trades, unions regulate entrance to the trade by controlling apprenticeship programs and referral services.

The following discussion will be concerned with a second broad category of discriminatory union practices. Here, the discriminatory conditions grow out of illegal seniority arrangements restricting blacks to inferior job classifications within the plant or job site.

Before beginning our discussion, we shall review the concept of seniority and the role it plays in determining a worker's position in a plant vis-á-vis his co-workers.[18] By seniority, we generally mean a set of rules which give workers with longer years of continuous service a prior claim to a job over others with fewer years of service. The use of seniority to determine one's employment status in relation to others has been called "competitive status seniority." Competitive status seniority has normally been used to govern competition of employees for promotion, layoffs and recall, transfer and shift preferences.

Seniority rules are also used to determine the benefits to which employees are entitled by virtue of their continuous service with a company. This is called "benefit seniority"; it is applied to such items as vacation time, sick leave, and pension benefits. These are benefits which employees accrue by virtue of the number of years they have worked for a company.

Racial discrimination by unions usually involves competitive status seniority, and it is with this area that this study is concerned. Although discrimination can occur in the application of benefit status seniority, where, for example, a union negotiates inferior job benefits for black workers, no cases of this type appeared in the study.

In applying competitive status seniority arrangements, companies will differ as to the unit within which seniority operates. In some, the department will be the unit for purposes of applying seniority; in others, it will be the plant. In still others, it will be a group of functionally related jobs within a department which are organized into a separate progression line. Generally, the more homogeneous the work unit, the broader the seniority unit is likely to be.

It should be emphasized that a seniority system by itself is racially nondiscriminatory. It applies equally to whites and blacks, allocating jobs on the basis of length of service in the unit within which seniority operates. Indeed, it is this nondiscriminatory feature of a seniority system that gave rise to its introduction. Unions demanded the establishment of seniority systems to eliminate favoritism; the call for a seniority system to replace the foreman's complete authority in the areas of promotion and layoff is one of the union organizer's principal and more effective appeals in unionizing a plant's work force.

For the union itself, a seniority system can be viewed as an internal device for allocating job opportunities among members; it helps to immunize the union from the criticisms of disgruntled employees denied promotion or laid off.[19]

Yet, seniority systems have become significant instruments for racial discrimination. This has occurred where they have been superimposed upon restrictive hiring practices of companies. In many instances, especially in the South, employers deliberately excluded blacks from jobs specifically defined as "white men's jobs." In so doing, they were either motivated by their own prejudice or sympathized with the discriminatory attitudes of their workers out of fear of causing dissension. Typically, blacks would be hired in classifications designated as "common laborer," "yard laborer," "nonoperating," or "maintenance department." In fact, these categories were euphemisms for the establishment of all-black work units or departments. Where this has been practiced, the seniority systems that were institutionalized through collective-bargaining agreements are discriminatory because they operate to freeze black workers in the job classifications into which they were originally hired. Thus they perpetuate the original discriminatory hiring patterns.

Dual Seniority Groups for Similar Jobs

The cases involving discriminatory seniority systems can be grouped into three classes.[20] The common ingredient in the first group of cases is that although black and white workers perform the same work, they are placed in separate seniority groups. A consequence of this dual seniority arrangement is that black workers are precluded from advancing into better-paying positions, since residency in the white seniority group is a prerequisite for promotion. To conceal this discriminatory setup, the employer may assign black and white workers different job titles. Where this occurs, blacks probably receive lower wages and inferior benefits than those earned by their white counterparts.

While cases of this type are relatively rare, they occurred in the post-1964 period, particularly among the operating railroad crafts. Consider the following situation which existed until 1967 on the St. Louis-San Francisco Railway Line.[21] On this railroad, black train porters performed essentially the same duties as white brakemen; porters performed braking duties on the front end of the passenger trains and on freight runs. At times, train porters served as replacements for brakemen and vice versa. Notwithstanding the similarity in job functions, porters and brakemen were classified as holding different jobs and placed in separate seniority units. While brakemen were in line for promotion to conductors, porters were not and, in fact, could not advance into any other jobs. Thus the collective-bargaining agreement between the railroad and the Brotherhood of Railway Trainmen (BRT) provided that advancement to the position of conductor would be on the basis of a person's length of service in the brakemen classification. At the same time, porters received less pay than brakemen. When passenger service was finally terminated, black porters were allowed to transfer to brakemen vacancies, but in doing so, had to surrender the seniority they accumulated as porters.

Of the five seniority cases which can be described as Type 1 seniority problems (i.e., black and whites performing the same work but placed in separate units), two involved porter-brakemen issues. In a third case, the job of switchman commenced a two-job line of progression from switchman to conductors. The railroad maintained three separate seniority rosters, one for white switchmen, one for black switchmen, and one for conductors. All conductor vacancies were filled by promoting the white switchmen with the greatest seniority. Black switchmen were never considered for promotion to conductor. In practice, all white switchmen who were promoted to conductor were permitted to retain their seniority as switchmen, and, if laid off, could roll back into switchmen jobs, even if it meant the displacement of black trainmen.

These three cases are distinct from other seniority cases that we will examine subsequently in that the separation of black and white workers into separate seniority units was reinforced by the exclusion of black trainmen from the unions which represented white brakemen, switchmen, and conductors. Until the early 1960s, the constitutions of the principal operating crafts in the railroad industry barred the admission of blacks into membership.[22] In two of the three cases, black trainmen belonged to the International Association of Railway Employees, a small and feeble labor union consisting entirely of black workers. During the 1960s, the IARE had fewer than 1,000 members. In the switchmen's case, black workers were members of a steelworkers' local.[23] While formal bars to admission of black trainmen had been removed by 1964, the Commission found that in two cases the white craft local had systematically rebuffed the efforts of black workers to gain admission — even following passage of the act in 1964.

The representation of black trainmen by separate labor organizations, although necessitated by the operating crafts' exclusionary membership practices, was utilized by the unions and employers to justify maintenance of the separate seniority units. First, the railroads could claim that the lower wages and inferior fringe benefits earned by black trainmen were due to their representation by a less effective collective-bargaining representative. Second, the fact that "train porters" were under the jurisdiction of another labor organization "proved" that the jobs of switchmen, conductors, and brakemen were distinct job classifications. Therefore these jobs could not be incorporated legitimately within a single seniority unit for purposes of promotion and layoff. Thus one pattern of discrimination superimposed upon another restricted the employment opportunities of black trainmen.

Not all seniority cases of the Type 1 variety involved the exclusion of black workers from union membership.[24] In one case, the existence of separate seniority rosters was supplemented by the existence of segregated locals. Here, all black brakemen and switchmen belonged to an exclusively black local and were confined to one yard of a large terminal. Workers performing switchmen and braking duties in the terminal's other yards were represented by an entirely white local of the same international. The assignment of black workers into a separate seniority unit with promotion and layoff rights only within one yard meant that the employer could hire white workers to fill vacancies in other yards while laying off black workers. This event occurred and resulted in the filing of the unfair employment practice charge before the Commission.

Discriminatory Progression Line Seniority Systems

In the second class of seniority cases, black and white workers perform work closely related in skill or integrated in terms of the production process used. Under such circumstances, the jobs of black and white workers would normally and properly constitute a single unit for purposes of seniority. Thus, in many manufacturing plants work units are composed of grouping together functionally related jobs in an orderly line of increasing skills. Advancement within the progression line is then based upon an employee's length of service within the progression line or is made step by step on the basis of an employee's length of service on a given job within the progression line.

The unique factor in the following cases is that while black workers perform work functionally related to work done by white employees, they are not provided with an equal opportunity for advancement to the higher paying jobs in the progression line. This is accomplished in several ways. Typically, black workers are grouped together in a separate line of inferior jobs, while white workers occupy jobs in an all-white progression line. While the work performed in the two progression lines is functionally related, no transfer between lines is permitted. Thus black workers accrue seniority only with reference to jobs in their own unit and are excluded from the more skilled and related jobs in the white progression line. Alternatively, black workers are classified as holding nonprogression line jobs and, hence precluded from advancement.

The following examples are illustrative. Figure 2-1 shows the lines of progression that existed in 1965 in the stock preparation department of a paper mill. Black workers are isolated in a separate progression line consisting of three job classifications — hydropulper, pay loader, and helper. Vacancies in the white line of progression are filled by promoting employees with the greatest job seniority in the position below the vacancy. At the same time, the employer would fill the entry-level slot of broke-beater helper by outside recruitment; black workers had no opportunity to advance. This situation occurred despite the fact that in a nondiscriminatory promotion system, black workers in the hydropulper position could advance into the higher-paying positions of blend-tank man and beater engineer.[25]

Beater Engineer (w)
No. 7 Blend Tank Man (w)
Nos. 5 & 6 Blend Tank Man (w)
No. 2 Blend Tank Man (w)
Broke Beater Man (w)
Broke Beater Helper (w)

Hydropulper (b)
Pay Loader (b)
Helper (b)

Figure 2-1. Dual Progression Line in Stock Preparation Department[a]

In a case involving an electric utility, all black workers hired by the company were assigned to jobs carrying the classification of laborer, porter, janitor, or maid. By contract, these were nonskilled jobs cut off from line of progression positions which commenced in departments with the classification of helper.

As a result, black workers earned a monthly wage ranging from $381 to $414, while earnings on jobs in the white line of progression ranged from $473 to $785. Vacancies at the helper level were typically filled by hiring white workers from outside the plant. This policy was followed, although black workers were utilized to fill temporary vacancies in progression line jobs; black laborers were assigned on a temporary basis as both tractor and truck drivers, and even as light equipment operators.

Black workers excluded from white lines of progression may face added barriers to their advancement. Frequently, all black laborers have to pass written examinations testing their mechanical and verbal abilities. While this requirement is mandatory, the company's own validation studies may reveal no significant

[a]The purpose of this department was to blend stock for eventual feeding into the paper machine.

statistical correlation between passage of the tests and job performance. At the same time, whites already in the line of progression had never been tested. Second, in moving to the white line of progression, the black laborers are forced to surrender the seniority they had accrued in the black line of progression. These two obstacles — passage of nonvalidated tests and loss of seniority rights upon transfer — appear in nearly all cases where black workers had been excluded from white lines of progression.

In some cases, discriminatory seniority arrangements are reinforced by the existence of segregated locals. Here, each local bargains for the jobs which it considers to be exclusively under its jurisdiction; advancement of the black worker into the white progression line is then blocked on the grounds that such movement would encroach upon the jobs "belonging" to members of the white local. This situation existed in cases involving several paper plants and an iron foundary.

Discriminatory Department Seniority Systems

In a third class of cases involving discriminatory seniority arrangments, two or more groups of jobs are organized into separate seniority groups, with the jobs in the different groups having no close functional relationship. In these cases, "departmental" or "group" seniority restricts black job opportunities. Typically, blacks are restricted to departments where the work is low-skilled, and perhaps performed under unpleasant conditions. Several examples are illustrative. In one rubber plant, the overwhelming number of blacks were restricted to the hot compounding rooms where the rubber was processed. In a tobacco firm, 226 of the 231 workers who worked in the leaf-processing department were black. In this department, work was seasonal and low paid, with wages ranging from $1.69 to $2.12 an hour. On the other hand, in the fabrication department, where the work was regular, involved more skill, and paid wages ranging from $1.80 to $3.36 per hour, 90 percent of the work force was white. In another case, an employer who operated a truck maintenance firm restricted blacks to the three lowest-paying departments because Negroes were superior to whites in the jobs they held.

Departmental seniority reinforces the employer's hiring and placement pattern. Under it, vacancies within a department are filled by workers with the most seniority in the department. Additionally, one maintains his seniority only within the department where he works. When one transfers to another department, he loses all his accrued seniority. In one trucking firm, employees desiring to transfer from the maintenance to the driving department had to resign and apply for vacancies in the driving department as new hires.

This system limits the transfer of black workers into better paying departments by imposing upon them serious costs. In practice, the black worker will often be restricted to entry-level positions, since in seeking promotion to the "white department" he will be unable to compete for jobs on the basis of the seniority he accrued in the black department. Because he sacrifices his accrued seniority, the worker who transfers enters the new department least protected from layoff. In transferring, the black worker may even suffer a temporary loss in pay, if the job he holds pays more than the entry-level job of the department into which he transfers. Consequently, even where the employer removes the bars formerly excluding blacks from certain departments, the system of departmental seniority operates to confine the black worker to the departments to which he was originally assigned.

In the railroad terminals, black workers have been faced with a similar pattern of discrimination based upon a system of "group seniority." Here, blacks were hired as porters, laborers, and janitors. These jobs, which cut across several departments in the terminal, were organized in a separate seniority district. Generally, the jobs were classified as Group 3 positions. At the same time, whites were hired to fill the more skilled clerical and office positions at the terminal such as messengers, train announcers, gatemen, and clerks. These jobs were organized in a separate seniority district, generally known as Group 1 or 2. Under the collective-bargaining agreement, black workers who desired to transfer from a Group 3 to a Group 1 position had to surrender the seniority accumulated in Group 3 and commence as new employees in Group 1. Given the present risk of being laid off on the railroads as a result of that industry's adverse economic situation, it is easy to perceive how the system of group seniority has operated to freeze black workers in the inferior Group 3 jobs.

In summary, the Commission has been faced with three categories of cases involving discriminatory seniority systems. In the first, blacks and whites perform the same work but are placed in separate seniority districts. In the second, blacks and whites work in functionally related jobs which normally might constitute one work unit for purposes of seniority, but which in fact are placed in dual progression lines. Alternatively, blacks are placed in the lowest level positions of laborer and barred from entry into the white line. In the third, blacks and whites are not in functionally related jobs and are placed in separate departments or district groups. In all three categories, the seniority system operates to freeze blacks into inferior job classifications. These three types of seniority cases form the basis of numerous decisions against labor unions and employers. Of the seventy-five cases examined in this study, twenty-seven were concerned with the seniority issue.

Segregated Locals

Historically, many unions have followed a policy of organizing black workers into separate locals. Among unions which traditionally established segregated locals in the South are the Carpenters, Longshoremen, Papermakers, Pulp and Sulphite Workers, Brotherhood of Railway Clerks, Tobacco Workers, and the Musicians.[26]

Throughout the decade of the sixties, local union leaders came under increased pressure to eliminate segregated locals. This pressure has originated from three sources: government, industry, and the international union leadership.

The National Labor Relations Board (NLRB) was one of the first governmental agencies to act against segregated locals. In 1962 the NLRB ruled that segregated locals could not take advantage of its contract bar rule. Under that rule, a labor union is immunized from an election challenge by a competing union during the first three years of the contract to which it is a party. Rivals are restricted to a sixty-to-ninety-day period at the end of the contract term within which to file petitions for elections. In *Pioneer Bus Co.*, the NLRB held that contracts executed by a segregated local would not bar the holding of a new election when requested either by competing unions or employees within the plant seeking decertification of the incumbent union.[27] Thus the Board had enunciated a policy that segregated locals would not enjoy the full protection of the act.

The NLRB strengthened its policy against segregated locals in another case when it rescinded the certification issued jointly to two segregated locals.[28] In effect, segregated locals were put on notice that they risked similar sanction. The loss of certification could be especially grievous to a local, since it implies that the employer would be relieved of his obligation to bargain with a discriminatory union, notwithstanding its majority status.[29] The Board's action similarly suggested that it would in the future refuse to certify newly established segregated locals. Undoubtedly, the decision was a strong influence in discouraging all internationals from chartering new locals that were racially segregated.

Following the enactment of the Civil Rights Act of 1964, the EEOC quickly took a strong position against segregated locals. In a statement circulated to AFL-CIO affiliates, the Commission advised that segregated labor unions violated Title VII.[30]

Yet the pressure on local unions to eliminate their segregated status did not originate solely with government and civil rights agencies. Federal contractors increasingly sensitive to public criticisms also sought the elimination of segregated locals. For example, some paper companies located in the South have made merger of locals a precondition for contract renewal.[31]

Finally, some internationals have intervened to consolidate segregated locals. The major factor underlying the actions of those unions has been an economic one. Thus the Carpenters in 1963 initiated a policy of integration having recognized that the segregation of blacks had been instrumental in lowering the wages of white union members.[32]

On the national level, the AFL-CIO signed a document, subsequently endorsed by 122 of its 125 international union affiliates, supporting fair employment practice efforts and promising among other items to promote the elimination of segregated locals.[33] Under the document, each international agreed to assign to an executive officer "the duties of administrative dissemination and implementation of the program for fair practice."[34] While the absence of data make difficult any evaluation, it seems that at least in theory the labor-union community was intent on eliminating segregated locals.

Yet, despite the progress that may have been made during the sixties, segregated unions still persisted.[35] The EEOC found that racially segregated locals existed in twenty of the seventy-five cases examined in the study. Unions in the longshore and railroad industries were involved in over half of these cases.

A study of these twenty cases reveals that generally the system of locals divided by race adversely affects the economic welfare of black union members. In the railroad terminals, segregated locals reinforce the pattern of job segregation wherein black workers are restricted to manual job classifications and are placed in separate seniority districts. Efforts of black workers to transfer to more skilled positions may be rejected on the grounds that these jobs are within the white local's exclusive jurisdiction. If allowed to transfer, the black worker will lose all seniority accrued as a member of the black local, working in a separate seniority group. In industrial paper plants, segregated locals helped perpetuate the dual lines of progression that locked blacks into all-black job classifications.

Segregation of locals in the building trades and other unions operating hiring halls has meant that blacks were not referred as often as whites nor referred at all to the higher paying jobs. Historically, the white locals have had contracts with a greater number of firms to which its white members would be referred, while the black counterparts would be restricted to work in ghetto areas. Consider, for example, the case of two locals of the same international which represented the motion picture operators employed in a large northern city. While the white local which had a membership numbering 300 had contracts with 193 theaters, the black local consisting of 30 persons had contracts with only 7 theaters, all of which were located in the black community. Under the contract, theater owners had to give advance notice of job vacancies to the respective unions. Since there was no interchange of information between the locals nor provision for the referral of blacks by the white local, black union members were normally restricted to employment opportunities in the seven ghetto theaters. The small size of the black local further weakened the black members' economic position. With only thirty members, the black local was unable to support a fulltime business agent to secure the contracts and obtain employment for members or even to maintain a union office. On the other hand, the white local's membership was able to achieve both.

Even in cases where segregated locals were parties to agreements to divide the work equally between them, in practice black locals received a disproportionately small share of available work. Segregated longshore locals in Texas present a striking illustration of the economic consequences of dividing work on the basis of racial considerations. There, the International Longshoremen's Association chartered locals in the ports of Houston, Port Orange, Port Arthur,

Orange, Beaumont, Freeport, Texas City, Galveston, Brownsville, Corpus Christi, and Port Lavaca. In these ports, the locals were totally segregated on the basis of race. Of the thirty-seven locals, nineteen were exclusively black, sixteen were all white, and two were composed of Mexican-Americans. Typically, for every white local there was a black counterpart, each having jurisdiction over the same type of cargo, performing the same job operations for the same companies, and under the same collective-bargaining agreements.[36]

Until 1964, the contracts under which these locals operated provided that work should be divided equally between the white and black locals.[37] Following this date, the work-sharing agreements were maintained, although not formally specified in the contract. While this arrangement on its face may seem nondiscriminatory, its effect was to deny black members an equal chance to gain work. This was true because dividing the work between locals neglected the fact that in most situations the black local was far larger than its sister-white local. Moreover, there were instances where notwithstanding the 50-50 division in work opportunities, the white local controlled 75 percent of all distributed work. For example, in the port of Beaumont, black workers made up 67 percent of the union work force but received only 52 percent of all work. In Brownsville, white longshoremen averaged twice as many hours per year as black longshoremen, although the black and white locals were of equal size.

Thus far, it has been noted that segregated locals promote a competition for jobs where the main criterion for success is race. In nearly all such instances, it is the black local which is unable to obtain a proportionate amount of work or employment in the better job classifications. There are other difficulties generated by the separation of locals. As indicated earlier, the limited resources of a black local may prevent it from operating a union office or maintaining even a skeleton staff to manage union business. This deficiency may be crippling where the black members must rely on the local union for job referral. In some situations, the black local lacks adequate leadership to represent the members. In several cases, the Commission found that the black local held meetings infrequently, its leaders were poorly informed, and as a result, important information on job openings and on criteria for advancement was never disseminated to black members. In a few cases, a black local had no record of ever having processed a member's grievance.

At times, the isolation of blacks into separate locals was so functionally artifical as to deny black workers any representation. This occurred in the case of a multiplant firm in Texas where in each plant a separate white local was formed. While these plants were each located in a different geographical area, the black workers were too few in number to organize plant locals, and consequently were grouped together to form one multiplant local. The one black local then had the difficult task of representing blacks who were scattered over a wide geographical area. Its problems of representation were heightened by the fact that workers in the different plants did not always face the same problems or seek the same types of job benefits. Coordinating bargaining efforts for the black workers of these widely scattered plants was virtually impossible.

Despite the generally adverse consequences of segregated local unions, there is a reluctance within many black locals to merge with their white counterparts. Of the sixteen cases in this study where the blacks voted on the merger issue, merger was approved in eight cases and rejected in eight others.[38]

There are several factors underlying a black local's opposition to merger. First, it must be noted that a segregated local system is not always devoid of beneficial characteristics. Segregated locals enable black union members to develop a trained local union leadership. Thus black members are forced to manage their internal affairs and, in some cases, must enforce their job rights in the plant independently of the white local. Additionally, the black local will normally obtain representation at the district and national level. Among the railroad and longshore unions, for example, leaders of black locals have been represented at the district level where they have participated in formulating collective-bargaining demands. In short, to those in positions of leadership, the black local operates as a source of prestige and power; merger may be opposed since it threatens their leadership status.

The rank and file in the black locals may oppose merger for different reasons. There are those who view with great pride the black local's achievements and are reluctant to give up control over what they have created. This problem can become especially serious where the black local has property assets. Finally, opposition may be engendered by the fear that however unfair the current distribution of work, a merger may actually decrease black job opportunities by destroying traditionally protected markets.

These apprehensions and concerns are expressed in the following testimony of an ILA local union president who opposed the merger of his local with its white counterpart:

I would say the first thing it [the Negro local] gave me [was] some security. I would say that it gave me a lot of hope. It has helped me to educate my family, my children. Politically I think it has been something outstanding in this community. By being a member of 872 you can get people to stop and listen to you where if you wasn't. . . . I am not against integration but I am against this amalgamation that 872 will lose its identity, and it has never been proven to me by the Philadelphia Plan or any other plan that any government who wants to be fair to me is offering me something better than what I have. . . . If I'm not mistaken, I have been reading where there is something that the government has that they call the Small Business Administration, and I think I read a few months ago where here in the city of Houston that a member of my race was assisted through this Administration to open up a tailor shop or something similar to that on Main Street in this city. To help to put my people in business. To me 872 is a big business, and we built this business from our boot straps, back in the days when it wasn't popular. And now we have built it up into a big business. And I don't think it is fair that you come along and destroy this in order to force integration on us.[39]

Another black local union official indicated that he favored the continued existence of all-black locals because:

we can defend ourselves and sit there and help make those contracts and the same grievance machinery and everything and see that it is carried out properly. . . . If you merged those two locals together we are going to lose something. . . . The black people going to lose in Houston, Texas. . . . We are going to lose because we are not going to have the same number of officers in 872; say for instances they have got 12 officers in each one of those locals. You are not going to carry 24. We are going to lose something there. These things that we are talking about, what the I.L.A. mean to the black community, as far as prestige and some influence and to help other black people in that community, we are going to lose that. So consequently I wouldn't be in favor of merging.[40]

While these ILA representatives from black locals opposed merger, other ILA locals have gone on record as favoring merger with their white counterparts. In part, the conflict between these ILA locals is based upon their conflicting interpretations of the advantages and disadvantages of integration. To the black local in Brownsville which in 1968-1969 received only one-third of all work, merger is an economic necessity. If implemented fairly it will provide blacks with the same referral opportunities as enjoyed by white longshoremen. On the other hand, a black local that is close to achieving what it sees as economic parity may lack sufficient inducement to sacrifice its separate identity. Thus the local 872 (black) in Houston which opposed merger accumulated in 1968-1969 a total of 1,737, 129 hours. This amount was only 100,000 hours or 3 percent fewer hours than were worked by its white counterpart. Such a local may view with great skepticism the notion that merger will improve the working opportunities for blacks.

The attitude of the leadership and rank-and-file toward merger will also be very dependent on the positions of blacks in the new locals. Where blacks will be a minority, there may be a strong reluctance to merge unless some members of the formerly all-black unit are given official positions in the new local.[41] In seven of the eight cases where the local voted against merger, the black local was smaller and its members expressed concern that a merger would destroy their representation.

Finally, it should be realized the decision whether or not to merge is often a hotly contested and divisive issue. Thus it is rare that a local will be united for or against consolidation. In all cases where the local's president opposed merger or where the local's membership itself rejected that option, there were members voicing their desire to transfer or to establish an integrated local. The bitter in-fighting that sometimes accompanies the issue casts doubt on the extent to which a local's official vote on merger reflects the membership's aspirations. There have been cases where the union officers are so concerned with maintaining their leadership positions that they misinform the membership as to the consequences of merger. In one case where the vote was six to five against consolidation, the local union president warned the membership that merger would result in the loss of jobs for black workers. In another situation, the local union president threatened that if merger occurred, workers would lose their cars, their homes, and their job classifications. Under such circumstances, it is not surprising that a local union may reject integration with its white counterpart.

In the final analysis, the EEOC's decision to merge segregated locals will not be scrapped as a result of a negative vote by members of either the white or black locals. Yet such votes are an important reflection of the fears and apprehensions which underlie union opposition to merger. Merger can only be achieved where attempts have been made to structure the merger agreement to ameliorate these concerns, and to safeguard the rights and interests of all members within the new local. How the EEOC has approached the problems of merger will be discussed in the next chapter.

Failure to Process Grievances

A labor union's authority to represent employees has been interpreted as carrying with it a concomitant obligation to represent fairly all employee members of the bargaining unit.[42] Where unions have accepted blacks as members, there is still a serious problem regarding the adequacy of the unions' representation. Union-employer agreements concerning seniority arrangements have been found at times to discriminate against the entire class of black workers in a plant.

The union's failure to represent black employees fairly manifests itself in another more limited fashion—the failure or refusal to process the grievances of individual black workers. Nine of the seventy-five cases involved this practice.

Seven of the nine cases involved a local's failure to process fairly a black worker's grievance that he had been improperly laid off or bypassed for promotion. In six of these seven cases, the Commission found, notwithstanding specific contractual provisions that the most senior qualified man should be given preference, the white worker awarded the disputed job was not any more qualified than the black grievant, and in fact, was junior to him in seniority.

Yet even where seniority clauses are weak and allow for wide management authority over promotion, the local union is obligated to protest management decisions which are racially motivated. In one promotion case, the contract enabled the employer to promote on the basis of merit as determined by supervisory evaluation. Here, the union refused to entertain a black worker's grievance on the grounds that the absence of a seniority clause left the union no basis for protest. The Commission rejected the local union's position, indicating that the union, under Title VII, has an affirmative obligation to protest and attempt to modify discriminatory company decisions and policies. To hold otherwise would allow the local union to escape its duty of fair representation on the possibility, however remote, that its efforts would be ineffectual.

In five of the nine cases, the local-union steward rejected the grievance, even refusing to take it up with the foreman. The union's conduct was generally based on specious grounds. In one case, the local union claimed that it thought the black worker was being represented by the NAACP. In the other cases, the local unions alleged either that the grievant had not been discriminated against or that racial discrimination was not the proper basis for opposing and seeking the reversal of a managerial decision. Somewhat surprisingly, one of the cases involved grievants who were members of a predominantly black bargaining unit, which had black workers serving as stewards. Here the inability to obtain proper representation was caused by the white business agent's refusal to act on the black stewards' requests. The stewards were inexperienced, and did not understand the procedures that had to be followed in processing grievances. Consequently, they were frustrated by the business agent's refusal to cooperate.

A business agent's refusal to process a grievance carries with it some risk. In another case involving a bargaining unit with a large black component, the white business agent's failure to seek a modification of the employer's promotion policy contributed to the union's decertification. On the other hand, in a predominantly white bargaining unit, the business agent's discriminatory handling of grievances is often supported by the white workers since they, as a result, become the recipients of preferential treatment. Indeed, such preferential treatment may be demanded by the white workers. In one case, a grievance committeeman sympathetic to the job aspirations of black workers was removed by the local union's president. In another, the local union membership voted not to proceed to arbitration.

Commission findings of union violations have occurred even where the union has taken some action in behalf of the grievant. The Commission has considered unlawful all grievance action falling short of arbitration where insufficient relief is afforded the discriminatee. For example, in a promotion case the local union declined arbitration when it obtained the management stipulation that the grievant would be "considered" for the next job vacancy. The Commission considered the union's termination of the grievance at the third step improper since the company had denied the grievant promotion on other occasions; therefore, the stipulation that it would only "consider" the employee for future openings did not adequately safeguard the black worker's promotion rights. Similarly in a discharge case, the union's shop committee voted not to go to arbitration because of the charging party's poor work record. The Commission ruled against the union for not proceeding to arbitration, on the grounds that white employees with equally inferior records had not been discharged.

Significantly, a union may not completely satisfy its duty of fair representation even where it has arbitrated the grievance. From the EEOC's perspective, a local union must raise the question of discrimination at an arbitrator's hearing where the grievant provides evidence that racial bias underlied or motivated the company's actions. Such an approach is necessary since arbitrators do consider questions of racial bias relevant in determining the legitimacy of employer discharges, promotions, and job assignment disputes when they are related to union claims of contract violations.[43] Thus a union's failure to allege employment discrimination limits, and may jeopardize, the black worker's chances of vindicating his rights. The Commission found cause in the second discharge case because the union failed to consider the grievant's contention that the discharge was racially motivated.

To be sure, whether or not a local union is discriminating when it fails to process a grievance through to arbitration is at times difficult to determine. A local union may sacrifice the job rights of one individual to gain other managerial concessions which benefit the entire membership. Yet, in a majority of these cases, no question of tradeoff in benefits was present. In five of the nine cases, the local union dismissed the grievance without even carrying it through the first step. In these cases, there is little doubt that the local unions were willing participants in the companys' unfair employment decisions.

Discriminatory Union Action Against Individuals

In the final group of cases, the local unions discriminated against individual black workers by contributing to or generating employer action which adversely affected the employment status of individual black workers. Two cases involved the union's role as an employer charged with discriminating against black applicants and employees, while three others concerned construction unions which had discriminated against individual minority workers. Table 2-1 illustrates the nature and consequences of the unions' discriminatory actions.

Most of these cases reflect efforts by the local unions to block the movement of blacks into better-paying, more skilled, and formerly "white only" job positions. Thus four cases involved the reassignment of black workers from a previously all-white job to the black unit following the local unions' protests. Similarly, in the two cases of unions acting as employers, blacks were precluded from advancing into jobs traditionally denied blacks. In one construction union case, the charging party was refused admission,[44] while in a second the charging party, although admitted into the union, was unfairly denied journeyman classification and placed in the classification affording him referral to only the lowest paying jobs.

An examination of these cases revealed the extent of the union's resistance to change. In one, the first black to occupy a position as fork-lift operator was replaced by a white worker following the local union's successful effort to convert the job into a permanent position. The black who held the then temporary job, by virtue of his departmental seniority, was replaced when the job's reclassification opened it up to plant-wide bidding. Significantly, the

Table 2-1.
Union Discrimination against Individuals

Case No.	Union Action	Consequences
BI68-4-844	Arbitration of white worker's grievance	Reassignment of black worker to inferior jobs
6-11-48	Employer-union job reclassification	Reassignment of black worker to inferior jobs
6-7-6194	Wildcat strike	Reassignment of black worker to inferior jobs
AU7-5-365	Filing of grievances	Reassignment of black worker to inferior jobs
6-1-322	Failure to apply contract uniformly	Discriminatory overtime assignments
68-8-202	Failure to apply contract uniformly	Layoff of black worker
6-8-7257	Union as employer	Refusal to hire black as business agent
CH7-5-276	Union as employer	Refusal to hire black as secretary
5-12-3217	Refusal to admit black as member	Restriction of worker's job opportunities
6-12-9560U	Refusal to refer black to alternative employment	Loss of earnings
6-2-792	Refusal to classify black as journeyman	Lower earnings

attempt to reclassify the position was first pursued vigorously following the appointment of the black worker.

In a second case, the local union which was predominantly white voted to arbitrate the grievance of a white employee whom the company had reassigned and replaced with a black worker whose original claim to the disputed job should have been recognized. The local union processed the grievance through to arbitration even though the company's actions were in response to a conciliation agreement that it had entered into with the Commission.

Union use of the grievance-arbitration process to block the advancement of black workers occurred elsewhere. In one plant, management had historically denied black workers entry into the checkers unit of the warehouse. Beginning in the late 1950s, the company decided to open up jobs in the checkers unit to plant-wide bidding. The company's objective was to afford black workers an opportunity to bid for and occupy the position of checker. As a result of its policy, black warehousemen were able to exercise their greater plant-wide seniority and displace incumbent checkers who were white. The displaced workers protested, and the local union processed their grievances. Under strong union pressure, the company resolved the grievances by reinstating the former white incumbents and adopting the policy that all vacancies within the checkers unit be filled on the basis of an individual's departmental seniority. This decision supported and demanded by the union effectively placed incumbents ahead of all black warehousemen, since the latter group never had had the opportunity to work in the checkers department.

At times, the membership will eschew the filing of grievances as a means of protest and take direct action. In one case, the company's promotion of a black to an apprenticeship position in an all-white unit led to a wildcat strike by the plant's 116 white workers. As a result, the company was forced to reassign the black worker to his former job.

In approximately half of these cases, the discriminatory activity was initiated and implemented solely by the local union. In two cases, the unions, acting as employers, denied qualified black applicants consideration for jobs as business agent and as secretary to the union business agent. In the three construction union cases, individual black workers were not admitted, referred as often, or placed in the proper job classifications.

In two final cases, the local union and management failed to abide by the contract which would have safeguarded the job rights of discriminatees. A black electrician was denied as much overtime as white electricians, although the contract provided for its equal distribution. In a second case, a black worker laid off from his job could not exercise his plant seniority to bump to other departments; at the same time, the contract allowed such bumping if the displaced worker could perform the work in the new unit.

All these cases involved discrimination against individual workers as opposed to all members of the minority class. Nevertheless, the fact that fewer individuals were involved in no way mitigated against the losses sustained by the discriminatees. For them, union discrimination meant placement in inferior jobs, less earnings, and higher risk of layoff. In some cases, it resulted in the failure of black workers to obtain or retain employment.

3

Remedies for Discriminatory Union Practices

The conciliation efforts of the EEOC commenced in October 1966. From that date until the latter part of fiscal year 1967, conciliation was carried out entirely by Washington, D.C. personnel. Beginning in late spring 1967, field-office personnel conducted independent conciliation efforts. Through 1968, however, settlements obtained by field-office conciliators were being approved by the chief of conciliation in Washington, D.C. Additionally, through 1968, the Conciliations Division of Washington maintained responsibility for the training of conciliators, standardization of procedures, and conciliation of significant cases.[1]

The centralization of conciliation activities during these early years was advantageous from two standpoints: first, it promoted the development of uniform procedures governing the conciliation process; second, it established the principle that the relief sought must go beyond the extension of aid to the charging party by eliminating the source generating the unlawful conditions.

This latter principle was especially significant in the establishment of a uniform remedial approach in cases of union discrimination. While the EEOC did not set forth official "guidelines" as to what the proper remedy must be in a particular case, there developed nevertheless a body of principles that were relevant to various kinds of cases. This is not to suggest that for each issue the conciliation proposal was the same; each case might have unique elements dictating modification in the conciliation proposal. At the same time, experience with particular kinds of cases enabled the EEOC's conciliation staff to ascertain those remedies that were essential to the eradication of a local union's discriminatory practices.

Remedying Exclusionary Union Practices

In this section, we will be concerned with the remedies the Commission has fashioned to eliminate four types of discriminatory union practices. They cover: (1) craft union exclusion of blacks from membership, referral, and apprenticeship programs; (2) operation of discriminatory seniority systems; (3) segregated locals; and (4) local union's failure to process the grievances of black workers.[2]

In remedying discriminatory practices of the building and printing-craft unions, the EEOC's policies were normally designed to achieve three objectives: (a) elimination of discriminatory barriers, (b) affirmative union action to promote minority entrance, (c) direct and immediate relief to the complainant and similarly situated individuals.

These objectives have been sought in all cases involving union exclusion of minority workers from either membership, apprenticeship-training programs, or from referral. In our discussion, we will examine separately Commission policy for each type of violation, since different remedies have been developed to meet the varying problems generated by each form of union exclusion. We will first examine Commission efforts to eliminate in membership admission cases union practices which, while neutral on their face, were utilized to restrict the admission of blacks.

Admission Problems

The exclusion of black workers from membership in the building-craft unions remains a serious problem. The utilization of discriminatory testing procedures, the requirement of membership sponsorship and approval, and the failure to process membership applications are tools of exclusion. To counter them, the EEOC has sought to modify the local unions' traditionally unlimited discretion in developing and administering admission standards.

In the typical case, the Commission attempts to have the union eliminate any of the following requirements for membership: (1) recommendation or endorsement by present members; (2) relationship by blood or marriage to present members; (3) election to membership by present members. In a union which has an all-white membership and has maintained a pattern of exclusion against blacks, such requirements are inherently discriminatory.[3]

While seeking to eliminate standards used exclusively to bar blacks, the Commission has traditionally not attempted to modify legitimate union requirements regarding age, experience in the trade, and ability. The Commission has recognized that examinations may be necessary to evaluate an applicant's ability to perform. Nevertheless, the Commission has tried to normalize both testing procedures and content to avoid their being utilized as exclusionary devices. Thus the Commission's policy is that journeymen's examinations are lawful only when they satisfy the Commission's guidelines on employment testing. Normally, a test is considered legitimate only if it has been shown to fairly measure a worker's ability to perform on the job.[4] Furthermore, the union must give applicants adequate notice regarding the dates of examinations and of any training classes that it holds to prepare workers for the examination.[5]

In cases where the evidence indicated that blacks and whites were graded disparately, the Commission has sought the establishment of an examination board consisting of a union, employer, and public representative. Such a board would then have responsibility for determining all testing results.[6]

There are two areas where the Commission has rejected he passage of a journeyman's examination as a valid admission requirement. The first involves cases where the journeymen applicants have already passed state or local governmental examinations and are licensed to engage in the craft. Here the Commission has maintained that such applicants must be admitted if they satisfy other qualifications regarding age, character, and experience as set forth in the union constitution.[7]

The Commission also rejected the passage of a journeymen's examination as a valid admission requirement where a craft union organizes a shop specializing in craft work, and enrolls the firm's white employees without imposing any testing requirement on them. Under such circumstances, the union's insistence that the firm's black employees can only become members upon the passage of journeymen's examination is blatantly discriminatory.

The second remedial objective in membership cases involves the union obligation to take affirmative action to promote entrance into the union. The exclusion of black from craft unions has been found to have a chilling effect on the number of blacks who apply for membership, referral, or entry into apprenticeship programs. The open preference given relatives and the cold reception afforded black applicants at union offices impress them with the futility of trying to gain admission.[8] As a result, the Commission has adopted as part of the conciliation agreement the requirement that minority organizations such as the NAACP, Urban League, black newspapers, and trade schools be informed by the union that its policy is to evaluate black applicants objectively and without regard to race. The union may similarly be requested to notify all applicants who have previously applied and been rejected and all journeymen licensed by the city of the union's policy of equal employment opportunity. Such affirmative action is considered necessary to dispel the union's discriminatory image which otherwise might stifle black efforts to gain admission.

The final remedial element in membership cases concerns the relief extended to charging parties. So far, the Commission's remedies are aimed at breaking down barriers that potentially discriminate against black workers as a class. At the same time, the Commission has sought to rectify the wrong suffered by individual black workers unfairly denied admission. The Commission's position is that all qualified black workers excluded from admission because of their race should immediately be admitted.[9]

Problems of Referral

As discussed in chapter 1, many craft locals in the building trades will for purposes of referral, divide their members and referral applicants into several priority groups. The criteria for selection and priority in referral are based upon a number of factors. These may include: possession of journeymen's license, membership in the union, experience in the trade, and record of working for a union contractor. Clearly, blacks who have been excluded from union membership cannot compete on equal terms with white union members when these factors determine one's position in a referral category. Having been barred from membership, blacks have had no opportunity to work under a union contractor. Where the craft is thoroughly organized, the nonunion status of black workers can result in their exclusion from the trade.

The Commission's position is that the union must modify the referral system to eliminate any differentiation in work opportunities based upon work for a union contractor, union membership, or experience in the trade. Additionally, it has rejected as a valid requirement for referral the passage of a journeymen's examination where the evidence indicated that it was used as a exclusionary device; thus successful completion of a test is not a legitimate prerequisite where the local union has referred whites who have never been tested or who failed such examinations.

Instead, the Commission recognizes "ability to do the job" as the general basis for a black worker's eligibility for referral.[10] This criterion is not without problems. How does the union evaluate one's ability to perform? Experience in the trade is one criterion. Yet the Commission is reluctant to utilize it since exclusion from membership has rigidly limited the amount of experience the black worker could gain. In practice the Commission has followed the courts in broadly defining the criterion of "experience in the trade" to include experiences in related construction work, schooling, training in the armed forces, and self-employment. Thus, if a local union requires that all applicants seeking referral must have three years experience *in the trade,* the Commission maintains that the local union must accept in fulfillment of that requirement the years of experience the black workers have gained from other sources similarly qualifying him for the job.[11]

The problem of establishing a viable referral system that will protect standards in the trade while affording black workers equal referral opportunities is illustrated by the court's remedial actions in *Dobbins* v. *IBEW, Local 212.*[12] In Dobbins, the union had established priority groups for referral based upon passage of a journeyman's examination, experience in the trade, and work under a union contractor. The court found that orders of preference in employment opportunities which were in fact predicated on union membership were unlawful. It ordered that the union's referral system be set aside, and that referrals be made on the basis of experience in any part of the trade. Specifically, no previous experience as a "wire-man" or in construction was deemed necessary, as experience in residential construction work could be substituted. Additionally, the passage of a journeymen's examination was set aside as a requirement for referral. The court permitted four priority referral groups with "experience in the trade," determining referral group assignment.[13]

While enabling black workers to be referred, the court's order generated several problems. Union representatives charged that the placement of workers who had passed journeymens' examinations on the same footing as others who had not done so and who had no real construction experience would seriously reduce the quality of the work force. They argued that union contractors do little residential work; consequently, the referral of workers on the basis of experience in home construction electrical work was inappropriate. The court-ordered referral systems allegedly had the following consequences. Apprentices found themselves working with less skilled men; thus, instead of learning from journeymen, the apprentices were "carrying" these higher paid workers. Apprentices further complained that there was little incentive to remain in the program. Instead of earning 60-70 percent of scale, they could drop out of the program and earn full scale on a referral basis. The local union contended that the only beneficiaries of the court-ordered referral system were low-skilled white workers. Thus, under the court-ordered referral system which was in effect from September 12, 1968 to April 4, 1970, several hundred white workers with mostly residential electrical experience were referred while only six blacks requested referral.[14]

Finding merit in the union's position, the court modified its order. The union had requested the reinstitution of its original contract referral system which gave priority to those who had passed a journeymen's examination, had worked under a union contractor, and had four years of experience in electrical construction work. The Court refused. Instead, it adopted the novel approach of allowing the local to return to the contract referral system for purposes of determining the eligibility of *white* applicants for referral; however, the court-ordered referral system would remain in effect for all *black* applicants.[15] In this manner, the court preserved the seniority rights of union members and protected the standards in the trade from dilution. At the same time, black workers were not penalized for their previous exclusion from the union.

The Commission's conciliation standards have been strongly influenced by the court's position. Thus, where a local union maintains a referral system which assigns applicants to various priority groups, the Commission does not demand that such a system be abandoned nor that all workers be referred on a first-in, first-out basis. Such a position fails to consider the realities underlying a union's referral operations. Moreover, by provoking intense union opposition, it tends to frustrate the Commission's conciliation efforts. The Commission seeks only as much change as is necessary to assure blacks a fair opportunity for referral.

The Commission also has sought to impose an affirmative action obligation upon the local union. To promote minority referral, the local union has been, as in membership cases, required to communicate directly with the minority community. This can involve contact with guidance counselors of high schools located in the black community, advertisements in black news media and periodic meetings with representatives of minority organizations in which the local would explain the procedures for referral and its desire to refer minority applicants. Additionally, the Commission has attempted to modify exclusive referral systems by allowing employers to hire minority workers directly. Once a man is recruited in this way, the employer notifies the union which then refers the worker back to the employer. This type of relief has been motivated by the realization that even following a conciliation agreement, members of the minority community may suspect the good faith of the local union and eschew utilization of the hiring hall. Therefore the Commission has attempted to open up work opportunities to qualified blacks who heretofore have been barred from employment with union contractors and who otherwise might still fail to obtain employment by their reluctance to use the union hiring hall.[16]

In practice, the Commission's efforts to allow black workers to be referred once they have been hired directly by employers are not without precedent. In many instances, local craft unions that refer workers out of priority groups based on their seniority on the out-of-work list make exceptions to the seniority rule. Often contractors can request a foreman by name without regard to his location on the out-of-work list. Generally, contractors have the same privilege with regard to persons possessing specialized skills. Finally, many locals may allow contractors to obtain the services of particular workers irrespective of their place on the out-of-work list if they have worked for the contractor within a given period of time. Thus the Commission has sought to broaden the contractor's right to hire directly in regard to black workers, viewing it as a potential way for easing black entry into the trade.

Regarding the relief extended to individuals denied referral, the Commission has required the local union to immediately refer the discriminatee. Such relief has been deficient in one respect. No effort has generally been made to obtain back pay for those not referred, primarily because of the difficulty in determining the extent of financial loss. Construction work is generally of short-term nature; yet duration varies, with some jobs lasting only several days and others lasting several months. There is consequently no precise method of determining for back-pay purposes the amount of work denied by the union's failure to refer an applicant. Most important, there is no certainty that the union's actions caused an individual to sustain a monetary loss. In the final analysis, it is the employer who judges one's ability to perform. It is possible that a worker referred by the union will nevertheless be immediately terminated by the employer for lack of qualification. For these reasons, the Commission generally has made no attempt to gain back pay relief for workers discriminatorily denied membership or referral.[17]

Remedial Policies Involving Union Apprenticeship Programs

In apprenticeship cases, the Commission's primary remedial objective has been the elimination of all discriminatory apprenticeship qualifications. Consequently, it has emphasized the need to institute objective and reviewable standards in the selection of applicants for training. Preference for relatives of union members or contractors must be eliminated. If an examination is required, it must accord with the Commission's guidelines on testing. Oral interviews are considered invalid.

During the period 1966-68, the Commission did not seek to insure a minimum participation of blacks in any program. Any such proposals would undoubtedly have met with strong and bitter opposition from the unions. It must be realized that during this period the courts had not yet ruled that the establishment of a black participation rate in referrals and job apprenticeships was either appropriate or necessary to provide blacks with employment opportunities and employment programs from which they had previously been excluded.[18]

The typical conciliation proposal required the nullification of all existing waiting lists for apprenticeships if they had been compiled during the time the local union and the joint apprenticeship committee were excluding blacks. A new waiting list was to be compiled after the local had notified the minority community that it was evaluating candidates indiscriminately and on the basis of objective standards.[19] Such a requirement is essential where the local union has a long waiting list composed exclusively of whites. If the union were to continue to draw applicants from this list, blacks would be prevented from entering into the program for years to come, even after the union had agreed to accept black applicants.

As with membership and referral, the Commission requires the labor organization to publicize and recruit actively in the black community. Finally, all minority applicants unfairly denied admission must be admitted to the next apprenticeship classes that were instituted.[20]

Some General Provisions

In remedying union exclusion of blacks from membership, referral, and apprenticeship programs, the Commission has had to deal with the frequent local union procedure of not even processing the applications of blacks. Often, blacks are unable to obtain the proper application forms, while those who have completed applications receive no response, or if rejected, obtain no information about the reason for their rejection. Such practices forcefully disclose to the black community the futility involved in seeking union membership or referral.

To eliminate these practices, the Commission normally requires the union to keep open its hiring, apprenticeship, and membership offices at regular time periods. Moreover, after receiving applications, the local is obligated to notify the applicant within a short period, advising him of the union's decision. If he is rejected, the union must inform the applicant of the reasons for his rejection.[21]

To check a local union's compliance, the conciliation agreement normally requires the union to submit to the Commission at periodic intervals all personnel records the union has compiled in processing its membership, referral, and apprenticeship applications. Additionally, the local union may be required to notify the EEOC of any action it takes in regard to minority applications.[22] These data enable the Commission to evaluate the degree to which the Commission's actions changed the union's policies and increased the number of blacks gaining entrance into the union.

The remedial policies developed by the Commission in craft union exclusion cases were designed primarily to eradicate all local union practices which restrict minority referral and admission into membership and apprenticeship-training programs. At the same time, it has not overlooked the remedial needs of individual discriminatees. The Commission directs the local to admit immediately into membership or refer those previously excluded on racial grounds. The Commission's remedies are not without limitations; no effort has been made to provide back pay to minority workers denied referral. Nevertheless, it is evident that the Commission has developed remedies which are sufficiently broad in scope and impact and which, if implemented, may have significantly promoted minority entrance into unions and the building-trades industry.

Seniority Cases – Development of a Remedial Policy

A common denominator in seniority cases is the concentration of black workers in inferior job classifications and restrictions upon their movement into "white" jobs. Many of these restrictions flow from the nature of the existing seniority arrangements governing promotion, layoff, and transfer. These restrictions may include: (1) the black worker's loss of accrued seniority in transferring to the white seniority unit; (2) inability to bump back into his original department upon layoff in the new unit; (3) reduction in pay of black workers who can transfer only into entry level classifications. Seniority arrangements may actually preclude any movement from the black to the white seniority unit.

In these cases, the Commission's primary remedial objective has been the movement of incumbent black workers into the formerly all-white seniority units. To achieve this goal, the Commission's remedies are two-pronged in nature, requiring (1) employer-union agreement to restructure the seniority system to enable black workers to compete for jobs on an equal footing with white employees, and (2) direct employer action to promote minority movement by providing them with the skills to handle more advanced jobs in other units and by eliminating the threat of wage reductions for those who move out of their former positions.

These remedial elements are generally sought in all three types of seniority cases: (1) black and white workers doing the same work but placed in separate seniority units, (2) black and white workers performing functionally related tasks but assigned to separate progression lines, (3) black and white workers performing unrelated tasks and placed in separate departments. At the same time, the Commission has varied some of its remedies in accordance with the type of seniority case. Consequently, we shall examine Commission policy separately for the three different types of seniority cases.

*Remedying the Maintenance of Separate Seniority Lists
for Similar Jobs*

In the first category of seniority cases, blacks performed the same work as whites but were segregated in separate seniority districts and thereby denied promotional opportunities. Additionally, where blacks were classified as holding inferior jobs, they received less pay and were more vulnerable to layoffs.

For remedial purposes, the Commission's policy is that the seniority lists of these white and black workers be "dovetailed"; that is, all black workers would be placed in the same seniority group as the white workers, with each worker's seniority based upon his length of service with the company. Figure 3-1 illustrates this formula.

Assume that the white seniority district has ten workers, each having been employed with the company from one to ten years, and that the seniority group

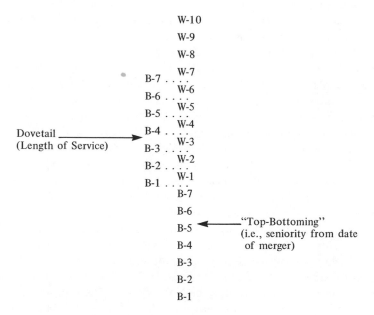

Figure 3-1. Methods of Merging Seniority Lists

for blacks consists of seven workers, each having from one to seven years of service with the company. Dovetailing of the seniority lists appears on the left-hand side of the table. It results in the integration of black workers into the white seniority district based upon each employee's length of service with the company. The Commission normally rejects as an appropriate remedy a merger of the black and white seniority lists in which the black workers' seniority commences from the date of the merger ("top-bottoming"). This procedure would not integrate the rosters in any meaningful way but would instead place all black workers below whites and thus continue to limit their employment opportunities. Over time, it may result in the promotion of some black workers. Yet on the railroads, where segregated seniority districts are found, "top-bottoming" would make black workers most vulnerable to the extensive layoffs occurring in that industry.

Additionally, the Commission breaks down any artificial distinction which may exist between the white and black seniority districts due to the assignment of inferior job classifications to black workers. Thus, for example, where black porters perform the same work as white brakemen, they are entitled to promotion to positions of "conductor" on the basis of their total employment seniority.[23]

It can be argued that black workers who have been isolated in separate seniority districts have sustained monetary losses. This is most evident where black workers performing the same work as white employees have been denied promotions that were afforded to junior white employees; in other cases, senior black employees were laid off while junior white employees were retained. In these situations the Commission has attempted to afford discriminatees back pay for the financial losses they have sustained.[24]

Typically, the Commission seeks back pay equal to the difference in the amount the black workers obtained and what they would have earned had they properly been promoted. Such a remedy is only appropriate, however, where there is an identifiable class of individuals which has unlawfully been denied promotion to positions they are capable of filling. In the case of porters and brakemen, the back-pay problem is easily resolved, since in fact porters performed the same work as brakemen but were nevertheless paid less.

At the same time, it should be noted that back pay has not constituted a standard remedial element in seniority cases. In only a few of the twenty-seven seniority cases have provisions for back pay been incorporated in the conciliation agreement. This has been the result of several factors. First, it is at times difficult to identify the individuals who suffered a monetary loss. Not everyone discriminatorily denied promotion would necessarily have been promoted if objective criteria had been utilized. Where black and white workers do not perform the same work, some black workers discriminated against may have lacked the ability to perform in a higher level job. More significant, however, if the fact that the seniority cases handled during the period 1966-68 involved in many situations management and union decisions regarding promotion and layoff that were made before the act was passed. Consequently, the nonretroactive nature of the act would have made back pay inappropriate. On the other hand, the discriminatory nature of the seniority system allowed for continued abuse as long as the system itself was in effect. Consequently, the typical conciliation proposal would concentrate on the steps a respondent had to take to modify seniority systems. Additionally, during the EEOC's early years, the courts had not yet authorized back pay as an appropriate remedy in seniority cases.[25] In the absence of such a decision the conciliator's efforts to achieve a back-pay remedy was rendered vulnerable by a challenge from a respondent that such a remedy was unlawful. This may have resulted in a tendency to compromise on back pay if other concessions were attainable. In the final analysis, the conciliator's primary objective is to eliminate discriminatory employment practices. No amount of back pay is able to accomplish this.

Remedies in Progression Line Seniority Cases

In a second class of seniority cases, black and white employees work in functionally related jobs but are placed in dual progression lines. Again, the Commission requires the merger of the segregated lines with black workers' seniority in the newly merged line to be based on their total employment with the company.

Crown-Zellerbach presented the Commission with one of its first opportunities for merging functionally related jobs that had been placed in separate progression lines based on race. In Crown, the Commission was initially concerned with separate promotion lines that existed in the Wood Room of the company's pulp and paper mill in Bogalusa, Louisiana. In these two departments black and white employees were assigned to jobs that were racially designated and were permitted to progress only to those jobs that were restricted to their respective racial grouping. Table 3-1 shows the segregated job classifications that prevailed in the Wood Room.

To eliminate the segregated lines, the Commission sought the horizontal intermeshing of white and black jobs according to the functional relationship each had with the other and on the basis of the responsibility and difficulty associated with each job. It was suggested that the wage rate related to each position be a measure of the job's significance and responsibility.[26]

The effect of the Commission's plan is illustrated in Table 3-2.

As the diagram indicates, black workers were dovetailed into the white line on the basis of their hourly wage rate. As a result, they were able to advance for the first time into formerly all-white positions.

In developing its merger plan, the Commission had previously rejected the merger proposal adopted by Crown which would have subordinated the jobs of

Table 3-1
Wood Room Progression Lines

White	Black
$3.60 – foreman	$2.74 – wood unloader
$3.27 – assistant foreman	$2.42 – screen room man
$3.18 – crane operator	$2.40 – belt and pit man
$2.92 – chip storage operator	$2.39 – drum man
$2.79 – assistant chip storage operator	$2.32 – flume man
$2.70 – No. 3 chipper man	$2.31 – utility wood room
$2.69 – Nos. 1 & 2 chipper man	$2.27 – wood room chain man
$2.29 – No. 3 chipper utility	
$2.23 – Nos. 1 & 2 chipper utility	

incumbent black workers below those of incumbent white employees. While willing to dovetail black and white jobs on the basis of their wage rates, Crown-Zellerbach Corporation sought to retain for the jobs in the newly merged lines their former white and black designations. This meant that employees already in the line at the time of the merger were to leap-frog to the job classification formerly restricted to their respective racial grouping. In effect, the company's proposal would have prevented blacks from obtaining a white job until all white employees had moved up. The company, however, accepted the Commission's merger plan with the result that the employees in the newly merged line moved up on a step-by-step basis without leap-frogging.

Crown-Zellerbach gave the Commission an opportunity to clarify its position on the merger of segregated progression lines. Still not fully settled, however,

Table 3-2
EEOC Merger of Segregated Wood Room Jobs

Job Classification	Race of Job Holders in Classification	Hourly Rate
Foreman	W	$3.60
Assistant foreman	W	$3.27
Crane operator	W	$3.18
Chip storage operator	W	$2.92
Assistant chip storage operator	W	$2.79
Wood unloader	B	$2.74
No. 3 chipper man	W	$2.70
Nos. 1 & 2 chipper man	W	$2.69
Screen room man	B	$2.42
Beet and pit man	B	$2.40
Drum man	B	$2.39
Flume laborer	B	$2.32
Utility wood room	B	$2.31
No. 3 chipper utility	W	$2.29
Wood room chain man	B	$2.27
Nos. 1 & 2 chipper utility	W	$2.23

was the question as to the seniority rights black workers could exercise in the new line. Since black workers had generally been relegated to the lowest paying jobs, merger of the lines on the basis of wage scale, even when the wage structure per se was not discriminatory, placed most if not all formerly "white only" jobs above the formerly black jobs. An examination of Table 3-2 showing the merged Wood Room progression line reveals that even under the Commission's plan most black jobs were below those of incumbent white workers. The subordination of black workers is reinforced when a system of progression line seniority is maintained. Here, incumbent white employees were given preference in filling vacancies. Even more serious, however, is that in time of layoff, white workers can bump down the line on the strength of their job or line seniority and displace black workers who had recently entered the all-white line.

To prevent this, the Commission in merging segregated progression lines requires that, for purposes of promotion and layoff, the seniority of black workers in the new line be computed on the basis of their total employment with the company. This approach was developed early in 1966 as a result of a case involving separate but functionally related black and white lines of progression in the stock house of a steel facility. Here, black workers in what was designated as Line 1 selected material on railroad cars and delivered them to the blast furnace; at that point, Line 2, consisting of all white workers, commened with lifting the materials by a hoist and dumping them in the furnace. While the two lines were in the same department, and promotion within the same departments was standard plant procedure, black workers were confined to Line 1 jobs.

Following charges against both the company and local union, the respondents attempted to rectify the discriminatory condition by a merger which allowed black workers to become the junior employees in the white line, as vacancies occurred. They also provided that blacks could roll back into the former black line if laid off from the white line. In effect, the company and union had endorsed the *Whitfield* doctrine wherein black employees who transferred to the white line began as new employees and could not utilize the seniority they had accrued in the black line for purposes of promotion and layoff.[27] The only concession they made was to allow blacks to bump back into the black line, if necessary.

In reviewing the company-union offer, the chief of conciliation noted that there existed at least five alternatives, ranked in order in which they provided relief to the black workers. These were:

1. Merge the two lines in the literal sense, and allow all employees to carry their seniority from the segregated lines into the merged lines. This would permit the more senior black employees to immediately displace (or bump) junior white employees up in the previously all white line, to the extent that the black employees were (or could become) qualified.

2. Allow the black employees, on the basis of their seniority, to fill vacancies which develop anywhere in the white line, not only at the bottom, and to utilize their full seniority in the event of a layoff. This would be use of full seniority for promotions when vacancies developed, and in the event of layoffs.

3. Allow senior black employees to enter the white line at the bottom, for promotion purposes but use their plant age in the event of a layoff, so that the senior employees would remain in the white line while junior white employees were laid off, or bumped down.

4. Allow senior black employees to fill vacancies anywhere in the line of promotion, but, in the event of layoff, to be returned to their seniority position in the previously all-black line (Leap in — leap out).

5. All senior black employees to bid into the bottom of the previously all white line, and, in the event of a layoff, treat them as the most junior employees in the white line, allowing them to exercise their full seniority for layoff purposes only with respect to the previously all black jobs.[28]

The fifth alternative which gave black workers the least protection represented the company's and union's positions.

The Commission rejected the company and union offers and resolved to continue to meet with the respondents, recognizing that the second alternative represented the approach it would favor.[29]

Reflecting the Commission's position, Executive Director Herman Edelsberg wrote to the respondents officially rejecting their offer, and noting:

The Commission's deliberations identified two broad areas where it believes that the revision is not adequate to the requirements of the statute. First, it does not give adequate weight to seniority in permitting Negro employees to move up in the previously all white lines of progression. Second, it fails to allow Negro employees who have moved up in the line of progression to utilize their seniority in cases of further promotion or in cases of reduction in force.[30]

Instead, he insisted that an acceptable provision would have to "provide Negro workers with the opportunity to fill vacancies anywhere in the line on the basis of their company seniority. Additionally, company seniority would govern their status in the line for layoff purposes."

While the Commission's establishment of the principle that plant-wide seniority should be the unit governing minority workers' job rights grew out of the 1966 steel case, there were even earlier cases where plant-wide seniority had been sought on an ad hoc basis.[31] Even in 1965 the chief of conciliations recognized the necessity for broadening the transfer and promotion rights of minority employees previously restricted to segregated job classifications. In November 1965, Professor Blumrosen outlined the following steps which should be taken in seniority cases:

1. Integration of seniority lines and departments on a nondiscriminatory basis, such as length of plant service

2. Removal of barriers to worker mobility, such as risk of loss of seniority rights on transfers to a new department

3. Provision for on-the-job training where there has been a discriminatory refusal in the past to allow minority members to secure work experience

4. Immediate transfers and promotions where appropriate[32]

These principles laid the foundation for subsequent conciliation efforts. From a remedial standpoint, it is obvious that the decisions in *Quarles*[33] and *Crown-Zellerbach*[34] did not create new remedies, but adopted remedial policies espoused by the Commission in the previous years.

Some General Remedial Provisions

In promoting the movement of blacks into formerly all-white units, the Commission has faced another problem. In many situations, the beginning wage rates at the entry-level jobs in the formerly all-white unit were lower than the rates black workers enjoyed at the upper strata of the black unit. As a result, blacks may decide to remain in their original jobs rather than transfer and suffer an immediate reduction in income, although the entry-level job in the white line may lead to higher paying positions in the future. In these cases, the Commission has adopted the practice of "red circling" the initial rate in the formerly all-white unit. Under this procedure, the black employee who transfers is allowed to maintain his former wage rate until he advances to a position where the wage rate for the job in the formerly all-white unit matches that in the black job.[35]

There is still another and more difficult barrier to the movement of blacks out of their segregated seniority units. The Commission's policy has been to accord black workers seniority rights on the basis of their total employment seniority. At the same time, it has recognized that workers exercising such seniority rights must have the ability to perform the job to qualify for promotion. As a result, in plants where past experience in entry-level jobs provides the training necessary to the satisfactory performance of higher-paying jobs in the progression line or department, black workers may in practice be restricted to filling entry-level slots. To overcome this problem, the Commission has sought the establishment of plant-training programs through which black workers may become qualified for the higher-skilled, better-paying positions. These training programs compensate black workers for the experience they would have acquired had they not been denied entry into the all-white unit and make possible the promotion of blacks to jobs to which they are entitled by virtue of their company seniority.[36]

In some cases, it is possible to identify particular jobs in the progression line for which experience in entry-level jobs is not essential. Here black workers can skip over the entry-level jobs and obtain higher-level jobs on the basis of their company seniority. This procedure was followed by the courts in *Crown-Zellerbach* when it allowed black workers in several departments to bypass certain jobs when bidding for higher-level jobs in the progression line. Experience in the bypassed jobs was not considered essential for the training of workers for upper-level positions.[37]

Remedying Discriminatory Departmental Seniority Systems

In the third category of seniority cases, the seniority system restricts black workers to exclusively or largely all-black departments or seniority districts. In these cases, the jobs performed by black workers do not bear a close functional relationship to those of whites in the other departments or work districts. To integrate the segregated departments, the Commission requires that blacks be able to transfer and compete for promotion on the basis of their company, and *not* departmental, seniority.

In remedying a discriminatory seniority system, the Commission's efforts are aimed at eliminating only those features that generate the discrimination. Thus, in the case where departmental seniority operates to confine blacks into dead-end inferior jobs, the Commission does not attempt to eliminate the use of departmental seniority on an across-the-board basis. Typically, only black workers hired during the period the company was discriminating against them are given the opportunity to transfer and compete for jobs in other departments on the basis of their company seniority. In this manner, the conciliation agreement minimizes any changes that may upset employee expectations and other rights the workers have.

Commission Remedial Policy in Seniority Cases: A Summary Review

In all three types of seniority cases, remedies developed by the Commission included several common elements: (1) right of incumbent black workers previously restricted to all-black seniority units to compete for jobs in other units on the basis of their total plant-wide seniority; (2) red-circling of wage rates of black workers who transfer into previously all-white units. The latter prevents a reduction in the black worker's wage if his starting rate in the white seniority unit is lower than the rate he had enjoyed in his former job.

In cases involving functionally related but separate progression lines, the Commission would require a merger of the two lines. Similarly, it would require the merger of separate seniority units where both black and white workers are performing the same job functions. Cases involving the separation into different units of black and white workers performing the same work were unique in that only in these did the Commission seek back pay for black workers. Thus one could argue that the Commission failed to compensate many black workers for the losses they previously sustained. This is true. Yet one must temper this criticism with the recognition that calculating such losses is difficult in the other seniority cases,[38] while the legal questions concerning a back-pay remedy were not fully resolved until 1969. In fact, most court orders in seniority cases do not provide for back pay to black workers.[39]

While not compensating black employees for monetary losses they sustained, the Commission's remedial elements were effective in eradicating those features of the seniority systems that penalized blacks who sought entry into previously all-white units. Additionally, by requiring employers to institute training programs for minority workers, the Commission laid the foundation for the movement of blacks into the more highly skilled jobs from which they were previously excluded. In this manner, black workers would be compensated for the experience they had missed as a result of their segregation in inferior jobs. Had the Commission been able to execute settlement agreements incorporating its remedial policies, it would have eliminated the cause of the complaint while providing some direct relief to affected minority workers.

Remedial Standards – Segregated Locals

The Commission has held that segregated unions constitute a per se violation of Title VII.[40] Both the locals which segregate and the parent internationals which allow their affiliates to operate on a segregated basis are held responsible for the violation. As a remedy, the Commission generally requires that segregated locals be merged. By merger, it meant the actual consolidation of two locals and not an agreement providing only for the transfer of members of the black local into the white local. Such a remedy would be incomplete since it allowed for the continued existence of two locals separated on the basis of race alone.

While adopting merger as an appropriate remedy, in the absence of special circumstances, the Commission would not seek to specify in the conciliation agreement the ways in which the international was to implement a merger. Frequently, it would accept an agreement simply specifying that the international had effected or was planning a merger within a specified time period.[41]

It is evident that a simple merger proposal is an inadequate remedial device in certain cases. It may not achieve fair representation for black workers nor may the prospect of merger by itself be sufficient to induce them to liquidate their own local. As was examined earlier, the suggestion of merger raises considerable apprehension among both the union leadership and rank and file of the black locals. They may oppose integration unless guaranteed official positions in the new local. This is considered at times necessary since the maintenance of discriminatory policies by the white union majority may leave the black membership in the new local bereft of all representation. Similarly, black members as a matter of pride may be unwilling to give up their charter to join the white local when the black local has been in existence longer. In these cases they may demand that an altogether new local be chartered by the international. Both white and black locals will also be concerned with disposition of union property. In short the Commission's remedy of merger may generate economic and political consequences that must be considered within any merger agreement to safeguard the interests of both white and black members.

The Commission was aware of these issues, and in its earliest cases demonstrated a sensitivity to the problems associated with merger. In *Crown-Zellerbach*, where a small black local existed side-by-side with a larger white local with a past history of intensive discrimination, Commissioner Jackson suggested that merger be achieved on the basis of allocating to black members positions on the bargaining and grievance committees during the first three years of the merger.[42] The chief of conciliations had in 1965 in fact suggested that special safeguards be established when black members constituted a minority of total membership in merging locals. It was recognized that there was the danger that the dominant white majority might continue its discriminatory policies following merger, and that this risk might lead black locals to oppose merger. To help resolve the difficulty, Professor Blumrosen suggested that the Commission's merger efforts should include specific safeguards. These would cover the following: (1) A guarantee of minority group participation in the management of the affairs of the union; and (2) a review of terms of any collective-bargaining agreements negotiated by the merged union to assure that the minority is being fairly treated.[43]

In its conciliation efforts, the Commission has followed the approach of seeking special protection of minority interests where it believes that such extra provisions are necessary to safeguard the rights of black workers.

The more rigorous approach toward merger is reflected in the following conciliation provisions which safeguarded the interests of minority union members of the all-black Local 991, which merged with the larger all-white Local 783.

- The merger shall take effect within thirty (30) days after this Agreement is approved by the membership of Local 783 and Local 991, and approved by the national office or . . . .
- The merged local shall be known as Local Union No. 783 . . . .
- From the date of the merger until the next scheduled election, December 1968, a protective board member, from dissolved Lodge 991, shall be vice-local chairman of Sunbeam Lodge Local 783 for the purpose of attending all meetings with local management, taking part in all discussions with local management, when grievances and working conditions are discussed.
- Every member of merged Local Union No. 783 shall be eligible to run for elective or appointive office in Local Union No. 783 at the next and all succeeding elections;

- All members of the merged Local Union No. 783 in good standing shall be arranged on a single Seniority List in accordance with the date of their admittance into a Local Union.
- Locals 783 and 991 shall prepare a financial report as of December 31, 1967. This shall include the regular report submitted to the United States Department of Labor, plus a statement of assets and liabilities as of December 31, 1967. Copies of each shall be turned over to the merged Local Union No. 783.
- All benefits applicable to present members of Local 783 shall become applicable to present members of Local 991.
- All members in good standing in Local 991 as of the time of merger, shall not be obligated to pay any additional initiation fees, dues of financial obligations.
- No member of either Local Union will lose his position with the company because of this merger.[44]

Several provisions afforded minority workers special representation. First, a board member from the former black local was to occupy the position of "vice-local chairman," with authority to participate in all negotiations with management. Second, black members would carry over their accrued seniority. This particular clause was essential to preserve union benefits such as pension payments which varied with the length of union membership. Additionally, merger of seniority lists breaks down the separate work jurisdiction that each local may have previously maintained, thereby allowing each employee to compete for jobs on the basis of their total union or company seniority, and not on the basis of racial considerations. The problem of the disposition of assets is handled by subjecting both locals to an audit before merger has occured. The intent is to have both locals surrender their assets to the new local formed by the merger.

In September 1968, the Justice Department obtained a consent order merging segregated locals of the United Papermakers and Paperworkers which represented employees of Crown-Zellerbach Corporation in Bogalusa, Louisiana.[45] The consent order significantly expanded upon the privileges afforded to black local members at the time of merger of the segregated locals. Instead of providing one or two union positions to members of the former black local, the court order placed five black members on the Executive Board of the new local. Even when these five-added offices ceased to exist following the three-year transition period, two officers of the local's Executive Board and Grievance Committee were to be elected from the Wood and Yard Department. Since these departments were heavily black, former members of the black local were assured continued representation. Regarding the handling of grievances, the general vice-president was authorized to process through to arbitration grievances filed by members of the former black local which were not approved by the local's full grievance committee. The cost of such grievances, however, was to be borne by former members of the black local. Finally, all committees appointed during a two-year transition period had to include representatives from the former black local. In summary, the order provided numerous measures to allay the concern of black workers that in merging with the numerically larger and once hostile white local, their interests would be protected.

The legitimacy of a Crown-Zellerbach type merger was challenged in an earlier case involving the Musicians Union.[46] Here the international adopted a merger plan whereby the black local was authorized to elect three of eight Executive Board members, an administrative vice-president, two of the eleven Trial Board members, one of the three members of the Examining Board, and a number of individuals who would represent the merged local at various conventions. The merger agreement would operate for a transition period of six years.

The court dismissed the argument that the plan violated Section 101(a) (1) of the Landrum Griffin Act.[47] It noted that the right of members to vote for union officers was not absolute, but was qualified by the right of the union to establish "reasonable rules and regulations" in its constitution and bylaws. First, the court pointed out that the classification of voters by race in this situation was to become part of the local union's bylaws. Second, it was a reasonable limitation since it was the only practical method of merging the two segregated locals.

Juxtaposing the requirements of the Landrum-Griffin Act against those of Title VII, we can observe that an international has great flexibility in merging segregated locals. In merger, it may adjust the interests of both white and black members, for otherwise merger may be impossible. From the standpoint of Title VII, the allocation of various union positions to black members is a logical remedial measure justified under certain circumstances to guarantee black union members the minimum representation previously denied them by the white local's failure to admit black workers. It is this approach that the Commission pursued when seeking merger, and which, if implemented, would have laid the framework for the proper representation of black workers in merger situations.

Remedial Policy in Cases Involving Discriminatory Actions Against Individual Minority Workers

The Commission developed a uniform remedial policy for grievance cases and for cases involving direct union action against individual minority workers. Both types of cases produced the same discriminatory consequences. The union's failure to process the grievances of all workers indiscriminately enables management to implement personnel policies and decisions that severely limit the employment rights of blacks. As a result, black workers were laid off, discharged, or bypassed for promotion. Similarly, in the cases concerning direction union discrimination against individuals, black workers were laid off, demoted, or not referred as often or hired because of union pressure or as a result of decisions made by the union when acting as an employer or in the capacity of a referral union.

In conciliation, the Commission's remedial objectives are two-fold: (1) to provide relief to the discrimantee, and (2) to insure that in the future the local union will process the grievances of black workers and/or represent their interests fairly.

Regarding the first objective, the Commission normally seeks an agreement whereby the respondents make whole the discriminatee for his losses. For example, in the cases of a discriminatory discharge, layoff, or demotion, the relief sought is back pay and reinstatement. In promotion and hiring cases, it is instatement to the disputed job and back pay to cover all wages lost.[48]

In implementing the second objective, the Commission's conciliation proposals typically provide that the local unions will represent all members fairly when negotiating for and administering the collective-bargaining agreement.[49]

In the case of a local union with a history of rejecting the grievances of black workers, the Commission has at times sought to strengthen its conciliation proposals. The mere statement that the local union will process grievances fairly provides by itself little assurance that the union will comply. Thus, in the absence of reporting requirements, there is no method of determining, other than by the filing of new charges, whether the union is processing the grievances of black employees. To assure compliance, the Commission has in some cases required local unions to report periodically the actions it has taken in response to black grievances. By continually examining the reports, the Commission makes more difficulty and hazardous union grievance decisions which unfairly and adversely affect the rights of black workers.[50]

There are additional remedial measures that the Commission could implement to enhance black workers' chances of having their grievances processed. Where the evidence documented a severe pattern of nonrepresentation, the Commission could seek the allocation of a number of positions on the local's grievance committee to black members. Black grievance committeemen could act as stewards where necessary, thus insuring that the black workers' grievances would be considered at the lowest level – discussion between the stewards and plant foremen or lower-level supervisors. The settlement proposal should also authorize the black members of the grievance committee to take up to the arbitration stage any grievance initiated by a black member without the approval of the local's grievance committee provided, however, that the expense of a hearing be approved and borne by the black members. This remedy would remain in effect only temporarily, after which time full authority over grievances would be given to the local's grievance committee.

Such a proposal at first glance raises serious questions. While appealing as an instrument for safeguarding employment rights of black workers, affording blacks in the bargaining unit the power to compel arbitration notwithstanding the decision of the local union's grievance committee seems foreign to existing statutory and legal concepts of the arbitration process. Thus the courts have held that normally the union is the sole agency empowered to arbitrate grievances.[51] It is argued that to hold otherwise would undermine the grievance arbitration procedure.

If the individual employee could compel arbitration of his grievance regardless of its merits, the settlement machinery provided by the contract would be substantially undermined, thus destroying the employer's confidence in the union's authority and returning the individual grievant to the vagaries of independent and unsystematic negotiation. Moreover, under such a rule, a significantly greater number of grievances would proceed to arbitration. This would greatly increase the cost of the grievance machinery and could so overburden the arbitration process as to prevent it from functioning successfully.[52]

While these arguments are perhaps pursuasive when applied in the context of the traditional union-employer relationship, they are not as compelling when applied to a union-employer grievance structure which has prevented blacks from having their grievances processed fairly. First, it should be noted that the individual black worker would not have the unlimited right to seek arbitration; only those grievances approved by the black members of the local union's grievance committee and subsequently endorsed by the black membership would go to arbitration. Many grievances may be settled through negotiation between the black grievance committeemen and the shop foremen at the first step of the grievance process. Furthermore, since black workers would bear the cost of arbitrating cases rejected by the local union's grievance committee, there need be little concern that affording black grievants the right to go to arbitration would bankrupt the local union or employer by flooding the arbitration process with a host of frivolous grievances. The limited resources of black members would act to screen out all but the most meritorious charges upon which the local union had failed to act. Indeed, the most powerful argument against such a proposal is that the local will purposely defer action on black grievances and thereby impose on black grievance committeemen and black members the responsibility to pursue their own grievances.

There is the contention that such a proposal conflicts with the statutory principle of Taft-Hartley, which provides that the local union is the exclusive bargaining representative of all employees in the unit with respect to negotiations over contract issues and grievances. Thus the ability of black members to compel arbitration despite a contrary recommendation of the local union's grievance committee negates the exclusive bargaining status of the local union. Perhaps this is true. Yet the validity of the exclusive representative concept rests on the notion that the union protects the interests of all unit employees. Where, however, there is the danger that a union which has repeatedly ignored the interests of a group of workers will continue its policy of neglect, a modification of the union's authority is appropriate.[53]

The Commission has not sought in any of the grievance or union discrimination cases special representation for minority workers on the local's grievance committee. Nevertheless, the Commission's remedial design is structurally sound, providing extensive relief to the individual discriminatee. The Commission attempts to compensate the discriminatee by both restoring him to his rightful job and by reimbursing him for his monetary losses. Concerning the local union's remedial obligation, the Commission in routine cases has secured a declaration of its intent to represent fairly all workers. In the more serious cases, the Commission has imposed a reporting requirement. Given the remedial framework of Title VII, and the non-class-related aspects of these cases, it is not likely that either the Commission or even the courts could have achieved much more.

4

Efficacy of the Conciliation Process

Having presented the various types of discriminatory union practices and the remedial policies fashioned by the Commission, we can now examine the central question of this study: how effectively has the Commission remedied union discrimination? Have the Commission's conciliation efforts proven successful, or has the entire relief process been a chimerical exercise?

One primary standard will be used to evaluate the effectiveness of the Commission's conciliation efforts: Has it executed the basic remedial measures for the various types of union discrimination? If these have been implemented, the Commission would achieve its two principal objectives: (1) elimination of the discriminatory situation underlying the complaint, and (2) extension of relief to charging parties and affected class members. Consequently, the degree to which the Commission has been able to secure agreements implementing its remedies provides a critical basis for evaluating the efficacy of the conciliation process. In addition, follow-up studies have been utilized to gauge the degree of local unions' compliance with a settlement agreement and the impact of the respondents' settlement position on the employment status of minority workers. We will begin with an analysis of the Commission's settlement record in twelve building-craft union cases.[1]

Remedying Exclusionary Union Practices

Remedial Efforts in Union Membership Cases

In eight cases craft unions were found to have excluded black workers from admission. Table 4-1 lists the total number of black and white union members in each of these locals at the time of the EEOC's investigation and for the time period following the conciliation effort.

In seven of the eight cases, agreements were not executed, and in these cases union rejection of the EEOC's settlement proposals generally meant continued exclusion of blacks. Thus in the first five cases cited, the local unions refused to implement any remedial measures, taking the position that no discrimination had occurred. Data on the racial composition of the membership of these local unions for the period following the conciliation effort showed the continued absence of blacks from membership. The continued exclusion of blacks is

59

Table 4-1
Black Membership in Selected Building-Craft Unions

Case No.	At Time of Investigation		3-12 Months Following Termination of Conciliation Effort	
	Union Memb.	Black Memb.	Union Memb.	Black Memb.
1	224	0	230	0
2	551	0	517	0
3	618	0	682	0
4	773	3	780	7
5	6000	1%[a]	6375	23
6	72	0	81	4
7	300	0	345	35
8	329	0	340	3

[a]The local union failed to maintain membership records by race, contending that state laws prevented any record-keeping whereby blacks and whites would be counted separately. The Commission found that no such state law existed. The figures for this union on black and total union membership are based upon a rough estimate by the local's business agent.

Source: EEOC Regional Investigation Reports and EEO-3 Union Membership Reports, Interviews with Charging Parties.

highlighted when we note that the conciliation effort typically occurred over eighteen months after the initial investigation had been made. In none of these cases were the charging parties admitted into membership.

In two cases where agreements were not obtained (cases 6 & 7), some limited progress was achieved. In both, charging parties were admitted into the union following the settlement effort. In the sixth case, however, the local refused to validate its admissions test which had had a disparate effect on minorities and was unwilling to contact minority organizations to encourage minority entrance.

The seventh case was unique and somewhat of an anomaly. Here, conciliation was attempted even before a cause decision had been rendered. Following the field investigation, the conciliator met with the union officials and verbal agreement was reached to have the local union process fairly the applications of black workers. Two of the four charging parties were immediately admitted, and two others were promised admission once they passed the journeymen's examination. Within a twelve-month period following conciliation, additional black workers were admitted, raising the minority component to 35 out of a total membership of 345.

In the single agreement case (case no. 8), the Commission initially succeeded in achieving two of its three remedial objectives. The local union agreed to admit the three charging parties and to establish contact with minority organizations. However, the Commission failed to eliminate significant institutional procedures which promoted the exclusion of blacks. A non-job-related admissions test was left intact. Additionally, the union failed to abide by the agreement's requirement to file with the Commission reports on its efforts to recruit minority journeymen. A year following the execution of the agreement there were still only three blacks in the local out of a total membership of 340.

Remedial Efforts in Apprenticeship Cases

There were eight cases in which blacks had been excluded from apprenticeship-training programs.

In conciliation, the Commission's remedial objectives paralleled its remedies in admission cases: (1) elimination of barriers, (2) relief to charging parties, (3) affirmative union action. No success was achieved in obtaining these results. In all eight cases the local unions rejected the Commission's settlement efforts and refused to make any real concessions. For example, they defended their use of oral interviews and nonvalidated tests as legitimate admission criterion and made no effort to eliminate preferences afforded relatives of union members or to promote minority admission. The continued exclusion of blacks from these unions' apprenticeship programs is revealed in Table 4-2.

In seven of the eight cases for which postconciliation data is available, it is evident that the blacks were present in only token numbers over a year after the EEOC had determined that these unions' apprenticeship practices were discriminatory. In the one case (no. 6) where some improvement is noted, the

Table 4-2
Black Apprentices in Selected Building-Craft Unions

	At Time of Investigation		3-12 Months Following Termination of Conciliation Effort	
Case No.	Total No. of Apprentices	Black Apprentices	Total No. of Apprentices	Black Apprentices
1[a]	26 14	1 0	34 13	2 0
	23	0	38	1
2	100	0	139	2
3	64	0	64	0
4	111	2	121	2
5	96	0	124	2
6	NA[c]	1	240	18
7	NA[c]	1%[b]	NA[c]	NA[c]
8	94	0	97	0

[a]In this one case, the EEOC processed complaints against three craft unions.

[b]Estimate of local union.

[c]Data on this union was unavailable.

Source: EEOC Regional Investigation Reports and EEO-2 employer-union apprenticeship Reports; Bureau of Apprenticeship and Training Apprenticeship Reports.

local union began to admit blacks in significant numbers only after the Justice Department had instituted a Title VII suit against it.

Remedial Efforts in Hiring Hall Cases

In five cases, unions were found to have excluded blacks from referral. In these, the locals either refused to process the referral applications of black workers, failed to inform them of the proper referral procedures, or maintained criteria for referral by which preference was given to union members. The Commission failed to execute agreements in all five cases. Table 4-3 reveals that following the conciliation effort, black workers were still not being referred.

Table 4-3
Referral of Blacks by Unions Operating Discriminatory Hiring Halls

Case No.	At Time of Charge		3-12 Months Following Termination of Conciliation Effort	
	Total Ref.[a]	Black Ref.[a]	Total Ref.[a]	Black Ref.[a]
1	_[b]	1%[c]	542	3
2	203	2	109	5
3	134	0	102	0
4	287	1	395	5
5	_[b]	0	1200	0

[a]Referral figures reflect the numbers referred within a given monthly period.
[b]Data not available.
[c]Estimate of EEOC investigator.
Source: EEOC Regional Investigation Reports and EEO-3 Referral Reports.

Some Concluding Observations

Overall twelve cases were examined in which building-craft unions discriminated against blacks by refusing them admission into membership, by excluding them from apprenticeship training programs, and by denying them equal referral opportunities. It is obvious that the Commission's remedial efforts met with little success. In the apprenticeship and referral cases, the local unions refused in all cases to execute agreements whereby they would agree to terminate the use of procedures which restricted minority entrance. These practices included preference to relatives of union members, utilization of nonvalidated tests, sponsorship requirements, and dissemination of information in apprenticeship and referral openings to union members alone. The charging parties in the apprenticeship and referral cases received no relief; they failed to obtain apprenticeship admission or referral. Similarly, little success was achieved in the union membership cases. Settlement agreements were executed in only one of eight membership cases, and that agreement, while affording relief to the charging parties, failed to eliminate the discriminatory union practices underlying the complaint. Relief to charging parties was also generated in two nonagreement admission cases. Overall the Commission's intervention failed to bring about any change in the local union's discriminatory practices in nine of the twelve cases.

Other Craft Union Cases

At times black workers have been denied admission into the printing crafts. In two cases black workers in a printing plant were barred from apprenticeship positions because they were denied admission into the craft union exercising control over the positions. What were the results of the Commission's conciliation efforts? In both, it was unable to execute an agreement.

In the first case, however, the local union refused to conciliate because the charge of discrimination had been rendered moot. Subsequent to the filing of a charge, it had admitted the complainant to membership. Additionally, it amended its bylaws which previously had allowed a negative vote of five members to result in the rejection of the applicant to provide for the admission or rejection of applicants on the basis of a majority vote. Following this modification, the local increased its minority membership from zero to six.

In the second case, the union had also denied black workers admission into membership and thereby prevented them from occupying positions as apprentice press helpers. There were twenty-one charging parties, nineteen of whom worked as packers and were members of a bindery union. In the same department where they worked, there was an all-white unit of twelve packers who worked with the pressmen and who were in line to become apprentice press helpers. The white packers were members of the craft union controlling all skilled positions in the press room. Efforts by the black packers to gain access to the more skilled positions were systematically blocked.[2]

The Commission's conciliation efforts did not materially alter the discriminatory situation. The local craft union made some concessions, but these in reality operated to conceal the continuation of the local's discriminatory policy. For example, the local and the company admitted twelve black packers into the white packers unit. At the same time, they negotiated an agreement which established job seniority within the packers unit as a prerequisite for promotion to apprentice positions. Thus all black packers were placed below white packers for purposes of promotion. Additionally, black packers were afforded only provisional membership status. Until they had been promoted to the position of apprentice press helpers, they could not vote. At the same time, black packers who were incorporated into the white packers unit received pay increases to equal the general salary level of the white packers. One year following the EEOC's termination of its conciliation efforts, black packers had failed to gain entry to apprenticeship positions.

Remedial Effectiveness in Seniority Cases

As noted in chapter 2, one type of discriminatory seniority arrangement involved a system of departmental or group seniority which restricted black workers to the department into which they were originally hired. Transfer to jobs in exclusively white departments was in practice precluded by contractual provisions which either prohibited transfer between departments or allowed it at the expense of the black workers' accrued seniority. Thus a black who moved into a new department had his seniority commence from the date of transfer. This loss of seniority tended to deter the interdepartmental movement of blacks, since the worker who transferred — as the junior man in the department — would be most vulnerable to layoff and least eligible for promotion.

The Commission's standard remedy in this type of case consisted of four measures: (1) the utilization of plant-wide seniority to govern the eligibility of incumbent black workers for purposes of transfer, promotion, and layoffs; (2) bump-back rights for black workers to their original departments; (3) red-circling of black workers' wage rates; (4) establishment of employee training programs. The last provision would be sought where black workers were historically locked into inferior job classifications and deprived of the opportunity to participate in in-plant training programs. As a result, they could not qualify for promotion absent some on-the-job training in the new position.

The evaluation of the efficacy of the Commission's settlement efforts will utilize as its point of departure the standard seniority remedies. Thus, as a first step, all conciliation agreements will be evaluated to determine whether or not these remedies were incorporated into the agreement.

Remedial Efficacy in Discriminatory Departmental Seniority Cases

There were only five cases in which conciliation agreements were executed where the issue concerned a discriminatory departmental seniority system. Six cases were unsuccessfully terminated. Table 4-4 outlines the basic remedial provisions incorporated in the agreements obtained. These will be compared with the Commission's remedial objectives previously discussed.

As the table indicates, all five conciliation agreements failed to allow black workers to compete for vacancies on the basis of their plant-wide seniority. Additionally, the red-circling of a black worker's wages to assure that he would not suffer a reduction in earnings upon transferring was not implemented. The

Table 4-4
Conciliation Agreements in Department Seniority Cases

Case No. and Type of Plant		Relief to Class
AT 6-4-26 Mineral Processing	(1)	Instruct in writing all supervisory personnel to treat all employees without discrimination.
	(2)	Desegregation of washrooms and lockers.
	(3)	Modification of apprenticeship tests.
6-4-2641 Foundry	(1)	Desegregation of shower and locker facilities.
	(2)	Modification of apprenticeship qualifications.
	(3)	Maintenance of departmental seniority; employee transferring to new department retains seniority in old department for purposes of layoff until time he has served in a new unit equals time he has served in the old department.
	(4)	Employer will immediately integrate machine shop, and attempt to integrate all other departments through future transfers and hires.
AT 6-11-861 Textile	(1)	Update employees' personnel records to determine the nature of workers' job interests and their job qualifications for promotions.
	(2)	Afford advice and guidance to those meriting further advancement.
	(3)	Agree not to hire any new workers until and unless first consideration in filling vacancies has been given to present employees.
	(4)	Advise black workers of their rights to seek promotion and transfers.
	(5)	Integrate restrooms.
	(6)	Adoption of EEOC guidelines in testing.
	(7)	Workers who transfer to new jobs will be given same instruction and training that would be afforded new hires.
6-4-3988 Bakery Plant	(1)	Desegregation of showers, lockers, and eating facilities.
	(2)	Maintenance of departmental seniority, but employee who transfers to new department retains his seniority in former department for purposes of layoff.
6-1-46 Railroad Terminal	(1)	Top-bottom seniority lists of black and white work groups.
	(2)	Creation during Christmas season of three temporary positions in white seniority district to be filled by black workers.

absence of the latter provision cannot be defended on the grounds that a reduction in wages was not probable; in three of the five cases, the highest hourly wage rate in the primarily black departments was higher than the initial wage rate in the all-white departments. Because of the black worker's inability to compete for jobs on the basis of his plant-wide seniority the vacancy he would most likely fill would be the entry-level position in the white department. Consequently, the lack of a red-circling provision would operate to restrict the interplant movement of minorities.[3] Regarding bump-back rights, employers and the unions in two situations agreed to allow workers who switched departments to retain their seniority in the original department for layoff purposes. Finally, in only one case did the agreement provide for the training of workers who transferred. Here (AT6-11-861), the employer indicated that he would afford transferring workers the same on-the-job training as was given new hires.

When we contrast the Commission's remedial objectives in seniority cases with the remedial measures implemented in these agreements, we are compelled to conclude that less than adequate relief was provided the black class. This is not to suggest that the Commission's efforts were in vain. Some progress was made in the movement of black workers out of dead-end departments and in the integration of formerly all-white units. Yet it is clear that the relief afforded black workers in dead-end departments was extremely limited.

Why then did the Commission execute these agreements? The answer is partly revealed by the previous table which shows that the Commission was not only dealing with problems of seniority, but also with other forms of discrimination. For example, in four of the five cases, the agreements provided for the desegregation of washroom, locker, and cafeteria facilities. Typically, the agreement provided that lockers be assigned on an alphabetical basis, and physical barriers between black and white washrooms be removed. At the same time, the employer would instruct all employees that facilities were open to the use of all workers. Interviews with the charging parties revealed that the facilities had been integrated.

In two cases, employers agreed to modify apprenticeship qualifications that had discriminated against blacks. One eliminated the reading comprehension part of the apprenticeship examination that the Commission had found objectionable.[4] Another agreed to eliminate the age restriction imposed upon workers seeking apprenticeship positions. This was necessary since some blacks who had been restricted to the helper job category and who still wanted to train as apprentices were no longer of apprenticeship age. A third employer agreed not to utilize any tests unless they were validated in accordance with the Commission's guidelines. Thus concessions were made by respondents that went beyond the seniority issue and which provided a basis for the execution of an agreement.

The conciliation agreements contained some remedial measures that would alleviate the seniority problem: bump-back rights in two cases and promises in three others, to integrate the all-white units (6-4-2641, 6-1-46, AT 6-11-861). This statement of employer intentions to integrate can be viewed in two lights: in one as a very limited response and in another as a broad concession. Judged against the needs of the black class, the employers' promises are wanting; their agreement to consider for promotion to current vacancies incumbent employees before hiring from the outside in no way enhances the promotability of black workers who eschew transfer because of the costs involved — loss of seniority and possible wage reduction. At the same time, success in obtaining agreement to transfer black workers and promote from within was no small feat. In effect, the employer was indicating his intention of abandoning a policy whereby blacks were bypassed from promotion and restricted to dead-end departments.[5] It is this accomplishment which provides the basis for the Commission's acceptance of these agreements, notwithstanding the relatively weak remedial provisions concerning the seniority problem.[6]

Given the execution of these agreements, what progress did black workers make in transferring into formerly all-white departments.[7] Table 4-5 examines the increase in the number of black workers employed in the formerly all-white units following the execution of the agreement. When examining table 4-5 one should remember that changes in black employment in the formerly all-white units could have been generated by two sources: (1) interdepartmental transfers, and (2) employer recruitment and hiring. For the purpoes of analyzing the relief afforded black workers locked in dead-end departments, we are primarily interested in the degree to which the former generated the increase.

In four of the five cases, black workers were admitted to formerly white-only departments. But this was achieved largely by the hiring of blacks to these departments and was not a result of their movement from black departments. Only in the mineral plants case was the increase of black workers in all-white departments generally due to the transfer of incumbent black workers. Of the eleven blacks added to the milling and mining departments, eight had moved out of largely black departments. By contrast, only three of the nine additional blacks in "white" jobs in the iron foundry had transferred from within; similarly the presence of an additional 118 blacks in white job classifications in the textile plant over a year after the conciliation effort resulted entirely from employer hiring and placement.

Interviews with black workers in the iron foundry and textile cases help explain why few blacks moved out of dead-end departments. Several factors were involved. Some workers, especially those near retirement, were content to remain in their original jobs and were not interested in undertaking new responsibilities. Others would transfer but felt they lacked the aptitude to learn a new skill. For these workers, the prospect of the difficulties they might encounter in acquiring a new skill inhibited their willingness to transfer. There were some who did desire to transfer and who were confident of their ability to handle the job. Yet even they failed to transfer. Here, the basic element retarding their movement was the existing seniority arrangement whereby transfer meant a loss of seniority and a possible wage loss.[8] In general, workers with at least five-to-ten years were reluctant to switch.

In the iron foundry case it would seem that the relatively stable employment and, in some instances, the actual employment decline in the "generally white" departments would limit the movement of black workers out of the all-black departments. To some extent this is true. However, the fact that net employment does not change, or even decreases, does not mean that opportunities for advancement and transfer do not occur. Normal turnover can create job openings and this in fact did occur. An examination of a current printout of this company's work force shows the presence among production employees of twenty-one white and only two black workers who had been hired following execution of the agreement. At the same time, only one black moved out of an all-black department to become an apprentice machinist in the white machine department. Yet in this same department, five white employees had been hired from the outside to fill vacancies in the apprentice and semiskilled helper categories. Similarly, in the core room, pattern, and maintenance departments, thirteen new employees were hired – twelve of whom were white – to fill existing vacancies. Certainly, not all of these vacancies could have been filled by incumbent blacks, but it is reasonable to assume that had the Commission's policy of transfers been promoted and pursued, some could have moved out of the lower-paying departments.

Two cases exemplify agreements which ironically benefited white more than black. In both, incumbent white employees in danger of losing their jobs were able to transfer to formerly black-only jobs. In the bakery plant case, two white workers who were then employed in the formerly all-black sanitation department had transferred out of the bread-production department, where the work was more arduous. Before the Commission's intervention, transfer between departments was actually prohibited. The agreement did, however, benefit black workers as well. Two of the five black sanitation department workers transferred to better-paying jobs in other units. One became an engineer helper, the second highest paying job in the plant; the other, the chief stock clerk. Significantly, these two employees indicated that they would not have transferred if they had not been allowed the right to bump back to their original departments.

The final case involved a railroad terminal operator and a railroad craft which represented clerical, office workers, and porters. The Commission's agreement top-bottomed the dual seniority rosters. Hence, all black workers assumed seniority rights in the clerical and office units from the date of the agreement; the converse was true for white employees. In effect, the agreement placed blacks below all whites for purposes of promotion and layoff in competing for clerical and office vacancies.

Given the declining employment in the railroad industry, top-bottoming proved to be an illusory remedy. As Table 4-5 indicates, the clerical and office unit declined to an all-white contingent of five workers. Ironically, the agreement proved to be of more help to the white rather than to the black workers. Several whites in the clerical group took advantage of the seniority rights they received in the black seniority group and, when faced with the loss of their clerical positions, transferred to formerly black jobs.

On a short-term basis, the Commission's agreement did provide some relief to the charging party and two other black workers. It provided that during the Christmas season, the employer would fill temporary clerical slots with three black workers from the porter unit. This provision was limited, however, to one

Table 4-5
Integration of All-White Work Units in Successful Department Seniority Cases[a]

AT 6-4-26 — Minerals Plant

Traditionally Black Departments

	Processing Plants			Milling
At time of charge:	66(53)	101(74)	25(15)	25(15)
15 mos. after conciliation:	102(71)	132(99)	66(38)	30(15)

Traditionally White Departments

	Prospecting	Milling & Mining	Milling & Mining	Electrical & Plumbing
At time of charge:	8(0)	28(1)	16(2)	11(0)
15 mos. after conciliation:	9(0)	35(3)	42(11)	14(0)

6-4-2641 — Iron Foundry

Traditionally Black Departments

	Cleaning	Shipping	Foundry	Milling
At time of charge:	59(59)	8(8)	50(50)	12(12)
15 mos. after conciliation:	43(41)	6(6)	51(50)	13(13)

Traditionally White Departments

	Core	Pattern	Maintenance	Machine	Molding
At time of charge:	15(5)	9(1)	10(2)	50(5)	58(23)
15 mos. after conciliation:	12(5)	9(1)	12(3)	39(7)	36(18)

6-11-861 — Textile

Traditionally Black Departments

	Shipping	Grey Bales	Laundry	Yard	Stockroom
At time of charge:	81(62)	14(13)	4(4)	39(39)	13(11)
15 mos. after conciliation:	97(79)	14(13)	7(7)	32(30)	12(11)

Traditionally White Departments

	Mechanical	Inspection	Lab	Production	Printing	Packing
At time of charge:	216(13)	104(2)	30(0)	1,174(69)	453(27)	550(7)
15 mos. after conciliation:	203(14)	122(14)	27(1)	1,089(129)	388(59)	497(19)

6-4-3988 — Bakery

Traditionally Black Departments

	Sanitation
At time of charge:[b]	All black
15 mos. after conciliation:	5(3)

Traditionally White Departments

	Bread Production	Bread Finishing	Maintenance	Stockroom
At time of charge:[b]	All white	All white	All white	All white
15 mos. after conciliation:	29(1)	12(2)	2(1)	3(2)

6-1-46 — Railroad Terminal

Traditionally Black Departments

	Laborer and Porter Unit
At time of charge:	87(87)
15 mos. after conciliation:	93(86)

Traditionally White Departments

	Office and Clerical Unit
At time of charge:	33(0)
15 mos. after conciliation:	5(0)

Key: Numbers in columns outside of parentheses refer to total employment in a department. Numbers within the parentheses refer to the departments' black component.

[a]Data is based on departmental breakdown of work force supplied by respondents to author.

[b]The original investigations failed to give a numerical breakdown of the company's departments other than to indicate that they were either exclusively white or black.

Christmas season; as clerical positions dwindled, the opportunity for black workers to be promoted to such jobs was effectively nullified.

To summarize, in the five cases where the Commission executed agreements, the scope of relief that was implemented to eliminate the effects of a discriminatory departmental seniority system was limited. This is certainly not to suggest that no progress was made. The reverse is true. In four of the five cases, some traditionally white-only departments were integrated. Additionally, conciliation efforts generally led to the integration of work facilities and the modification or removal of such employment barriers as nonvalidated tests and apprenticeship qualifications. Yet most of the increase in the number of blacks in these departments was due to employer recruitment of new workers. For incumbent black workers who had been assigned to inferior jobs in largely all-black departments, only limited progress was achieved. The failure to allow such workers to carry over their seniority and hourly rates (when necessary) operated to restrict their movement into other departments. This was most sharply illustrated in the third case analyzed where, of 129 black workers who constituted five nearly all-black departments, not one had transferred.

Departmental Seniority Cases – Unsuccessful Conciliation Efforts

In the six cases in which departmental or group seniority systems operated, the employers refused to take any remedial actions consistent with EEOC guidelines. As a result, little progress was made in integrating traditionally white-only work units. The situation is amplified in Table 4-6.

In all six cases, the companies and unions refused to allow for the transfer of black workers without loss of their accrued seniority. Some companies continued even more stringent restrictions against blacks. Both trucking companies reserved the right to fill vacancies in all departments by hiring, rather than giving consideration to incumbent blacks in other departments.

The effect of these policies is evident. In the trucking cases there was only a token increase in the number of blacks in the formerly all-white city driver and over-the-road units. Furthermore, the negligible increase was not produced by the transfer of incumbent blacks, but resulted from employer recruitment of new workers. In hiring outside workers, both truckers bypassed considerable numbers of blacks employed in maintenance departments who possessed valid ICC driving licenses and who previously had requested transfers.

In the two railroad terminal cases, black workers remained locked in their porter and laborer classifications. There the reduction in the number of white-unit jobs, combined with the failure to allow blacks the right to compete for vacancies on the basis of their company seniority, stifled entry into clerical and office jobs.

Table 4-6

Integration of All-White Work Units in No-Agreement Department Seniority Cases[a]

Case No. and Type of Firm	Departments from which Blacks Excluded at Time of Charge			Minority Employment in Departments 7-15 mos. after Conciliation Effort	
		W	B	W	B
AT7-4-371	Over the road unit	471	1	471	5
Trucker	City drivers unit	55	0	55	0
AT6-11-8683 Trucker	City drivers unit	25	0	26	1
AT7-1-49 Railroad terminal operations	Interdepartment clerk unit	–	–[b]	13	0
	Office unit	–	–	19	0
6-6-596 Railroad terminal operations	Interdepartment clerk unit	64	0[c]	131	2
	Office unit	121	0		
6-4-3638 Rubber manuf.	Stock Room	3	0	3	0
	Quality Control	12	0	12	0
	Mill Room	250-300	1	308	21[d]
6-7-374 Tobacco manuf.	Fabrication Division	1,719	235	1,582	228

[a]Data based on EEOC investigations and subsequent examination of Justice Department and OFCC records.

[b]The original Commission investigation did not contain a numerical breakdown by race of the employees working within these units, other than to indicate they were exclusively white. The statistics in the adjacent column are based on subsequent government investigations.

[c]These groups were later merged by the railroad and union.

[d]Changes occurred only after filing of court suit.

The last two cases involved industrial plants manufacturing rubber and tobacco products. In both, black workers had been restricted to the physically more burdensome and lowest-paying departments. Both cases culminated in court suits when the Commission was unable to secure agreements to any modification of the existing seniority arrangements. In the case of the rubber plant, the initiation of the court suit did generate changes in the plant's seniority system. Following the filing of the suit, the company and the union amended the collective-bargaining agreement to provide that when vacancies within a department were not filled by employees within the same department or division in which the vacancy occurred, employees with the most plant-wide seniority would be given preferential bidding rights. Under the modified seniority arrangement, approximately twenty black workers transferred into the generally all-white mill room.[9]

To summarize, eleven cases concerned the existence of departmental seniority arrangements which restricted the movement of black workers out of all-black departments. The Commission executed agreements in five of the eleven cases. The settlement rate of 45 percent would seem to suggest that its conciliation process achieved a modest share of success. Yet a close examination of the five agreement cases demonstrates that the Commission failed to execute agreements which incorporated the remedies it viewed as necessary in this type of case. Black workers were unable to compete for jobs on the basis of their plant seniority and had no guarantee that in transferring they would not sustain a wage loss. The only real progress achieved was the apparent modification of a policy wherein blacks were assigned into basically all-black departments. Thus, in several agreement cases, data secured from employers indicate that they had begun to hire blacks for placement into formerly white-only departments. In terms of the relief provided to incumbent blacks, however, the Commission's efforts were generally unsuccessful.

Efficacy of Conciliation Efforts in Cases Involving Segregated Progression Lines

In the second class of seniority cases black and white employees work in functionally related jobs but are placed in dual progression lines. As in the case of a departmental seniority system, the collective-bargaining agreement may either preclude transfer between lines or enable black workers to transfer only to the entry-level positions in the white progression line. The worker who transfers will not be able to carry over his seniority and in the new line will be most vulnerable to a layoff. In some plants blacks are classified as "laborers" and hence barred from further promotion, although some of them perform on progression line jobs or jobs functionally related to progression line activity. As a result of these restrictions, black workers are locked into laborer and service job categories.

In analyzing the efficacy of the Commission's conciliation efforts, those cases where agreements were executed will be examined separately from those which were terminated without agreements. The major standard for evaluating the Commission's remedial efforts will be the degree to which the Commission was able to implement its remedies in this type of case. These remedies include:

1. Merger of all functionally related progression lines
2. The utilization of plant-wide seniority to govern the eligibility of black workers to fill vacancies anywhere in the lines and to govern their status for layoff purposes
3. Establishment of training programs to afford black workers promoted to formerly white-only jobs with the opportunity to learn the skills necessary in the performance of the job

In seeking an agreement, first consideration was given to achieving a merger of progression lines. Without it, the employer could continue to fill vacancies in the white line of progression by hiring workers from the outside. Once merger was effected black workers would at least have priority in filling entry-level slots in the white line. Thus, while the latter two remedies were important in facilitating the movement of blacks into white job classifications, merger was the essential element without which relief was blocked. Consequently, the Commission's success or failure to achieve a merger constitutes a partial test of the efficacy of its conciliation efforts.

It is possible, however, that having merged the dual lines, the employer could continue to deny advancement to black workers simply by not promoting them. Thus it is necessary to ascertain the degree to which black workers actually moved into white job classifications following merger. This analysis has been achieved by examining printouts of a company's work force that identify employees by name, race, job classification, and department. A comparison of such printouts for the periods before and after the Commission's conciliation efforts will document the extent of the integration. Additionally, the origin of any changes in the number of black workers in the formerly white job classifications will be evaluated. As in our earlier discussion of departmental seniority cases, increases can be generated from two sources: (1) through the upward movement of incumbent blacks; (2) from employer recruitment. Where integration was due entirely to the latter, it is obvious that merger has failed. In such a case, the employer has bypassed incumbent black workers and has perpetuated a dual progression line. In effect, a merger which does not generate movement of incumbent black workers is not a remedy, but rather a subterfuge for continued discrimination.

Settlement Cases

There were only three cases involving the existence of segregated lines of progression where conciliation agreements were executed. Five cases were unsuccessfully closed. Table 4-7 outlines the basic remedial provisions that were incorporated in the agreements.

Before examining the adequacy of the settlement agreements in terms of the seniority question, it should be noted that the cases involved other issues as well. In two of the three cases, the movement of black workers into white lines of progression was encumbered by the company requirement that workers desiring transfer first had to pass entrance examinations. These tests consisted of mathematical and verbal aptitude tests that had not been validated and which were found to have had a disproportionately adverse effect on black workers. Conciliation efforts in the case involving a steel company led to agreement that the company would not "routinely" administer such tests as a requirement to

Table 4-7
Conciliation Agreements in Progression Line Seniority Cases

Case No. and Type of Plant		Remedial Provisions
5-9-1178 Paper Plant	(1)	Integration of facilities.
	(2)	Elimination of testing as a requirement for entry into a line of progression. No postemployment testing program shall be reestablished without prior notification to the Commission.
	(3)	Merger of segregated progression lines.
6-6-5310 Iron Foundry	(1)	Merger of segregated locals.
	(2)	Consolidation of the separate seniority rosters of the two local unions.
	(3)	Employees advance to higher-paying jobs "when vacancies occur in their department in order of their seniority."
6-8-6955 Steel Mill	(1)	Integration of facilities.
	(2)	Elimination of routine testing of employees who bid for a vacancy in another line of promotion or who bid for transfer to other departments.
	(3)	The question of whether the charging party and others, by transferring from one department to another or from one line of promotion and demotion to another, shall, because of such transfer, forfeit occupational or other seniority held at the time of such transfer is not dealt herein and this agreement does not constitute a waiver of any right of the charging party (to sue).
	(4)	Back pay to workers denied promotion because of failure to pass ability tests.

transfer.[10] Following the issuance of a cause decision the paper company and union amended their contract to eliminate tests as a prerequisite for transfer. Additionally, the company agreed to review its policy of utilizing tests when recruiting for new employees.

Movement of black workers into white job classifications in the iron foundry case was blocked by the existence of segregated locals, each claiming exclusive jurisdiction over the jobs its members held. Here, the conciliation agreement eliminated the immediate barrier by merging the locals. A final issue concerned the elimination of segregated washroom, cafeteria, and restroom facilities. Thus, in executing a settlement agreement, the conciliators were coping with a variety of discriminatory practices. To the extent that some progress was made in each problem area, the conciliator would be more inclined to accept less that the complete remedy on any one single issue. This in part explains the narrow scope of the remedies that were incorporated in the agreements to resolve the seniority problem.

In regards to the seniority issue the agreements did not incorporate the standard remedial objectives. In no cases did the employer agree to institute training programs or to allow black workers who moved into the white line of progression to carry with them the occupational seniority they had accrued in the black line. At the same time, the agreements explicitly or by implication provided for the merger of the black and white progression lines. The agreement concerning the paper plant specifically indicated that the company and union had merged racially segregated progression lines. This action involved the relegation of black jobs, nearly all of which were in the laborer category, to the bottom of the white progression line.

The maintenance of dual progression lines in the iron foundry case grew out of the existence of segregated locals, each claiming jurisdiction over groups of jobs within the same department. The agreement thus required the merger of the locals and a combination of the unions' seniority rosters. The agreement is misleading when it touches on the seniority question, for it merely reiterated the language of the contract which provided that workers shall have the right to compete for jobs "in order of their seniority." Seniority is not further defined. However, in actual practice, the company and the union have recognized job seniority as controlling one's right to promotion and layoff within each line. Consequently, black workers have been permanently ranked below white workers.

The steel mill case basically concerned one large department where black and whites in functionally related processing positions were in separate lines. Here, too, the agreement was deficient. It did not require the merger of the segregated lines of progression. Nor did it prevent black workers' forfeiture of seniority upon transferring. Formally, the company only agreed to allow blacks to occupy jobs in the white progression line without having to pass a qualifying examination. In practice, these weaknesses were partially rectified by company and union's willingness to merge the segregated progression lines on a de facto basis. In implementing the agreement, the company and union agreed to give priority to incumbent blacks over new hires when filling vacancies in the white line. Moreover, to protect blacks against the risk of layoff, black workers who transferred were afforded bump-back rights to the black line. Consequently, eventual integration of the segregated lines was made possible by the potential movement of blacks into entry level slots in the white line of progression.

In summary, the agreements accomplished the major objective of merging the dual progression lines or segregated seniority rosters. Merger allowed black workers to begin occupying entry-level positions as vacancies developed. The agreements did contain serious shortcomings. For purposes of promotion and layoff either progression or job seniority was controlling. Consequently, blacks were initially restricted to filling entry-level slots and were vulnerable to layoff. The absence of any employer commitment to establish training programs for incumbent black workers meant that they would not be compensated for the experience and training previously denied them. Their capacity to move up the line was thus limited to a job-by-job progression. Thus, under the terms of the settlement agreements, the black worker with the greatest plant-wide seniority could be placed below the most junior white employee in the progression line.

Given these agreements, what progress did black workers make in moving into the job classifications of the formerly white-only progression lines? Table 4-8 indicates the degree of racial integration in the once exclusively white job categories.

As the table indicates, in each case black workers have moved into job classification that were once restricted only to whites. The progress, however, has been limited. In only one of the three cases were more than 10 percent of the formerly white-only jobs occupied by black workers. This occurred in the paper plant where eleven blacks had entered white job classifications. Of the eleven, eight were incumbents. In the iron foundry case, thirteen black workers had moved into white jobs, while in the steel plant, only four incumbent black workers had entered the formerly all-white divisions.

One factor limiting black gains was the reduction in the total number of jobs available in these plants in the period following execution of the agreements. In two of the three cases, total employment in the white job classifications also decreased. This is shown in Table 4-9.

As a result, there were fewer jobs into which black workers could enter. It is not surprising that blacks made their greatest gains in the plant where employment in the white job classifications had increased.

In the iron foundry, continued employer violations were also responsible for the relative absence of blacks from the formerly white jobs. Here, the evidence suggests that despite a 20 percent decrease in the number of production workers which occurred over a two-year period, vacancies in the white progression line occurred following execution of the agreement. Instead of filling these slots with blacks who had just entered the white progression line, the company hired new white employees. For example, in the molders' department, five white employees were hired as helpers, although fifteen black workers already in the jobs below qualified to fill the vacancies.

In the Link Belt Department, the company and union continued to maintain separate progression lines; when several vacancies occurred, these were filled by outside recruitment of whites. These practices which resulted in the filing of additional charges obviated the benefits that a true merger would have generated.

Unsuccessful Conciliation Cases Involving Segregated Progression Lines

Five cases were unsuccessfully terminated. The nature of the violations and the employer-union positions in conciliation are summarized in Table 4-10.

The facts in these cases are strikingly similar. The Commission found black

Table 4-8

Integration of White-Only Job Classifications in Successful Progression Line Seniority Cases

Case No.	At Time of Charge			At Least 15 Mos. after Conciliation					
	Number of Blacks in Black Line or in No-line of Progression	Number of White Job Classifications	Number of Employees	Number of Blacks in Formerly Black Jobs	Number of Job Classifications Remaining White	Number of Employees	Number of Integrated Job Classifications	Number of Job Classifications Blacks	Number of Whites
5-9-1178									
Paper Plant, Container Div.[a]: Total	62	26	141	50	17	64	9	11	72
Corrugator Dept.	16	4	14	23	2	7	2	3	11
Printing	0	9	66	0	7	60	2	2	7
Finishing	7	8	37	7	5	9	3	3	24
Shipping	6	1	9	12	0	—	1	2	7
Maintenance	0	4	14	0	3	3	1	1	10
Quality Control	0	1	6	0	1	6	—	—	—
Miscellaneous[b]	7	—	7	2	—	—	1	2	7
General[c]	26	—	5	5	—	—	1	5	1
6-6-5310									
Iron Foundry[d]									
Total for 4 depts.[e]	229	—	286[f]	168	—	—	246[g]	13	233
Centrifugal	67	—	110	80	—	—	98	7	91
Bench Molders	63	—	85	15	—	—	73	—	73
Link Belt	80	—	33	62	—	—	23	—	23
Core Room	19	—	53	8	—	—	52	6	46
6-8-6955									
Steel Hoop Mill Dept.	107	8	55	79	6	31	2	4	11

[a] All black employees in the Container division were not in any line of promotion and were considered in effect nonpromotable.

[b&c] The general and miscellaneous departments contained no-line of promotion, and consisted basically of unskilled blacks and a few white employees.

[d&e] Data on progression lines were available for only four departments. The printout failed to identify workers by each job classification, and classified groups of jobs as being under the jurisdiction of either the black or white local. Thus there are no figures for columns 2, 5, and 6.

[f&g] Figures in column 3 represent the number of employees in jobs under the exclusive control of the white local. Figures in column 7 indicate, for the period following merger of the locals and following conciliation, the number of workers in jobs formerly restricted to whites. Adjacent columns give a further breakdown by race.

Table 4-9
Total Employment in Firms by Race

	At Time of Charge			At Least Fifteen Months After Conciliation		
	Black	White	Total	Black Jobs	White Jobs	Total
Paper plant	62	141	203	50	147	197
Iron foundry	229	286	515	168	246	414
Steel division	107	55	162	79	46	125

workers to be generally restricted to laborer categories and hence cut off from the white progression lines. In the latter, the entry level was that of helper and would be filled by the employer's outside recruitment of white workers. In three of the five cases, blacks who wanted to transfer had to pass qualifying examinations.

Unvalidated tests formed a major barrier to the advancement of black workers. In some cases they were first introduced following the passage of the Civil Rights Act of 1964. This meant that white workers already in the line had not taken any tests to gain entry nor were they required to take any as a condition of remaining in the line.[11]

A final violation found in four of the five cases concerned the segregation of plant facilities. Black and white workers generally used separate locker, shower, toilet, and cafeteria facilities. The separation was de facto in that formal signs restricting races to particular areas were not present. While such signs had been removed, the segregation of facilities was no less rigid and absolute.

The Commission's conciliation efforts were unsuccessful in eliminating the institutional or structural barriers to the advancement of blacks in the plants. In three of the five cases where dual progression formally existed, the employers and unions refused to allow the consolidation of black jobs even to the bottom of the white lines. In rejecting merger, they upheld the policy of recruiting white workers to fill entry-level slots in the white progression line.

Integrally related to the maintenance of separate lines was the employers' refusal to eliminate all nonvalidated tests. By upholding their reliability, the employers justified the existence of separate progression lines by maintaining that minority workers who could not pass the examinations did not deserve to be considered part of the white line of progression. The response of the unions was that testing fell within management's domain and that they were not responsible for the companies' use of tests.

Transfer of Blacks into White Job Classifications

Given the respondents' general refusal to conciliate, one would expect that few incumbent black workers would be able to transfer into white job categories.

Table 4-10
Employer-Union Response in Unsuccessful Progression Line Cases

Case No. and Plant Type		Scope of Violation	Employer-Union Concessions
6-10-8187 Electric Utility	(1)	Restriction of Black workers to nonline of progression laborer positions	Rescheduling wage rates of Black workers
	(2)	Use of nonvalidated tests as requirement for entry into line of progression	None
	(3)	Segregated lockers and toilet facilities	Assignment of new lockers on alphabetical basis
6-5-4508 Paper Plant	(1)	Restriction of Blacks to laborer nonline of progression jobs	None
	(2)	Use of nonvalidated tests and high school diploma as requirements for entry into line of progression	None
	(3)	Segregated locker, toilet, and cafeteria facilities	Reassignment of all lockers on alphabetical basis
6-5-5170 Paper Plant	(1)	Dual progression lines	None[a]
	(2)	Tests as prerequisite to hire, promotion, and transfers	[b]
	(3)	Segregated facilities	[b]
6-11-8752 Paper Plant	(1)	Dual progression lines	Top-bottoming
	(2)	Segregated facilities	Integration of facilities
4-10-1773 Steel Plant		Dual progression lines	None

[a]Here, the company and union had previously merged dual progression lines. The effect of the merger was vitiated, however, by the company and union practice of allowing white workers who were on layoff on the call boards doing temporary work to exercise recall rights and leap in the white progression line ahead of senior black employees who had just entered the line.

[b]The case file lacked information on the positions of the respondents.

Whether or not any movement did occur is unfortunately indeterminable since in the five unsuccessful cases data were not available on the racial composition of the companies' progression lines. At the same time, we can ascertain through EEO-1 data whether or not various occupational classifications have been integrated following the Commission's intervention. Table 4-11 presents the EEO-1 data.

In all five cases only a marginal improvement occurred in the percentage of black workers in the craftsman category. In the power facility case (6-10-8187), blacks remained excluded from even operative classifications. From observing the data, one might attribute the limited movement of blacks into craftsman jobs to low plant turnover and overall reduction in jobs. Generally, however, this

Table 4-11
Movement of Minority Workers in No-Agreement Progression Line Cases

Case No. and Plant	EEO-1 Data	Laborer	% Black	Operatives	% Black	Craftsmen	% Black	Service Workers	% Black
6-10-8187 Electric Utility	At time of charge	70	100	338	1%	376	0%	14	100
	At least 6 months after concil. effort	67	100	319	1	358	0	14	100
6-5-4508 Paper Plant	At time of charge	211	52	227	20	321	1	22	64
	At least 6 months after concil. effort	133	55	212	22	332	3	24	63
6-5-5170 Paper Plant	At time of charge	622	31	538	14	557	1	43	42
	At least 6 months after concil. effort	299	38	722	20	582	2	31	42
6-11-8752 Paper Plant	At time of charge	61	78	260	42	285	3	21	57
	At least 6 months after concil. effort	64	69	228	51	306	3	17	47
5-10-1773 Steel Plant	At time of charge	2,088	83	3,387	44	4,470	9	263	45
	At least 6 months after concil. effort	1,319	87	3,446	52	4,316	9½	176	28

was not the case. For example, during an eighteen-month period following the termination of the conciliation effort involving the power facility, a total of 154 white employees were hired into the entry-level position of helper. Black workers in laborer positions were categorically bypassed.

In the final four cases, the data reveal a pattern of limited upward mobility by blacks combined with continued employer violations. The number of black workers in operative classifications increased by two, six, seven, and eight percentage points respectively in these cases. In two cases (6-5-5170, 6-5-4508) subsequent investigation revealed that during the year following the termination of the conciliation effort, entry-level positions in white progression lines were filled by white employees, although black workers in the jobs below should have been promoted. Similarly, in the final paper company case, the company and the union continued to maintain dual progression lines in the storeroom, paper mill, wood preparation, and shipping and finishing departments. Integration finally came only after the Justice Department instituted a suit against the company and union.

The final case involved charges against a large steel facility. In contrast to the previous cases where the Commission had found the plant's entire progression line structure to have been discriminatory, its findings here were restricted to several particular progression lines. The company and unions involved had merged nearly all existing racially segregated progression lines in the 1950s. That black workers were not isolated in laborer and service categories is revealed in the EEO-1 reports, which showed that even at the time of the charge, they constituted 44 percent of all operatives and 9 percent of all craftsmen.

While any overall pattern of discrimination was lacking, the Commission did find that in some instances black workers were barred from entry into certain progression lines, although their jobs were functionally related to craft positions occupied by whites. In one situation, blacks employed as millwright helpers were prevented from advancing to the position of millwright. In another, black laborers in the boiler area were severed from the progression line leading to boiler operator. Conciliation failed when the company and locals rejected the Commission's contention on the functional relationship of the jobs of the black and white workers, and as a result, refused to incorporate the blacks' positions into the white line of progression. Interviews with several of the charging parties in this case indicated that blacks are still barred from the appropriate line of progression and that the classifications of boiler room operator and millwright have remained white.

To summarize, the Commission's efforts to eliminate segregated lines of progression met with only limited success. Of eight cases, agreements were executed in only three instances. In one of the three cases, new charges were filed which revealed that following the execution of the agreement, the employer had bypassed black workers in the newly merged line and filled vacancies in the formerly white job classifications by recruiting white workers.

The conciliation agreements themselves were imperfect instruments of relief as they provided only for merger and did not allow blacks to advance on the basis of their plant-wide seniority. As a result, the movement of black workers was restricted to the filling of entry-level slots.

All five unsuccessful cases later became the subjects of Section 706 or 707 suits. Viewing these cases as a group, substantial improvement was not generated by the Commission's intervention. In four of the five cases, the segregated progression lines remained intact. Even following the closing of the conciliation effort, the evidence suggests that employers continued to hire white workers into white job classifications, while blacks remained locked into their laborer categories.

What progress they would have made had the Commission's remedies been implemented is difficult to determine. Yet it is clear that because the Commission's remedies were not adopted, the conditions which would have promoted transfer remained nonexistent. Thus, given the existence of dual progression lines, employers were free to by-pass black workers. Black workers who wished to transfer could do so only by sacrificing their accrued seniority in the black line with no guarantee of bump-back rights to their former line. In several cases, blacks faced the added burden of passing nonvalidated tests which placed a premium on numerical and verbal skills not shown to be related to the mechanical prerequisites of the jobs. Under these conditions, it is not surprising that EEO-1 reports which reflect two-to-three-year time intervals between the filing of the charge and the closing of the conciliation effort show no gain in the percentage of craftsmen positions occupied by blacks and only moderate gains in the percentages of operative jobs held by them.

*Efficacy of Commission Efforts in Cases Involving Dual Seniority
Arrangements for the Same Jobs*

In a third class of seniority cases, blacks performed the same work as whites but were placed in separate seniority rosters and thereby denied access to better-paying positions. In some situations, the employer and local union attempted to justify the existence of the dual seniority rosters by assigning black and white workers different job titles, although in practice both groups performed the same work. A common example is the assignment in the railroad industry of black workers to porter classifications and white employees to the brakeman category.

The Commission's remedial efforts focused upon two objectives. First, it required the "dovetailing" of separate rosters; for purposes of layoff, transfer, and promotion, black workers would then be able to compete for jobs on the basis of their total length of service with the company. This would eliminate the distinctions between white and black workers arising from the assignment of the latter to artifically inferior job classifications. Second, the Commission sought back pay where it was shown that as a result of the separate rosters the company had failed to promote or had laid off blacks with greater seniority than white employees.

There were five cases involving dual seniority rosters; in four a railroad craft was the respondent. Two cases embraced the porter-brakeman problem. Here, black porters consituted a separate seniority roster and, as a result, were barred from the brakeman progression line leading to the position of conductor. In both cases, conciliation efforts failed. The unions involved refused to consider even the top-bottoming of the seniority rosters, contending that porters and brakemen were functionally disparate groups and under the jurisdiction of separate internationals.

The refusal of the unions to admit proters as brakemen spelled disaster for the porters. This was because black porters were generally restricted to passenger service, the lines most affected by employment cutbacks. Unable to transfer to brakeman positions in the freight lines, porters were laid off. In one case, all thirty-four porters lost their jobs when the company terminated its passenger lines. The same outcome would have occurred in the second case if the black porters had not brought suit against the company and the local. The suit culminated in an out-of-court settlement that provided for the top-bottoming of the porter-brakeman rosters. Since the settlement, 60 of approximately 100 porters have transferred to the brakeman position.[12]

A similar case to the porter-brakemen situation occurred in an industrial setting. Black workers classified as "hookers" performed essentially the same work as whites classified as rigger helpers. Hookers were excluded from the line of progression leading to the position of rigger. In conciliation, the union and the company refused to reclassify hookers with the result that hookers are still precluded from advancing into rigger jobs.

In the final two cases, black and white workers performing the same work and possessing the same job titles were still placed in separate seniority rosters. The first case concerned black switchmen who were excluded from the white switchmen's progression line which advanced to the position of conductor. In the second case, black brakemen were restricted to one section of the railroad yard, while white brakemen had transfer rights throughout the entire yard, except for the section of the yard under the black local's jurisdiction. Restricted to one yard, their access to employment opportunities was severely curtailed. Reinforcing the separate seniority rosters were membership barriers. Black switchmen were forced to join a separate international union, while the black brakemen constituted an all-black local.

Both cases were unsuccessfully terminated, as the unions rejected the Commission's demands that the rosters be dovetailed. The unions and the company subsequently top-bottomed the switchmens' rosters six months following termination of the conciliation effort. All black switchmen regardless of their length of service with the company were for promotion purposes placed below white switchmen. As the result, no black switchmen has as yet been appointed a conductor, although many of them outrank white conductors in terms of overall company seniority.

In the brakeman case, the white local's offer to top-bottom the seniority roster was rejected by the black local, since it would have meant that blacks desiring transfer would have had to give up their accumulated seniority. Thus, although top-bottoming would have allowed them to transfer to other yards, it carried with it the price of severe risk of layoff.

In all five cases the Commission's efforts to eliminate the dual seniority roster were totally defeated. Its inability to provide relief is most pathetic when we note the consequences in an industry of declining employment — the layoff of blacks locked into nonskilled categories.

Other Seniority Cases

Three additional seniority cases illustrate a serious administrative problem within the Commission. Charges were filed against three railroad firms and one railroad brotherhood alleging that the seniority arrangements blocked the advancement of black workers into craft positions. The charging parties in these cases were members of the International Brotherhood of Firemen and Oilers (IBFO), a union which traditionally has accepted black workers on the basis of full equality.[13] Through confusion and misunderstanding by the complainants and later by the Commission representatives, charges were filed and processed against the IBFO as the local union responsible for the exclusion of blacks from craft positions. Charges were not filed against the operating craft unions which exercised jurisdiction over the jobs in question and which historically maintained policies of racial exclusion. This failure to cite the proper respondents rendered futile the conciliation effort. In the three cases, the IBFO was not in a position to eliminate the discriminatory situation, while the local unions which should have been charged refused to participate in the conciliation attempts on the grounds that there was no Commission finding that they were guilty of discrimination. In all three cases, the error concerning the respondent local unions was not discovered until after the decision had been written and conciliation attempted.

Efficacy of Remedial Efforts in Segregated Local Cases

Twenty of the seventy-five cases studied concerned the existence of segregated locals. As noted earlier, the Commission's remedy is a bona fide merger of the locals. Additionally, where there is a danger that following merger black workers would not be represente'd adequately, the Commission attempts to safeguard the rights of minority members by allocating official union positions to black members of the newly merged local.

Of the twenty segregated local cases, the Commission executed agreements in four cases. The terms under which these segregated locals were merged are amplified in Table 4-12.

Table 4-12
Scope of Merger Agreements

Case No.	Main Features
5-11-2870	Lodge 45 represents that it will accept for membership those members of Progress Lodge No. 2 who present authorized transfer cards.
6-7-6158	As stated by Respondent's International General V. P., Local Lodges 2013 and 10 agree to merge. The merger shall become effective not later than October 30, 1967.
5-7-162	(1) Assets of both locals combined after independent audit; (2) Election date scheduled; (3) For one-and-a-half year transition period, member of former black local appointed to executive position of financial-secretary; (4) All members arranged on single seniority list in accordance with their date of admission into either local.
6-6-5310	Union represents that locals have combined and held elections in which "members of each of the formerly separate locals have been elected as officers" of the new local.

In the first case, the settlement agreement was not satisfcatory because it did not remedy the per se violation of segregated locals. It only specified that black members be allowed to transfer to the all-white Lodge 45. Under this procedure, the black lodge would cease to exist only after all members had transferred. In practice, the segregated locals continue to exist. Some blacks opposed transfer because they feared a loss of representation; others wanted to retain their own chapter for prestige purposes. The charging party himself did not transfer because the white local following execution of the agreement had raised its dues for all carmen helpers, a job class in which most black workers were placed.

In the three other cases merger was achieved although the process of implementation was different in each. In the first, no special representation rights were demanded by the black local or thought necessary by the Commission. Consequently, a simple statement of merger was provided by the agreement.[14] In the final two cases, the procedures for achieving the mergers were formalized. Both settlements grew out of the concern of the minority that its interest had to be protected following merger. In one (5-7-162), two measures were particularly significant in terms of safeguarding the rights of black members. The first provided that a former black member would hold the position of financial-secretary for a one-and-a-half year period following merger. This official would have the authority to participate in collective bargaining and grievance negotiations. This provision was felt to be crucial by the black members since they were merging with a white local ten times the size of the black local. Second, the seniority rights of each member were calculated in terms of the date each member had joined his former local. The dovetailing of membership seniority was essential since length of union membership determined a worker's priority in receiving job assignments. Following a transition period, a regular election was held in which a black member was elected financial-secretary and other black members were appointed to committee positions. Black members stated that they were fairly represented.

In most merger situations, it is the black workers who are in the minority and who, therefore, seek some guarantee of representation in the newly merged local. The fourth case (6-6-5310) involving a molders' local represents a departure from the normal situation. Here, the black local represented 65 percent of the work force and potentially could have controlled all union offices had a vote on strictly racial lines occurred. Such, however, did not occur. Following the issuance of the Commission's decision, both locals agreed to divide all elected positions among members of the two locals. Of the fourteen executive board members, seven were white and seven were black. The local maintained two full-time union officials, a business agent and a recording secretary; the former position being held by a white member, while the latter post was occupied by a member of the formerly black local. In effect, each local nominated candidates for selected union positions for which members of the other local could not vote.

The merger agreement was scheduled to operate for a three-year period. It did not fully resolve the problems of representation, however. Additional charges and later Commission investigation revealed that several progression lines were still restricted to white workers, and that the business agent had failed to negotiate changes with management that would have allowed qualified black workers to progress to jobs in the white line.

The execution of only four agreements in twenty cases suggests that the Commission's settlement efforts met only minor success. A fuller appraisal must, however, consider three other cases where merger occurred, notwithstanding the Commission's failure to execute a written agreement. In all three cases, merger occurred following a cause decision, but under very different circumstances. The terms under which these locals were merged are outlined in Table 4-13.

In the first case, the locals merged soon after the decision had been rendered and before the conciliation effort had been initiated. Interviews with the officers of the former black local revealed that in the newly merged local, blacks were being represented. Although no special rights were accorded black members, some were nevertheless serving as officers and committeemen within the local. In

Table 4-13
Merger in Nonsettlement Cases

Case No.	Terms of Merger
CC 6-8-6988	Inclusion of black members in larger all-white local No special representation Merger of assets
AU 6-12-301	Incorporation of black membership into white local No special representation Merger of assets
6-4-4125	Incorporation of black membership into white local Allocation of two seats on local's executive board to members of former black local

effect, the action by the locals, which was induced in part by the international whose policy was to eliminate all segregated locals, rendered moot the conciliation effort.

The second case (AU 6-12-301) presented greater difficulty from a remedial standpoint. The conciliator had demanded that black workers be afforded representation in union committees following merger. Such a request was made because of the local's past efforts to limit the job opportunities of blacks and because of the evidence that the local's leadership was controlled by militant segregationists. The international that participated in the conciliation effort rejected the Commission's agreement, but decided to merge the locals on a one man-one vote basis. Interviews with the charging parties revealed that they were often not informed of the time and location of membership meetings, were not represented in any official capacity within the union, and faced resistance from the union when they filed grievances against the company for limiting black workers to unskilled job categories.

In the third nonagreement merger case, the Commission was about to execute an agreement when its conciliation effort was terminated at the request of the Department of Justice. Justice was investigating the railroad crafts for possible "pattern or practice" violations, and sought the temporary suspension of the Commission's settlement efforts. Although an agreement was not executed, the locals nonetheless implemented a merger which gave special representation to black members in the newly merged local. Interviews with the black members revealed their satisfaction with the merger.

Even when we consider these last three cases, it is evident that the Commission's success in merging segregated locals was only marginal. The Commission succeeded directly through an agreement or indirectly by prodding the locals to initiate self-corrective action, in effectuating mergers in only seven of the twenty cases. Moreover, in two of these seven cases (6-6-5310, AU 6-12-301), follow-up interviews indicated that black workers failed to obtain adequate representation following merger. In another case (5-11-2870), the agreement itself allowed for the continued existence of the dual locals by providing only for the transfer of black members to the white local.

Remedial Efficacy of Commission's Efforts in Grievance Cases

Previously we examined discriminatory union practices which affected blacks as a class. In the next two sections the effects of union discrimination on individuals will be examined. Two groups of cases are involved. The first concerns the local union's failure to process the grievances of a particular black grievant. By failing to consider the grievance or process it fairly, the union tacitly supported the company's discriminatory action against him. The second largely involves union pressure on employers to discriminate against blacks.

When conciliating grievance cases, the Commission's remedial objectives were two-fold: (1) to make whole the grievant for his losses; for example, if he had been unfairly laid off, the Commission sought back pay and reinstatement; (2) to ensure the local's impartial processing of grievances in the future. Normally, the Commission sought an agreement in which the local union reaffirmed its intent to process the grievances of minority workers.

There were nine cases in which the unions had failed to process fairly black workers' grievances. Of these, settlement agreements were executed in five cases. Table 4-14 amplifies the particular issue generating the grievances, the local union's response, and the scope of the remedies incorporated in the agreement.

The Commission was moderately successful in rectifying the employers' discriminatory personnel action in the five agreement cases. In the discharge and layoff situations, the grievants were reinstated and afforded back pay. Where black workers had been denied promotions, they were now at least to be considered for promotion when new openings developed. However, the Commission's success was limited. While back pay would have been appropriate in all five cases, it was gained in only three instances. In only one of four cases (5-9-908) was the grievant compensated for the earnings he had lost by having been unfairly denied promotion. Full relief would have required, where possible, the immediate promotion of the grievant and not just the employer's promise to "consider" him for promotion (5-9-892). Additionally, in one case (6-4-3856), the black denied promotion to an all-white unit was not placed in that unit. Instead, he was assigned to a job in another unit where his starting salary was equivalent to the beginning rate in the white unit. The deficiency grew out of the fact that the white unit jobs (electricians) allowed progression to much higher paying positions than did the jobs in the unit to which the black worker was assigned.

In general, the agreements contain only promises of prospective relief or representations that relief had been provided prior to the execution of the agreement. The key issue is whether or not the agreements were in fact

Table 4-14
Union-Employer Discrimination in Grievance Cases

Case No.	Issue	Number of Grievants	Union Grievance Action		Agreement's Remedial Provisions
5-9-908	Failure to grant automatic step increase	1	None	(1) (2) (3)	Back pay Granting of step increase Union agreement to process grievances and to notify grievants of cause for delays
5-11-2571	Failure to promote to driver position; discharge[a]	1	None	(1) (2) (3) (4)	Offer to train charging party as tractor-trailer driver and to promote him to position at first available opening. If he fails to qualify, grievant will be allowed to continue in original job. Reinstatement and back pay for loss of earnings due to discharge Union agreement to process grievances fairly Union agreement to file reports to Commission on manner in which it disposed of black workers' grievances
5-9-892	Failure to promote	3	None	(1) (2) (3)	Employer agreement to consider charging parties for promotion when vacancies developed Adoption of policy of promotion from within Union agreement to process grievance fairly[b]
6-4-3856	Failure to promote	1	None	(1) (2)	Promotion to equivalent paying position Union agreement to process grievance fairly
6-2-869	Discriminatory layoff	1	None	(1) (2)	Union represented that it processed grievance and obtained back pay for charging party for period he was laid off.[c] Agreement to process grievances fairly.

[a]Subsequent to the Commission's decision, the charging party was discharged. In the conciliation effort, the promotion and discharge issues were combined.

[b]Following the issuance of a decision, the local union was decertified; it nevertheless signed the agreement, stipulating that if it should again obtain bargaining rights for the workers involved it would represent all workers fairly.

[c]Following the filing of the charge, the local union processed the grievance, which resulted in the grievant's reinstatement and his receiving back pay.

implemented. Interviews with the grievants disclosed that in three cases (5-9-908, 5-9-892, 6-4-3856), the company had carried out the agreement.[15] Full compliance was also achieved in the case where the company had agreed only to consider the charging parties for promotion. Here, the formerly all-white managerial and check-out positions in a grocery store were integrated by the promotion of the charging parties and other blacks shortly after the agreement had been executed.

A lack of compliance was suggested in one case (5-11-2571). Here the grievant indicated that while he had been reinstated and afforded back pay, he was never offered training promised him in the agreement. He added that following his reinstatement he was laid off so frequently that he was forced to resign. This case is presently being litigated.

In these five cases, the local union involved agreed to treat grievances of workers without regard to race. Additionally, in one case (5-11-2571), the union was required to report to the Commission on its disposition of black workers' grievances. This added requirement grew out of the Commission's awareness that the local had a record of failing to consider black grievances.

No general pattern was revealed from the interviews with the parties concerning union compliance.[16] In one case (5-9-892), the issue was rendered moot by the respondent union's decertification by the NLRB. Here, black workers revealed that the local's poor record of representation had been a significant factor in its loss of bargaining rights. It is apparent that when the local fails to represent adequately black workers who constitute a sizable proportion of the employees in the bargaining unit, it may suffer the ultimate penalty. It is not surprising that in most of these grievance cases, blacks constituted only a small percentage of the workers. In effect, the local unions were probably not concerned with any adverse consequences to themselves resulting from their improper representation of black workers.

In two cases, those interviewed revealed that the local union was fairly representing black workers. Union compliance was manifested in the appointment of black workers to the grievance committees. In one case, the charging party is presently serving as the chairman of the local's grievance committee.

Evidence in the final case (5-4-2571) indicated that the local had violated its conciliation agreement, failing to submit the required periodic reports to the Commission regarding its handling of grievances. The charging party also stated that the local union had not processed a grievance he had filed against the company for failing to train him as a truck driver. Other black workers suggested that the local union consistently refused to process grievances involving charges of racial discrimination. They claimed that the union's failure to support such grievances operated to immunize management's policy of restricting black workers to inferior jobs.

Unsucessful Grievance Cases

Four grievance cases were terminated as unsuccessful. In contrast to prior cases where the union involved had generally refused to even consider the black grievant's claim, the local union's actions were not so flagrantly unlawful. As Table 4-15 indicates, the grievances of blacks were processed in three of the four cases; one was even arbitrated.

Table 4-15
Scope of Violations and Nature of Union-Employer Action in Unsuccessful Grievance Cases

Case No.	Issue	Number of Charging Parties	Union's Grievance Action	Resolution of Grievance
6-7-6289	Failure to promote	1	Processed grievance through third step	Company agreed to consider complainant for promotion in future
6-3-1297	Discharge	1	Processed through third step	Management's decision accepted
6-3-2253	Discharge	1	Arbitrated	Against grievant and upholding company
6-12-361	Laid off	1	None	Agreement between charging party and company whereby charging party waived rights to sue and he received back pay of $1,500.

These cases involved factually complex situations; aside from having to determine the legality of the employer's conduct, the Commission had to judge whether the local union in processing the grievance had gone as far as it could have on behalf of the grievant. Only in the fourth case was the factual situation simple; there, so far as the discriminatee was concerned, the local union had failed to even consider the grievance at the first step.

In the first two cases, the local union had stopped short of arbitration. Arbitration was not invoked in one case because of the employer's agreement to consider the charging party for future promotion to new vacancies. In the other, the union's grievance committee voted not to arbitrate because its review supported the employer's contentions that the discharge was for "cause." In both, the Commission ruled that the local union in failing to seek arbitration had mishandled the charging party's grievance.[17] The Commission also found cause against the local union which had arbitrated the black worker's grievance. Its decision was based on the the local's refusal to raise in arbitration the charging party's contention that the employer conduct had been racially motivated.

Of the four cases, relief was afforded the charging parties in only the fourth (6-12-361). There, the company had entered into an agreement with the complainant whereby he waived all claims against the company in return for a monetary award. This settlement was executed shortly after the Commission's conciliation effort had commenced. It, was not, however, a party to the settlement which was precipitated by the charging party's demand for a right to sue notice soon after the conciliator had contacted the parties.

In the three remaining cases, the companies rejected all efforts at conciliation, insisting that the issue had been settled through the grievance process. The unions involved in two instances (6-7-6289, 6-3-1297) were willing to discuss settlement; only in the third case (6-3-2253) did the local union strongly support management's position that the grievance had been fully adjudicated. Indeed, the Commission's settlement efforts here were condemned strongly by the union as unwarranted interference with the grievance arbitration process.

When we juxtapose these four cases against the previous five, we can make this observation. In contrast to class action cases, the Commission enjoys a moderate success in remedying employer violations against individual black workers. In over half of these cases, relief was afforded or promised the charging party.

The response of the unions to the Commission's settlement efforts was similar. In a majority of the cases, the unions executed agreements, and in two of the four unsuccessful cases expressed their willingness to discuss a settlement. In the last, only the employer's firm opposition precluded a settlement. What factors are responsible for the local's seeming willingness to settle, in contrast to the general record of unions in the other cases? The answer essentially had already been given. The Commission's conciliation demands upon local unions were extremely limited. They were directed toward obtaining a local union's declaration that it would process grievances, or in effect a statement that the local would agree to do what is required under the 1964 Civil Rights Act. Put another way, the costs the local union faces in executing an agreement are minimal. Significantly, it is the employer, and not the union, which must bear the brunt of the relief required − reinstatement, back pay, or promotion. The employer's heavier remedial burden is, however, the result of the employer's responsibility for generating the discriminatory action against the black worker.

At the same time, when the local union itself has been the primary agent behind the discriminatory situation, the local union's willingness to settle is sharply reduced. This is observed in the next section where, although the cases do not involve class issues but only single black workers, the Commission's efforts to execute agreements have been completely ineffective.

**Efficacy of Commission Efforts to Remedy Union
Discrimination against Individual Minority Workers**

In the previous section, the employer was primarily responsible for the adverse and discriminatory treatment of blacks. The local union's role was passive; by not processing the grievances of black workers, it acquiesced in the employer's unlawful conduct. In the final group of cases, it is the local union which has precipitated the discrimination against individual blacks. In some cases, unions have caused the employers to discriminate; by resorting to various tactics ranging from the filing of grievances to wildcat strikes, they have succeeded in pressuring the employer to pursue discriminatory policies. In two cases, the union itself, when charged as a respondent, was acting in an employer capacity. In several construction industry cases, the union denied blacks equal admission and referral opportunities.

Table 4-16 summarizes the nature and consequences of the unions' discriminatory actions. To remedy the discriminatory treatment of black workers, the Commission's major remedial objective is to make the discriminatee whole for his losses. Additionally, the Commission has the local reaffirm in the agreement its intent to represent all members of the bargaining unit fairly.

The Commission's remedial efforts in these cases met with almost complete failure. An agreement was executed in only one of the eleven cases. This occurred in one construction case (5-12-3217) where the local had unfairly denied admission to a minority applicant. The agreement was effective in terms of remedying the complaint, providing that upon payment of the normal initiation fee, the complainant would be admitted with all rights and benefits made retroactive from the date he originally filed for membership.[18] In one nonagreement case (6-7-6194), the Commission's intervention nevertheless generated some relief to the complainant. Following the filing of the charge, the company reinstated the black worker who had been demoted as a result of a wildcat strike. Intervention by the business agent contributed to the rank-and-file acceptance of the company's action. No back pay was provided, however.

No relief was forthcoming in three other cases where blacks had been reassigned to inferior jobs as a result of the local union's protests to management. These cases presented serious conflict situations making conciliation difficult since they concerned the job rights of white versus minority workers. The extent of the union's opposition can be seen in its willingness to process grievances in two cases (AU7-5-365, and BI68-4-844) in order to protect the job rights of white union members. Interviews with the charging parties in these demotion cases revealed that they remained locked in their original and inferior job classifications.

In only one of the remaining six cases was relief afforded a complainant. As a result of successful suit action, the local union was compelled to hire a black

Table 4-16
Union Discrimination against Individual Minority Workers

Case No.	Union Action	Consequences	Number Affected
AU7-5-365	Local union processing of white workers' grievances	Demotion of minority worker	4
BI68-4-844	Union-employer arbitration	Demotion of minority worker	1
6-11-48	Union-employer job reclassification	Demotion of minority	1
6-7-6194	Wildcat strike	Demotion of black worker	1
6-1-322	Failure to apply contract uniformly	Disparity in overtime assignments	1
68-8-202	Informal union-employer agreement on layoff procedures	Layoff of black worker	1
CH7-5-276	Union as employer	Refusal to hire black as business agent	1
6-8-7457	Union as employer	Refusal to hire black as secretary	1
5-12-3217	Refusal to admit	Limitation of job opportunities	1
6-12-9560U	Failure to refer as frequently as white members	Limitation of job opportunities	1
6-2-792	Improper classification	Limited referral opportunities	1

worker as business agent. The consequences of the Commission's failure in the other cases were severe; two black construction workers continued to face difficulties in obtaining referrals; a black woman denied a job as secretary suffered a long period of unemployment before gaining employment elsewhere; a black worker was laid off and forced to find another job, while the complainant in the overtime case decided to quit his job rather than be subjected to further discrimination.

In human terms these are some of the costs of the Commission's failure to achieve compliance: lower earnings, inferior jobs, limited advancement, a higher risk of layoff and discharge for minority workers. The overall settlement record of the Commission is revealed in Table 4-17.

The table indicates two marked patterns. First, the Commission generally failed to execute settlement agreements. Thus agreements were executed in only nineteen of the eighty-one situations involving one of the five types of union discrimination. Moreover, the failure to execute an agreement was generally associated with the union's refusal to correct the discriminatory practice. This was particularly true in craft union exclusion, seniority, and union discrimination cases. Of those nonagreement cases where remedial action was taken by the local union, the relief implemented extended to the charging parties alone, and did not eliminate the potential for future discrimination.[19]

Second, a majority of the agreement cases did not contain the measures considered essential by the Commission to provide adequate relief to the charging party or members of the affected class. This failure was most apparent in craft union exclusion and seniority cases. Only in segregated local and grievance cases did the agreements generally contain the standard Commission remedies. The Commission remedy of merger was implemented in three of the four segregated local agreement cases. In the grievance cases, complainants generally received some compensation for the losses they sustained, while the local unions did agree to process fairly the grievances of minority workers. The overall weakness of the conciliation process is further evident in the fact that in five of the nineteen settlement situations, subsequent investigations revealed that the respondents had not complied with the settlement agreements.

The compliance picture is brightened when we remember that the settlement agreement did produce positive results in nonunion-related areas. As previously indicated, employers agreed to recruit blacks into formerly white-only departments, integrate plant facilities, and eliminate the use of nonvalidated tests. At the same time, in terms of remedying discriminatory union or joint employer-union practices, the effect of the conciliation process was one more of illusion than reality.

Table 4-17

Summary of EEOC Efforts to Execute Settlement Agreements (Total Number of Cases: 75)

Remedial Issue	Number of Cases Involving This Issue	Standard Remedy Provisions for This Type of Discrimination	Number of Cases Where Agreements Executed Covering Issue	Number of Agreements Incorporating Standard EEOC Remedy
Craft union exclusion from membership, apprenticeship, or referral by building and printing crafts	14	(1) Elimination of discriminatory barriers (2) Affirmative action to promote minority entrance (3) Relief to charging party	1	—
Seniority	27	(1) Seniority rights to black workers to be computed on basis of their length of employment with company (2) Red-circling of black workers' wage scales (3) Establishment of training programs (4) Merger of functionally related progression lines	8	—
Segregated local unions	20	Merger	4	3
Grievance Cases	9	(1) Compensation of charging party for losses (2) Union agreement to process grievances of minority workers	5	3

Discriminatory union action against individuals		11	1	1
	(1)	Compensation of individual		
	(2)	Union stipulation to represent fairly all bargaining unit members		
Total		81[a]	19[b]	7

[a]The total number of cases examined was 75; 6 cases involved both seniority and segregated local issues and were counted twice. This is the reason why the number of separate issues exceed the number of cases examined.

[b]The actual number of agreements executed was 18. The total in the table is 19 because one agreement involved both seniority and segregated local issues.

5

Constraints upon the Conciliation Process

Factors Underlying Union Noncompliance

Of the seventy-five cases in this study, the Commission executed agreements in only eighteen cases, or a conciliation rate of 24 percent. Clearly, the Commission was unable to achieve compliance in approximately three-fourths of all labor-union cases. Moreover, when the Commission does not execute an agreement, little, if any, relief will be provided the charging parties or members of the affected class. Generally, the discriminatory situation underlying the complaint will persist. To what factors can we attribute the Commission's apparent inability to achieve compliance with the act in labor-union cases? This question can be divided into two related questions: (1) What factors underlie a local union's unwillingness to accept the Commission's remedial proposals? (2) Are there elements within the Commission's conciliation process which inhibit its settlement efforts? These questions help focus upon those variables which are both within and beyond the Commission's control, and which should help explain the reasons for its poor compliance record.

A major factor underlying a local union's resistance to the Commission's settlement efforts is the high cost that settlement agreements may impose upon the local's membership and subsequently upon the union leadership and management. The mandate of the Commission is the elimination of discriminatory employment policies. This normally requires significant changes in plant practices and union policies. When such changes operate to adversely affect the job status of white workers vis-à-vis minority workers, strong resistance is generated. It should be noted that discriminatory practices are not based upon feelings of prejudice alone, but are rooted in economic considerations. The exclusion of black workers from membership and referral will result in a greater number of job opportunities for white union members. A discriminatory seniority arrangement protects young white workers in competition for jobs with minority workers with greater seniority. In effect, discrimination against minorities offers white employees economic advantages they are reluctant to give up.

The opposition to change was fiercely and dramatically noted in several seniority cases where the local union threatened to strike if the company modified the existing job seniority system. In one case, the company's promotion of a black worker to an apprentice position in a previously all-white department precipitated a wild-cat strike by white workers. Worker resistance to change places serious constraints upon both management and union representatives who are involved in settlement discussions. Management is reluctant to institute any changes which generate significant rank-and-file discontent; it must be concerned about the possibility of wild-cat strikes, slow-downs, and even physical disturbances between white and minority workers. One respondent objected to government efforts to restructure the seniority system because in his view "to deny incumbent employees their earned rights to progress to higher jobs in accordance with established progression, or to deny them earned job security rights (recall rights) would as a practical matter create a serious risk of labor strife."[1] When the union representatives also oppose any concessions, management will be under greater pressure to reject the Commission's settlement efforts. Thus, where the discriminatory practice in question is governed by the contract, then any unilateral change by management can precipitate the filing of grievances as well as unfair labor practice charges alleging management violation of its bargaining obligation under the Taft-Hartley Act.[2]

While the costs to the company of accepting the Commission's terms are economic, the costs to the union negotiator are political in nature. If the union leadership accepts an agreement that antagonizes the great majority of white workers, it may face defeat in the next election. To the extent that the Commission's remedy calls for a reallocation of job opportunities that may frustrate the job expectations of a significant number of white workers, the union's ability to accept the Commission's agreement is impaired. As a result union negotiators seriously consider the political implications of an EEOC settlement agreement. Indeed, union leader resistance to governmental demands may be a device to gain popular support, while, conversely, accusing opponents of bowing to governmental pressure may be an effective means of discrediting them. The following letter sent by a business agent to the membership shortly before the local union election vividly illustrates the union leader's use of the civil rights charge for political gain:

Dear Sir and Brothers:

By this time I am reasonably sure you have heard or read in the newspapers of a decision rendered by the FEPC ordering me to have J.R.H. as a business representative solely on the basis of H. being Negro. . . .

Since this decision was made July 21, 1967, . . , I have been flooded with telephone calls, telegrams, and letters from our members protesting the decision of the FEPC demanding I appeal to a higher court. . . .

Local . . . is being used as the goat in this so-called civil rights action and I would appreciate the full support of our entire membership at this particular time in objecting to the FEPC decision and directing me to file an appeal.

I respectfully request you also to mark and mail your ballot for me and your team. I am of the considered opinion other candidates for the office of Business Manager would take the line of least resistance and sweep this matter under the rug.

You know where I stand in the contemptible decision of the FEPC. I will appeal it to the highest court in the land before I will give in to unloading this person on you as a Business Representative. . . .

I will appreciate your comments (written) as I will need them for the appeal. Your position will be supported to the fullest extent. . . .

P.S. Brothers, please do not write on your ballot and do not sign your ballot. If your ballot is defaced in any way, your vote will not count. Write to me separately — not on your ballot.[3]

In summary, the Commission's settlement proposals, when adopted, generate political and economic costs for the membership, the union leaders, and the employer. Changes in long-held, deeply-rooted policies are not modified without some individual or group of workers being affected adversely. These costs often underlie a respondent's refusal to settle. The problem with the Commission's remedial process was it's powerlessness to impose equal or greater costs upon management or union respondents for rejecting a settlement agreement. From a bargaining theory framework, a respondent will settle when the costs of rejecting a settlement agreement exceed the costs of acceptance. The bargaining power of the Commission can be increased by two means: (1) increasing the costs to the respondent in rejecting an agreement, (2) decreasing the costs to the respondent in accepting an agreement. These two means were not equally available to the Commission. Furthermore, whereas the first could promote the implementation of an effective remedial policy, it was beyond the capacity of the Commission to exercise. Conversely, if it did have the capacity to lower the cost of agreement to the respondent, such a policy conflicted with the objective of securing the necessary remedial changes.

How could the Commission have imposed costs upon a respondent who rejects a settlement agreement? As indicated in chapter 1, under the 1964 act the Commission possessed no enforcement authority; it had no cease-and-desist authority, nor could it file law suits to curtail unlawful employment practices. The sole leverage that it exercised under Title VII consisted of the potential threat of a private or public suit. The costs the respondent might have faced in such an event were potentially high: an injunction backed up by the court's authority to fine and imprison for contempt, the possibility of large back-pay awards, adverse consequences of unfavorable publicity on public relations of the company, and heavy litigation costs. To the extent that numerous law suits were filed, respondents' willingness to settle could have been increased. The fact remains, however, that the threat of litigation was more theoretical than real. The EEOC has reported that private law suits were initiated in less than 10 percent of all cases in which agreements were not executed. Nor was intervention by the Justice Department a real threat. The number of law suits initiated by the department was so limited as to almost eliminate the leverage a conciliator could have exercised by that threat. As a result, it was likely that many respondents were not concerned about the prospect of a law suit.

Respondents involved in EEOC conciliation efforts were probably also not concerned that their failure to settle would make them vulnerable to the sanctions of the Office of Federal Contract Compliance (OFCC). Between 1964 and 1970 the EEOC and the OFCC failed to coordinate their compliance efforts. EEOC investigations and conciliations were in most cases carried out independently and without knowledge of past, current, or prospective OFCC action. As a result, the conciliator was in no position to utilize the sanctions available to the OFCC as leverage for inducing respondents to settle. In summary, then, the conciliation process functioned in an economic and political environment wherein the costs to respondents for settling were high, while the probable costs for rejecting a settlement were often low. Consequently, respondents had little incentive to settle.[4]

In addition, there are cases in which under no circumstances would respondents settle unless compelled to do so by governmental edict. For the memberships of some local unions, resistance to the admission of minorities is a matter of such strong principle that the costs of litigation diminish in significance. Business agents in five construction union cases acknowledged that in refusing to settle they felt that the chances of a court suit were high. Yet the attitudes of the rank-and-file prevented them from settling. One business agent remarked that the membership voted not to settle although the business agent supported by officials of the international warned the local membership that its policies of rigid exclusion would be attacked in federal courts. A similar situation occurred in several seniority cases where the memberships had voted not to modify their seniority systems, despite Commission directives. In effect, employee opposition to change was often so intense as to forestall voluntary compliance on the part of the local-union leadership.

A third element contributed to respondents' unwillingness to execute settlement agreements. These cases were conciliated during the 1966-68 period when the Commission's remedial efforts had not yet secured judicial support. In rejecting the Commission's remedial proposals, some respondents felt that its objectives went beyond the scope of the act. For example, while agreeing to merge segregated progression lines, respondents resisted the effort to restructure movement within the merged progression line. As one stated:

The earned rights of incumbent [white] employees should be granted to them both as a matter of propriety, and as a matter of legality arising under existing union contracts. We further stated that in our opinion there was no conflict between this concept and the requirements of the applicable Executive Orders or applicable sections of the Civil Rights Act of 1964.[5]

In seniority and building-craft union cases, respondents argued that Title VII is not retroactive. This meant their sole remedial obligation was to eliminate practices that discriminate presently and overtly, but that they were not obligated to eliminate the effects of past discrimination.[6] Some respondents may have felt that if a suit would occur to modify referral and seniority arrangements, they would be able to challenge them successfully.

The Commission had one other means which it used to increase its chances of executing an agreement — decreasing the costs imposed upon the respondent for settling. How could the Commission have achieved this end? The stronger the remedial program, the greater the costs inflicted upon respondents; thus, to the degree that the Commission compromised on its demands, the greater the likelihood that its offer would have been accepted. For example, its requirement that minority workers be allowed to compete for jobs on the basis of their plant-wide seniority was strongly resisted by the local union since it may have disadvantaged white workers who, under the current seniority arrangements, would have had preference for higher-paid jobs. Agreement to the proposal generated costs — dissatisfaction and discontent at least among junior white workers who would rank below minority workers if a plant-wide seniority arrangement were instituted. On the other hand, if the Commission accepted the current seniority arrangement in return for an agreement that in the future all job classifications would be open to members of each race, the cost to the respondent for settlement would have been reduced significantly. In the latter situation, the job expectations of incumbent white employees were not affected, although some resistance might have been displayed by the white employees who were opposed to the integration of previously all-white progression lines or departments.

Thus, in moderating its key demands, the Commission had a better opportunity of gaining a settlement. This tactic was adopted frequently. A conciliator would relinquish demands in some areas to gain concessions in others. This process is reflected in the agreements examined in this study. The problem with this procedure is evident. There is the serious risk that concessions will be made which will preclude the adoption of remedies fully making whole complainants or eliminating the source of discrimination. Substandard or soft agreements were negotiated in the craft union, seniority, and grievance cases examined in this study. From a remedial standpoint, then, this procedure of inducing agreements is unsatisfactory. Unfortunately, the inability of the Commission to compel enforcement made it often the only option available to conciliators.

The effect of the Commission's nonexistent enforcement powers upon its ability to compel compliance with Title VII should not be cause for surprise. Following passage of the act, one commentator referred to the Commission as "a poor enfeebled thing . . . [with the power to conciliate but not to compel]."[7] Recently, a former chairman stated, "We're out to kill an elephant with a fly gun."[8] Until passage of the Civil Rights Act of 1972, the Commission was the only regulatory agency that operated without enforcement powers. Past experience has demonstrated that an agency without enforcement powers will face severe difficulties in achieving compliance. Before the passage of the Wagner

Act, Congress had established Labor Relations Boards to implement Section 7(a) of the National Industrial Recovery Act; this section had given employees the right to organize and bargain collectively free from employer interference. Neither the National Labor Board, nor its successor, the first National Labor Relations Board, possessed independent enforcement authority. Like the Commission, its powers to settle disputes were generally limited to the processes of mediation, conciliation, fact-finding, and (voluntary) arbitration.[9] The Labor Relations Boards were also similar to the EEOC in the respect that ultimate compliance depended upon other sources. If a respondent refused to abide by a Board award or decision, its sole weapon was to refer the violation to the Compliance Division of the National Recovery Administration (NRA) or to the Department of Justice. The sanctions of the NRA involved the potential removal of the Blue Eagle. The Justice Department had the authority to bring suit against violators of Section 7(a) of the National Industrial Recovery Act. Neither forum provided an effective alternative means for enforcement. The Department of Justice hesitated to bring suits against violators, while the NRA was extremely cautious in exercising its sanctions.[10] Thus employers could refuse to abide by the decisions of the Board without serious fear of being prosecuted or penalized. This circumstance manifested itself in the Board's compliance record before the Wagner Act. Between March 2, 1935 and July 9, 1935, the Board obtained compliance in only thirty-four of eighty-six cases in which violations were found.[11]

The major lesson drawn from the compliance record of the early Labor Relations Boards was that the elimination of unfair labor practices could only be achieved if the agency charged with this task were given the powers to compel enforcement and provide relief. The passage of the Wagner Act, which provided the NLRB with cease and desist powers, corrected this deficiency. The same lesson can be drawn from the compliance record of the EEOC.

Internal Commission Problems

Given the absence of enforcement powers, the Commission was unable to remedy discriminatory union practices. The lack of such authority was beyond the control of the agency. There are, however, factors of an internal nature which are within its powers and which contribute to its inability to execute settlement agreements. Consequently, the burden falls upon the Commission to make the necessary adjustments to facilitate the conciliator's remedial efforts. The two factors examined below are interrelated — the first involves the excessive time delays permeating and burdening the conciliation process; the second concerns the existence of serious staffing problems within the agency.

Time Delays in Conciliation Process

One factor limiting the Commission's ability to obtain agreements was the excessive time delays occuring between the date a complaint was filed and the date the conciliation effort was initiated. This delay was generated by two elements, the first of which grew out of the Commission's compliance procedures. Under Commission regulations in effect from 1964 through February 1970, conciliation could begin only after an official Commission decision finding cause had been rendered. While statistics are not available, it is general knowledge that a lengthy time lag evolved between the date of the charge and the date of the decision. Since conciliators could not initiate settlement effort before a decision was issued, this meant that in a typical case, over a year could pass before the conciliator could begin to resolve the case. In 45 percent of the cases studied in this project, the decision was made at least thirteen months following the filing of the charge.

Table 5-1 presents data on the complaint-decision time intervals in seventy-five cases.

Table 5-1
Time Lags in Processing Complaints

Interval between Filing of Charge and Decision	Number of Cases Decided within this Period	Percentage of Total Cases	Number of Agreements
1-6 months	13	17.3	5
7-12 months	28	37.3	7
13-18 months	28	37.3	6
19-24 months	4	5.3	1
25-30 months	2	2.7	—
	75	99.9%	19

Another factor further increases the length of the time lags. While the conciliator can officially initiate his settlement efforts once a decision is rendered, he is not always able to do so. The shortage of trained conciliators, excessive turnover within their ranks, and a heavy caseload result in the development of a backlog of cases scheduled for conciliation. The Commission itself has reported that it takes a minimum of eighteen to twenty-four months to process a job discrimination complaint from receipt through conciliation.[12]

Significantly, Table 5-1 suggests that speed in undertaking conciliation action is important to success. When the interval between filing and decision is greater than six months, a significant decline in the rate of agreements secured is registered. Moreover, after eighteen months, the prospects appear to be all but hopeless. Several factors are responsible for this situation. First, the greater the time delay, the more likely it becomes that the charging party's status has significantly changed. The complainant whose job has been terminated is forced to find substitute work and may even have moved to a new area. Where he has found a new job elsewhere, his interest in the conciliation effort is muted.[13] These facts are not unknown to the respondents who may view the long delays as indicative of the decreased interest and significance that is attached to the cases by both the Commission and charging party. For example, in several construction union cases, business agents were aware that the charging parties had found other employment and openly admitted their skepticism as to the liklihood of a private suit.

Second, lengthy delays can abort the conciliation effort. At times, complainants will become so frustrated by the long delays that they will request a right to sue notice without waiting for the Commission to commence settlement efforts. This occurred in one case in this study, and it is more likely to happen when the charging party is represented from the outset by counsel. If the charge is well documented, the complainant's counsel may see no point in waiting for the conciliation effort, especially when he feels that the chances for a voluntary settlement are limited. In some cases the charging party may ask that the conciliation effort be terminated. This also occurred in one case where the settlement attempt had been initiated over a year past the date of the complaint. Believing that the conciliation effort would produce additional delays, the complainant demanded a right to sue notice.

In some cases, critical issues may be rendered moot by the time the conciliator meets with the parties. At times, the respondent will take steps to correct the grievance, but will subsequently refuse to sign a settlement agreement. While the informal settlement may satisfy the charging party, it may constitute less than the Commission considers adequate from a remedial standpoint. In one discharge case, the charging party agreed to a bilateral settlement with the respondent whereby in return for a monetary award, he would waive his rights to reinstatement and to file suit. At the same time, the union which had been a co-respondent for failing to process his grievance was not a party to the bilateral settlement. From the Commission's standpoint, full relief required an offer of reinstatement and steps to assure the fair processing of grievances by the union. Neither of these objectives could be achieved since the execution of the bilateral settlement terminated the respondents' incentive to participate in conciliation discussion.

The extent to which lengthy delays in the conciliation process inhibit chances for executing agreements is difficult to gauge. Yet most conciliators in the field would agree that cases scheduled for conciliation which are over one-and-a-half years old present serious difficulties.[14] The fact that the charging party has lost interest, the mootness of issues, and the diminishing prospect of private suits create serious obstacles to the conciliator's attempts to execute agreements.

Additional Administrative Problems – Errors in Case Handling

Earlier we examined three cases in which it was found that charges had been filed against the wrong unions. Conciliation failed because the charged union was not in a position to eliminate the discriminatory practices while the proper union respondents refused to participate in settlement discussion on the ground that no finding had been made against them. In these cases, the error was not discovered until after the decision had been issued and conciliation efforts initiated.

While this type of imbroglio was not common, it reflects a serious problem within the Commission – the presence of staff members with insufficient legal or industrial relations background to adequately handle investigatory and conciliation assignments. The following case illustrates the problem.

In October 1968 the Commission found cause against a building-craft union for excluding blacks from membership. The mechanism of exclusion was the union's refusal to refer blacks since membership in the union was predicated on persons being referred and working on a job for a period of seven days. The Commission's finding was based on the local union's repeated failure to refer a qualified black journeyman and upon statistical data revealing the complete absence of blacks within the union.

Following the issuance of the decision, the conciliator assigned to the case by the regional office, met and reached a tentative agreement with the local union. The local union agreed to a settlement agreement which basically provided for the following remedial provisions.

The Respondent agrees to undertake a scan . . . of the metropolitan area in an effort to determine if there are any qualified minority group equipment operators. Should the aforementioned scan reveal that such minority group members exist, Respondent will, upon application of such minority group members, admit said persons into Local . . . as journeymen, under the same qualifying standards applied to all other applicants.

Respondent agrees to notify Mr. Robert C. T. . . . that he . . . will be admitted to membership in Respondent's Local Union . . . within thirty days following his application for membership. . . .

Provided, however, it is understood . . . that the continuation of Robert C. T.'s membership shall be conditioned, as is that of all other members, upon his adherence to and compliance with the provisions of the Constitution of the International Union . . . the By-laws of Local Union No. 101 and the collective bargaining agreements negotiated by said Local Union . . . and provided further that it is . . . agreed that . . . Robert C. T. will be referred as a Group C applicant for employment. . . .[15]

The Conciliations Division which reviewed the proposed settlement agreement returned it to the region because of its serious deficiencies. In rejecting the proposed agreement, Headquarters (HQ) Conciliations made the following comments.

The [first] provision leaves unanswered issues of signal importance. First, how is the local to "scan" the area for minority applicants? Will it contact legitimate minority organizations such as the National Urban League and State Employment Services to obtain information on the location and number of minority journeymen? Certainly the agreement should contain this modest requirement. Additionally, if [craft workers organized by the local] are licensed by the city, the local should be obligated to examine the city's licensing records and to compile from them a list of Negro journeymen eligible for membership. At present, the provision established no guidelines for the task of seeking out Negro journeymen and simply allows the local to fulfill the requirement by following procedures utilized in the past. These may well consist of scanning the yellow pages of the telephone book.

The second provision in paragraph [2] wherein T is placed in group C for purposes of referral raises more serious questions. . . . Local 101 operates an exclusive hiring hall and has excluded Negroes from referral. Yet, the agreement . . . fails to consider the possible existence of a discriminatory hiring hall structure. Thus, for example, does [the local] in referring workers give preference to union members and to those who have worked under union contractors. T is placed in group C, but what are the standards by which the union places workers in group A and B and gives them priority in referral? Our concern is twofold: (1) T has 18 years experience in the trade; it is likely that if non-discriminatory referral criteria were utilized, T would be placed in group A and thereby be given priority over other who have just entered the trade. (2) If the structure of the hiring hall is itself discriminatory, then the local's past policy of exclusion will be perpetuated. If the latter is true, then appropriate remedial measures must be taken.[16]

Following this critical analysis, a review of the files confirmed HQ fears. The local union's referral procedures did in fact institutionalize discriminatory procedures. Workers with experience working for union contractors were given preference in referral. This explains why the union sought to place the complainant who had eighteen years of experience in the C group, from which he would be dispatched only after all workers on the A and B lists had been referred. Additionally, the local was affiliated with an international union whose bylaws provided that individuals receiving membership had to be approved by a majority of the membership. Thus, although the complainant may have gained admission, he was denied equal referral opportunities while membership requirements existed which could be used to block the admission of other minority candidates.

In this case, HQ instructed the regional office to reinstate settlement efforts and attempt to execute an agreement correcting these deficiencies. It is cases of this type that are hardest to conciliate. The respondent had agreed to a tentative agreement and is then informed that it is insufficient. Here a respondent typically will charge the Commission with negotiating in bad faith; the suspicions created combined with the natural unwillingness and difficulties involved in making further concessions seriously jeopardize the subsequent settlement effort. In the above case the union refused to modify its original proposal, and the conciliation effort was terminated.

This case raises two questions of importance (1) how significant are the staffing problems within the agency, and (2) what factors are responsible? The first is the more difficult to answer, and indeed would require an independent study to achieve an objective answer.

In three of the seventy-five cases it is clear that administrative error precluded the successful execution of the agreement. Here, the wrong union was charged. If these cases were the only evidence of error, it would perhaps be an overstatement to talk in terms of an internal Commission problem. The data suggest, however, that they were not the only cases where mistakes occurred. The problem of poor workmanship was revealed in several settlement agreements where the "remedies" incorporated in the agreement were so minimal as to render them valueless or even of negative value since they operated to prevent the charging party from filing suit.

In a construction case a craft union was not obligated to suspend the use of an admissions test which was not job-related and which had a disparate effect on minorities. Failure of a conciliator to require the merger of segregated locals and his willingness to resolve the issue on the basis of a transfer policy exemplified the disparity that developed at times between Commission policy and practice.[17] In these cases, the agreements operated to conceal continued policies of nearly complete discrimination and exclusion of minorities.

Thus it can be seen that a problem did exist within the Commission; moreover it was not restricted to any one regional office. The five cases examined above occurred in different regional offices. Does such a problem exist today? The problems relating to the midwestern construction union case was of recent occurrence (1971). The fact that no one in the entire regional office could point to the deficiencies of the proposed settlement agreement is perhaps suggestive of the scope of current difficulties.

Significantly, the factors responsible for the serious staffing problems within the Commission are not unknown; nor are they insoluble. Governmental reports have noted that the Commission has suffered from a high turnover rate and an almost unmanageable caseload.[18] With an excessive caseload, mistakes are unavoidable. Internal systems of personnel evaluation may also have a detrimental effect on the quality of the settlements executed. During the 1966-68 period, the Commission introduced a policy of evaluating a conciliator's work in terms of the number of agreements he executed and the number of cases he handled. The system placed a premium on numbers rather than upon the substantive merit of the conciliator's work output and specifically on the scope and effect of the agreements he executed. Conciliators were under the strong incentive to obtain agreements, with or without strong remedial provisions.

A third factor contributing to an erosion of work standards concerns the failure to provide personnel with adequate training programs. Throughout the first five years of the Commission's existence, no uniform or systematic training program was ever developed for new field investigators or conciliators.[19] New investigators and conciliators in practice may begin the jobs with little more than on-the-job training afforded them by the overtaxed field-office personnel. When one considers that those newly hired may be without legal or industrial relations background, it is easily seen that the potential for error is great.

Intervention of the Labor Union Community

We have observed that the Commission's inability to execute settlement agreements was in large part due to local-union opposition to any modification of existing practices. To the degree that the scope of the changes required were great, the local union will be more inclined to resist. Reinforcing any tendency not to settle was the realization that even in the absence of a settlement, court action was not automatic, for both the charging parties and the Justice Department would fail to act. Finally, there was the additional possibility that even in the event of a suit the court may refuse to order the local to adjust its practices, if the practices on their face were racially neutral.

These elements set the stage for a sharp conflict between the local union and the Commission. When the Commission was organized, it was not unaware that it would meet resistance from local unions, and it was with this awareness that it began to establish formal contact with the major organizations of the labor community, specifically with the AFL-CIO Civil Rights Division and the international union leaderships. The Commission felt that a close working relationship between it and the leaders of the labor movement would facilitate resolution of charges against local unions.

Intervention of AFL-CIO Civil Rights Division

Early in its existence, the Commission formally decided to notify the AFL-CIO Civil Rights Department (CRD) when it received complaints against labor unions. This step was authorized by the Commission's first chairman, Franklin Delano Roosevelt, Jr., on September 30, 1965, and was taken following such a request by Donald Slaiman, the director of the AFL-CIO's CRD.[20] In setting up this procedure for notification, the Commission believed that through the good offices of the CRD, the Commission could more easily rectify discriminatory union practices.

The Roosevelt memorandum specified only that copies of charges would be sent to the CRD. The record indicates, however, that soon other steps were taken to provide the CRD with more information. In March 1966, the Commission's executive director was recommending to the director of compliance that copies of the decisions should be sent to the CRD.[21] While no formal understanding between the Commission and the AFL-CIO was reached regarding the forwarding of the decisions, the Commission began to forward copies of decisions to the CRD in 1966. Professor Blumrosen, then the Commission's chief of conciliation, writing about the 1966 compliance procedures, stated: "The first step after the reasonable cause finding is notification to the parties. Notification is also sent to the AFL-CIO Civil Rights Division, the Construction Industry Joint Council, and to the NAACP in appropriate cases."[22]

Under Professor Blumrosen's direction, the Conciliation Division also began at the end of 1966 to transmit to the Civil Rights Department copies of conciliation agreements involving unions affiliated with the AFL-CIO. Thus, in a little over a year from the date of Chairman Roosevelt's agreement to transmit charges, the interchange of information between the CRD and the Commission has expanded considerably with the result that the CRD was aware of the various stages of EEOC involvement with their local union affiliates.[23]

Having noted the creation of an informational exchange between the Commission and the CRD, two questions merit analysis: (1) How did the CRD utilize the information supplied by the Commission? and (2) What role did it play in the Commission's conciliation efforts? In asnwering the second question, we shall have some understanding of the extent to which the Commission's expectations on the critical nature of AFL-CIO involvement were justified.

Of the seventy-five cases examined in this study, sixty-eight concerned local unions which belonged to international unions affiliated with the AFL-CIO; the remaining seven cases involved local unions affiliated with independent unions. In twelve cases, the Commission failed to provide the CRD with copies of either the charges or the decisions. Consequently, the potential for AFL-CIO CRD intervention was limited to fifty-six cases.

In the fifty-six cases where it received notification, the CRD routinely forwarded copies of the charges and the decisions to the relevant union international, and specifically to the international union representative designated to handle civil rights matters.[24] In a form letter to the internationals, the CRD indicated its willingness upon request to provide assistance.

The value to the Commission of this secondary interchange between the CRD and the international unions depends in large part on the willingness of the latter to cooperate with the Commission's conciliation efforts. Conversely, international union antagonism may severely reduce the Commission's chances of executing an agreement. At the very least, notification to international unions of charges filed against their locals has facilitated the Commission's investigative work. At times, when local unions refused to supply Commission investigators with union documents the internationals have generally intervened in the Commission's behalf, often successfully.

Notification of internationals by the CRD and the latter's help in arranging for an international's participation in the conciliation conference can be of critical significance. In some cases, the implementation of the Commission's remedy may conflict with an international bylaw. By waiving the local union's obligation to conform to a particular bylaw, the international enables the local to execute the agreement. This type of international union support is particularly relevant in merger cases where an effort is made to allocate union positions to former members of the black local.

At times, notification of the international can produce dramatic results. The following case is illustrative.

The EEOC investigator could not get all the information he needed from the local [ironworkers] union. The [AFL-CIO] Civil Rights Department was asked for cooperation. It asked whether the international union had been notified. The answer was no. It then asked the EEOC to make such notification. The international union, when it heard of the complaint, sent a representative to the local. He interviewed the applicants, found they had knowledge of the trade, spoke to the local union officers and found they had no unemployed members. He convinced them to immediately give work permits to the complainants. They went to work at journeyman pay scales and conditions. Within a month they were given an examination by the local union, passed it and were accepted into membership.

There is no question that the cooperation of the international union following its notification had brought a rapid as well as satisfactory solution to this complaint.[25]

To be sure, such results are not typical; at the same time, they illustrate the potential benefit that arises from the interchange of information between the CRD and the international unions that is made possible by the Commission's policies of data-sharing.

Direct participation by the CRD in EEOC settlement conferences occurred in few cases. In only six cases did the CRD attend a conciliation conference where the Commission met with representatives of the local union and possibly the international to discuss settlement. Of these, an agreement was executed in only one case. The CRD also met with Commission representatives in three other cases. Of these, an agreement was executed in only one case. These statistics suggest rather strongly that the CRD has played only a minor role in the conciliation stage. Thus, in only nine of the fifty-six cases in which it received notification of charges and decisions did it meet with Commission representatives, and in even fewer cases did it participate in settlement conferences. Furthermore, the data implied that even when the CRD has intervened, the Commission's ability to execute an agreement was not materially advanced. In only two of the nine cases where CRD representatives met with Commission personnel regarding the charges were agreements executed. It seems that the CRD has not, as the Commission had expected, been a significant force in promoting the Commission's conciliation efforts.

To what factors can we attribute the low incidence of CRD participation in settlement conferences? Generally, both the Commission and the CRD share responsibility for this result. One contributing factor is the absence of any formal procedure whereby the field offices inform the CRD of their intentions to commence conciliation activities. All the CRD has is a copy of the decision; yet, conciliation may not commence for many months afterwards. In some cases, the CRD becomes aware of conciliation activities only after they have been concluded. Some offices, to be sure, make an effort to invite CRD participation, but they are the exception.

A second limiting factor has its origin within the CRD. Its functions are multiple: they include serving as a liaison with *all* government agencies charged with administering civil rights legislation, assisting its affiliates in civil rights matters, and working with local community organizations in the development of equal employment programs.[26] Clearly, only part of the CRD's resources can be devoted to liaison work with the EEOC, which is only one of the agencies enforcing civil rights laws. Other agencies such as the OFCC and Justice Department must also come within the CRD's purview. At the same time, the manpower resources of the CRD are extremely limited. Their full-time staff totals less than ten individuals. Thus, assuming that the CRD were given the full opportunity to participate in labor-union conciliation efforts, it is questionable whether its small staff would enable them to intervene in a significant manner.

It is also questionable whether the intervention by the CRD would materially affect the conciliation outcome. As indicated earlier, the rate of success was not enhanced in the cases where the CRD met with Commission representatives. Furthermore, it is unlikely that greater participation of the CRD in settlement conferences in these cases would have produced different results. The seventy-five cases in this study were decided in the years 1966-68. During this period there was still seriously lacking a firm body of court decisions to uphold Commission policy. In this vacuum the unions rejected the Commission's decisions that their activities were unlawful, insisting typically that they could not be held responsible for effects of their prior practices of discrimination if at present their procedures on their face were not discriminatory. Until the courts ruled in the Commission's favor, it would have been difficult for the CRD to support the Commission's conciliation efforts.

Even today when the courts have supported the Commission's policy by affirming broad remedial orders to rectify the effects of past discrimination, there is a limit to the support the Commission can expect from the CRD. It must be remembered that the CRD, as a department within the AFL-CIO, services international unions. It cannot coerce compliance on the part of internationals or their local unions. Like the Commission, its powers are those of conciliation and pursuasion. Excessive support of Commission views would place it, moreover, in a politically hazardous position. A policy of forceful compliance on its part would engender the antagonism of the internationals, and in the final analysis, it is the latter that it must assist to remain in business.

These comments on the value of CRD intervention in conciliation efforts should not be construed as an assertion of the nonutility of the EEOC-CRD data-sharing policies. The CRD plays a unique role as liaison between the internationals and the EEOC. It is able to perform this function because of the rapport it has established with both Commission personnel and the staffs of the internationals who handle civil rights matters.

Most important, CRD familiarity with, and knowledge of, the Commission's compliance efforts cases have enabled it to alert the Commission to serious internal problems. For example, during the 1966-68 period, the CRD warned the Commission concerning the adequacy of its investigations. In several cases, the CRD brought to the Commission's attention the fact that the wrong union had been charged. Similarly, it pointed out the Commission's failure to generally include local unions in conciliation conferences with employers where the settlement under discussion affected terms and conditions of employment in the plant. The absence of the local union could preclude chances for an agreement since the employer would have no legal authority to unilaterally change employment conditions. This problem was caused by the Commission's failure in many cases during the 1966-68 period to include not only employers but the local union as well, when the discriminatory situation was institutionalized by a collective-bargaining agreement. The CRD's awareness of this problem and its efforts to inform Commission field personnel concerning collective bargaining and labor-union structure and administration contributed to the Commission's growing sophistication in handling labor-union cases. This also is a by-product of the data-sharing policies of the Commission.

Involvement of International Unions

One of the primary functions of the CRD was to notify the international unions when charges had been filed and decisions issued against their local-union affiliates. Such notification laid the foundation for international union involvement in EEOC conciliations. Upon receiving copies of the decision, the international had the option to participate as a relevant party in all conciliation discussions, either at its own request or that of the conciliator.[27]

The international union in particular has also been viewed by the Commission as potentially increasing its chances of executing settlement agreements with respondent locals. There are several factors underlying this belief. International unions exercise varying but always considerable leverage with their constituent locals. Most internationals have the right to grant and lift charters, regulate the dispensation of strike funds, and approve or reject contracts. Such leverage can be utilized to compel local unions to modify practices or procedures that the Commission has declared unlawful.[28] Moreover, where local unions fail to respond to conciliation because of internal political considerations the presence of an international union representative may free them of such restraints. Under the guise that the international union is compelling the local union to change its practices, the local-union officers are better equipped to enter into an agreement without jeopardizing their local positions.

Assuming that international unions can exercise considerable influence with their locals, what roles do they play in the conciliation process? Have the international unions participated in the Commission's compliance efforts? Table 5-2 highlights the extent of international participation in the various types of cases.

Table 5-2
International Involvement in Labor Union Cases

Type of Case	Total Number	Number Notified of Decision[a]	International Participation in Settlement Discussions
Construction & printing	14	12	4
Segregated locals	14	14	10
Railroad seniority cases	10	9	9
Other seniority cases	17[b]	17	11
Grievances	9	7	3
Union discrimination against individuals	11	9	7
Total	75	68	44

[a]Notification from AFL-CIO, the local union, or from the Commission itself.

[b]Six seniority cases also involved the segregated local issue.

In forty-four cases, representatives of the internationals involved discussed settlement efforts with Commission representatives. This total represents 65 percent of the cases in which the international knew of the decision against its local. The total of forty-four cases should not, however, be taken as the absolute figure demonstrating the extent of international participation. It is conceivable that in the remaining cases the internationals were in contact with their locals although they eschewed any direct participation in negotiations. This happened, for example, in the four segregated local cases where no direct international involvement occurred in the conciliation proceedings.[29]

The extent of international participation varied with the types of cases and, concomitantly, with the union involved. International union participation occurred less frequently in construction cases than it did in seniority or segregated local cases. Several factors are responsible for this result. The negligible role of the international in the former can be attributed to the autonomous powers of craft locals in the building-trades industry. Here, power resides in the local. Thus it is the local which negotiates contracts and which provides jobs to its members. Union members tend to view their allegiance as primarily being owed to the local and not to the international. The chief concern of the nationals in local matters is with jurisdiction. Consequently the local is in a powerful position to resist international union demands that it considers antagonistic to its interests. Interviews with business agents in eight construction-union cases confirmed the extensive powers of the local in its involvement with the Commission. They indicated that the decision to settle was entirely up to the local, particularly the business agent. Typically, this decision was made with the assistance of the local's legal counsel. The role of the international was generally restricted to supplying legal assistance to the local. To these business agents, the international had no authority to dictate the local's position or settlement, and the locals would have resisted any such efforts had they been made.

Interviews with international officials of seven craft unions in the construction and printing crafts confirmed their generally passive role in conciliations. In four cases, they acknowledged a "hands off" approach; they would not participate unless requested to do so by the local. Representatives in the other cases indicated that while they actively sought to participate in conciliation conferences, this participation was predicated on acceptance by the local union. Significantly, there was uniform concurrence that the local union alone was responsible for changing hiring hall, joint-apprenticeship program, and admission standards not in conflict with international union norms.

A different power relationship exists within unions in the railroad industry, a circumstance which has led to a higher incidence of international union involvement. Ten of the twenty-seven seniority cases involved railroad brotherhoods, and in nine of these the international participated in settlement discussions. Traditionally the Grand Lodges have exercised a dominant position over their "subordinate" lodges. The structure of collective bargaining and the legal framework of industrial relations under the Railway Labor Act have contributed to the subordination of the local lodges. Historically, the local lodges have been deprived of collective-bargaining functions, except negotiations concerning the first steps of the grievance process. At its lowest level, collective bargaining has occurred between a single carrier and a single labor organization.[30] To facilitate this bargaining structure, the local lodges on a particular line are grouped together into a cohesive bargaining unit, the system federation, which is administered by a general committee whose full-time salaried officers (the general chairman, vice-chairman, and secretary) negotiated with the railway carrier.[31] Since amendments to the Railway Labor Act in the 1930s the scope of negotiations has steadily expanded until national bargaining over wages and employment conditions has become firmly established.[32] Thus the Grand Lodge has acquired control over the movement of wages and changes in employment conditions throughout the industry. Its directives must be followed by the local lodge.[33]

The broad scope of bargaining which has allowed the Grand Lodges to acquire considerable power over their subordinate lodges undoubtedly reflect economic forces — the desire of the unions to standardize employment conditions and of the carriers to present a united front. We must also note, however, that the legal framework developed in the administration of the Railway Labor Act has intensified the forces extending the structure of collective bargaining and the centralization of powers within the Grand Lodge. The policy of the National Mediation Board has been to refuse to certify a bargaining unit smaller in scope than an entire carrier.[34] The certified bargaining agent in these instances is the Grand Lodge. Consequently, while intermediate structures for bargaining may be set up in the form of system federations, their legitimacy emanates from the delegation of authority they have received from the Grand Lodge.

Ultimate decision-making powers for the union over negotiation of grievances is also vested with the Grand Lodge. Under the Railway Labor Act all unresolved grievances must be referred to the National Railway Adjustment Board which consists of the representatives of carriers and unions "national in scope." Selection of union representatives to serve on the Adjustment Board is made by the international union, generally by the Grand Lodge president. The Railway Labor Act thus establishes a legal basis for the centralization of collective-bargaining authority within the Grand Lodge.

The dominancy of the Grand Lodge in collective bargaining is paralleled in the role it assumes in the conciliation process. In the railroad seniority cases, settlement negotiations generally occurred between the Commission and the Grand Lodge, the latter represented typically, by a representative of the Grand Lodge's General Counsel's Office. It was not unusual for the Grand Lodge president himself to sign all statements concerning the union's position.

The participation of the Grand Lodge in the conciliation effort can be viewed as a routine extension of its authority and power in the collective-bargaining sphere. Seniority practices are defined in the collective-bargaining agreements. Since the Grand Lodge is the bargaining agent, the lodge would lack authority to modify the agreement on its own. Additionally, the Grand Lodges have traditionally defended the existence of separate seniority districts for white and black workers on jurisdictional grounds, even after they deleted exclusionary clauses from their constitutions. For example, they have argued that "porters" do not fall within the same jurisdictional classification as "brakemen." These classifications have in the past been affirmed by the Railway Adjustment Board.[35] Clearly, the local lodge lacks independent authority to modify these rulings. As a result, the Grand Lodge becomes an indispensable party to the conciliation effort.

In the remaining seniority cases, the international union's role as a party to collective bargaining also seems to have influenced its subsequent participation in the settlement effort. The international intervened in conciliations in eleven of the seventeen nonseniority railroad cases. In ten of these it had helped to negotiate and had signed the collective-bargaining agreement. Conversely, the internationals were not parties to the contracts in all six seniority cases where the local unions independently negotiated with Commission representatives. The determining factor behind the international's intervention is the local union's inability constitutionally to modify the agreement without obtaining advance approval of the international when the latter was a signatory to the agreement.

The international's concern over the outcome of the conciliation effort probably grows with the scope of the agreement under review. Where the international is party to a multiplant agreement which provides for similar seniority plans in each plant, Commission charges and remedial demands as applied to one plant have serious implications for the others. Of the eleven nonrailroad seniority cases where the international intervened, three concerned plants in which seniority arrangements under Commission attack had been implemented in other facilities. Thus international intervention is compelled by the need to present a uniform position to the question of seniority. This could be difficult if each local were to negotiate seniority arrangements with Commission representatives on a plant-by-plant basis.

Not all international involvement is motivated by the desire to protect international authority or safeguard existing seniority arrangements. In a case involving a rubber plant, the local had authority to modify seniority provisions without obtaining any prior approval from the international. Nevertheless, the international intervened pursuant to its general policy of participating in settlement discussions. Similarly, international union involvement in steel-company cases reflects the strong civil rights orientation of the steelworkers union. It has established at the international level a civil rights division with primary responsibility for resolving minority employment complaints. Once the international is notified of the EEOC charge, it directs an international representative to investigate the complaint, attempt to resolve it, and if necessary, participate in settlement discussions.

Finally, one should note that both personal and political considerations are important factors underlying international intervention. The support the United Papermakers extended to its locals against government attacks on the seniority system in southern paper mills has been explained as resulting from the personal views of its president who strongly defended the existing seniority arrangements.[36] Any international union officer with a large white southern membership would be cautious in moving against the locals' practices. Indeed, the ability of the international leadership to remain in office may depend upon its success in convincing its white membership that it is resisting governmental pressure. Such efforts might then be manifested in the assistance that the international afforded its locals in EEOC conciliations.

The involvement of international unions in segregated local cases reflects their position as indispensable parties to any conciliation. Generally, only the international has the authority to withdraw a charter and allow for a consolidation of two or more locals. Additionally, the existence of segregated locals has been found to be a violation not only by locals which restrict admission by race, but also by internationals which allow their affiliates to operate on a segregated basis. Thus, in six of the fourteen cases listed, the decision also named the international as a respondent.[37]

A further impetus to the international's intervention is the stated policy of the AFL-CIO against segregated locals. Since nearly all international affiliates have endorsed this policy, they are under added pressure to resolve the Commission's complaint.

There was little direct international involvement in the grievance cases. The three cases that witnessed such intervention involved internationals which had established special civil rights divisions to investigate charges of racial discrimination. In the absence of such a policy, it is doubtful that an international would intervene in the grievance cases since these typically involve minor problems affecting few workers. Moreover, regular union channels are also available for appealing the local's grievance decision.

Somewhat surprisingly, internationals participated in seven of the eleven cases involving union discrimination against individual minority workers. In two cases, intervention can be attributed to the international's policy of investigating such complaints and attending the settlement conferences. Intervention in the other five cases is more difficult to explain. Whether the issue was of peculiar international importance or whether the locals had requested assistance was indeterminable.

Having discussed the extent of international participation in the Commission's conciliation efforts, we can investigate the nature of this involvement. The Commission had hoped that the internationals would support its compliance efforts and thereby increase its chances of executing settlement agreements. While the evidence on the role of the international was not always available in the case files, it appears that the Commission's expectations were not realized.

In analyzing the international's position in conciliation, we can distinguish between several types of international union responses. At one end, there are cases involving international support for the Commission's remedial proposals. This is a basic test of an international's commitment to compliance for ultimate success of the conciliation effort is dependent upon the local union's willingness to adopt the remedies incorporated in the settlement proposal. Of the forty-four known cases of international involvement in settlement discussions, in only five was there evidence of such international support. Four of these cases concerned the international's willingness to implement a merger of its affiliated locals. In the fifth case, an international directed a craft local to grant retroactive membership rights to a complainant who previously had been denied admission.

While there were only five cases of specific international approval of the Commission's settlement proposals, there were six other cases in which the international attempted to resolve the charges against their affiliates. In these six cases, however, the records do not indicate whether or not the internationals accepted, rejected, or even took a position on the Commission's settlement proposal. Two cases concerned the operation of a discriminatory seniority system. In both, the internationals accepted the Commission's decision and directed the locals to resolve the Commission's complaint.

Evidence of more direct international intervention was present in two other cases, one involving a construction craft and the other a railroad brotherhood. Although not entering into an agreement, the building-trades international obtained the local union's consent to admit the charging parties into the union. In the second, the international negotiated an agreement with the EEOC providing for the transfer of black members to the white lodge.

The final two cases involved grievance issues in which the international's involvement was relatively minor. Here, both the locals and the internationals had informed the conciliator that they were willing to conciliate. Conciliation was, however, precluded by the company's refusal to reconsider its adverse personnel action against the charging party.

In only eleven cases was there evidence of positive international action; by contrast in twenty-five other cases the internationals either denied that their locals had engaged in any discriminatory practices or presented counterproposals that were totally unacceptable to the Commission. Thus, in nearly 60 percent of cases of international participation, the international's presence only hindered the Commission's compliance efforts. Clearly, a local union will be more inclined to resist the Commission's remedial demands when it is supported by the international. At the very least, this means that the international will supply legal assistance to the defendent local in the event of a court suit.

A full evaluation of the international's role in conciliation is made extremely difficult by the absence of data in seven cases concerning the international's response either to the Commission's decision or settlement proposals. The files reveal only that the international had a representative present in each case. In none of the seven was an agreement executed. It would, however, be misleading to infer from the failure of the conciliation effort that the international opposed the Commission's settlement proposals. It is conceivable that it favored a settlement but was unsuccessful in obtaining the local's consent and lacked either the power or the will to compel local acceptance. Yet even if we were to assume that in all seven cases the international had supported the Commission's remedial efforts, an admittedly unlikely prospect, we would still be left with the finding that in the majority of cases the international's position was one of opposition. This finding raises doubts as the extent to which the internationals can be viewed as vehicles for compliance.

We can also question whether an international which openly supports the

Commission's settlement proposals is in a position to reverse a local union's policy of discrimination. Earlier we spoke of the leverage that an international could exercise over its local-union affiliates. In practice, the international's power is limited, and its reluctance to utilize what powers it has further restricts its ability to compel compliance.

As noted earlier, many unions have authority to withhold strike funds in cases of unauthorized strikes, approve locally authorized strikes, and to make all collective-bargaining agreements or to authorize those agreements negotiated by the locals. The first two are relatively ineffective as sources of leverage because they can only be applied in a strike situation. Second, even assuming a local's request for strike authorization and assistance, it is not likely that the international would hold in abeyance such approval pending action by the local to purge itself of discriminatory practices. To do so would be to penalize the entire local for practices engineered perhaps by only a few individuals. Moreover, in failing to support a strike for a legitimate objective, the international might be bolstering the employer's bargaining position and considerably threatening union standards in the community.[38]

Regarding the international's ability to participate in contract negotiations as a source of leverage, we must note that many internationals (98 of 194) do not have any constitutional authority to veto contracts negotiated by their locals.[39] Yet even those internationals which exercise such authority face practical restrictions in using it. Rejecting an entire contract is surely an extreme measure and justifiable in only those cases where the discriminatory practices are pervasive and affect large groups of workers. Additionally, there are types of discriminatory union practices that are not amenable to contract reform, but which require changes in the local union's government. For example, a local union's policy of rejecting grievances of black workers cannot be corrected by changing the contract's language. It requires action on the part of the union leadership to remove or discipline union stewards and grievance committeemen who are guilty of discrimination. The use of its collective-bargaining powers is relevant only when the contract has expired and a new one is being negotiated. Consequently, during the life of the contract, the international cannot use its collective-bargaining authority to eliminate discriminatory employment practices that the international itself had previously sanctioned. To the worker who is the victim of discrimination, the prospect that relief must await the period of contract renegotiation affords him little solace.

There is another weapon the internationals can possibly exercise to effect changes in a local union's policies. Most labor organizations have extremely broad authority to establish trusteeships to protect the "best interests of the international."[40] Locals refusing to modify discriminatory policies could be placed in receivership, with international representatives subsequently implementing corrective measures.

Such an approach is rarely utilized. Thus, in none of the fifty-six nonagreement cases examined was there evidence of planned or actual international intervention to impose a trusteeship as a means of achieving local-union compliance. Although the authority is there, internationals are reluctant to impose a trusteeship because of its drastic and costly nature. If resisted by the local's officers and membership, litigation is necessary by the international to gain control over the local's office and assets. Additionally, there is the concern that a trusteeship may generate membership dissatisfaction resulting in changes of allegiances in favor of rival unions. Because of these factors, direct and forceful international intervention to compel local-union compliance is unlikely, limited at best to cases of extreme local-union abuse.

6

Sources of Relief to
Discriminatees

In this chapter we will be investigating the process by which discriminatees seek
and obtain relief from the EEOC. From interviews with charging parties, an
attempt will be made to determine a charging party's informational sources
concerning the EEOC, his understanding and knowledge of other forums of
governmental relief, and the nature of assistance he received from other
organizations, private and public, in processing his complaint. By contrasting the
discriminatee's ability to obtain legal aid from the Commission with the
availability and efficacy of other sources of relief, we can judge the ultimate
significance of the conciliation process.

Data Sources on EEOC

Table 6-1 lists the charging parties' data sources concerning the Commission in
forty-five cases.[1]

Table 6-1
**Sources of Information Concerning the EEOC (Some indicated more than one
source)**

Primary Source	Number of Cases
1. TV & Radio Commercial	4
2. NAACP & NAACP Legal Defense Fund	17
3. Plant Poster	7
4. Pamphlet and newspapers	12
5. Fellow Workers	9
6. Other Civil Rights Organizations	5
Total	54

Nearly 40 percent of those contacted learned about the Commission from the
NAACP branch in the community. This fact demonstrates the key role of civil
rights organizations in popularizing the Commission's compliance process. Other
organizations have also been instrumental in the filing of charges; they include
the Lawyers' Constitutional Defense League and the American Civil Liberties
Union.

The second most significant source was that of newspapers and pamphlets
that discussed the Commission. Often, the lead charging party was articulate and

obviously alert to printed material explaining the EEOC's functions. The charging party may not typify the average worker in the plant, but may in fact be a leader among his fellow workers in his efforts to eliminate discrimination. This is especially true in those cases where a segregated local had been in existence. Here, the black workers have a nucleus of black leaders with many years of industrial experience. Following the passage of the act, these leaders were quick to point out existing inequities and to press charges when management and the white union leadership refused to alter discriminatory employment practices.

The Commission itself helps to inform the public of its compliance efforts. Beginning in 1966, the Commission developed radio tapes which explained the Commission's complaint process. These tapes were subsequently circulated to the 1,000 leading stations throughout the nation which played them as a public service. In 1969 the Commission's Public Affairs Office developed commercials for television broadcasting which also notified the public of its right to file charges and identified for it the nearest regional office handling complaints. In four of the forty-five cases, the commercials were responsible for the charging party's knowledge of the Commission.

More important than the Commission's public service announcements are the posters that employers and unions are obligated to put up.[2] Seven of the forty-five lead charging parties learned of the Commission through this method. These posters announced that any individual who felt that he or she was discriminated against could file a charge. The address of the Commission's headquarters in Washington, D.C. was written on the bottom of the posters. Under the act, the posters had to be placed in a conspicuous place.

Fellow employees constituted a final source of information. The lead charging parties could not indicate in these cases how their acquaintances learned of the Commission, but it is probable that the sources previously discussed — commercials, contact with the civil rights organizations, posters, and newspapers — constituted the basis of a worker's knowledge of the Commission's complaint process.

Scope of NLRB Intervention

Besides the EEOC and the Justice Department, the National Labor Relations Board has jurisdiction to intervene against labor unions which are engaging in racially discriminatory practices.[3] In 1964 the NLRB held that a labor union, acting as exclusive bargaining agent, could not exclude, segregate, or otherwise discriminate among members of the bargaining unit on racial grounds.[4] The act has been interpreted to impose upon the bargaining agent a duty to represent all members of the bargaining unit fairly. Such discriminatory activity as (1) failing to process the grievances of blacks with the same diligence as those of nonminority workers, (2) bargaining for a contract containing a racially discriminatory provision, (3) excluding or bypassing minority applicants when referring workers from its hiring hall, and (4) causing an employer to discriminate against a worker because of his race violate the union's duty of fair representation and are subject to the Board's cease and desist powers.

The remedial authority exercised by the NLRB in *Hughes Tool* was applauded by civil-rights leaders. Most important, it was viewed as a precedent for applying the NLRB's more effective powers and procedures against employment discrimination. In contrast to the Commission's authority, the NLRB could enforce its remedial orders. Additionally, NLRB procedures removed from the charging party the financial burden of prosecuting his own complaint. Following *Hughes Tool,* it was expected that many new charges of employment discrimination would be processed, since it was apparent that the Board was ready to act decisively.

This expectation was not realized. Between 1964 and June 1969, the NLRB had been involved in only thirty-two cases in which charges of racial discrimination had been filed against labor unions. Of these thirty-two cases, sixteen involved a regional, Board, or court determination that the filed charges were meritorious.[5] The Board's meager caseload contrasts sharply with the greater number of similar charges filed annually with the EEOC. For example, in fiscal 1967 that agency received 884 charges alleging union discrimination on the basis of race.[6] What is responsible for this imbalance? Surely, we would expect that aggrieved individuals would go to the agency which has the greater enforcement and remedial powers.

To shed some light on this problem, the charging parties were asked whether or not they had filed charges with the NLRB and, if not, whether they knew the Board could also have handled their complaint. Of forty-five interviewed, only seven charging parties indicated their awareness of the NLRB's authority to handle civil-rights complaints. It seems that lack of information within the civil-rights community is a significant factor behind the NLRB's small employment discrimination caseload.

Of the seven who knew of the NLRB, two bypassed the Board because they felt they could obtain more expeditious relief from the EEOC. They felt that since the Board's authority was generally utilized to resolve union-employer labor disputes, their particular type of complaint would not be afforded the same priority that a purely civil rights agency could provide. In two other cases, the charging parties stated that they had intended to file with the Board, but were dissuaded by regional office personnel. In one case, the regional office advised the discriminatee to file charges with the EEOC, and in the other recommended to the grievant that he first exhaust his intraunion grievance procedures. Thus, in only three cases were complaints that ultimately were processed by the EEOC also filed with the NLRB.[7]

The data seem to suggest that not only charging parties, but NAACP representatives as well, remain uninformed about the NLRB. Civil-rights representatives were responsible for informing the charging party about the Commission in twenty-two cases. Yet, in only three of these cases had the charging party any knowledge of the NLRB as a possible forum of relief. On the other hand, it is conceivable that the failure of civil-rights representatives to inform a charging party of the Board may not represent their ignorance of the NLRB but rather a personal perference for the EEOC process. In this regard, it should be noted that the NLRB may face serious limitations in devising proper remedies. Frequently, provisions in collective-bargaining agreements have institutionalized and carried over into the present the effects of discriminatory employment practices which themselves have been terminated. Seniority arrangements present such a problem. On its face, a seniority provision may be neutral. Yet, where it has been superimposed upon a previous policy of restricting minorities to limited job classifications, the continuation and application of the seniority provision to minorities will operate to penalize them, although the employer has abandoned a policy of dead-ending blacks. As a remedy, the Commission requires modifications in the contract to allow blacks to compete for jobs on the basis of their total employment seniority.

At the same time, there is some doubt as to whether the NLRB possesses such authority. A previous effort by the NLRB to order an employer to agree to a dues check-off contract clause as a remedy for his refusal to bargain was rejected by the Supreme Court.[8] The Board was reminded that it had no authority to compel the inclusion of a particular substantive element in the collective-bargaining agreement. Rather, Section 8(d) of Taft-Hartley required that the parties be free to determine their own bargain. On the basis of this decision, it could be argued that the extent of the Board's authority is limited to setting aside unlawful contractual provisions and ordering the parties to bargain over new nondiscriminatory terms. Yet the NLRB would not be free to establish new terms that it felt were necessary to remedy the discrimination sustained by minority workers. To do so would be infringing upon the parties' rights under 8(d). Thus full relief would not be possible as a result of NLRB intervention.[9]

The absence of such remedial authority significantly weakens the efficacy of Board intervention, for an NLRB order requiring the parties only to bargain for a new provision contains inherent and obvious limitations. First, the discriminatory provision may have to remain in effect pending agreement on a new one. Second, there is no assurance that the parties will succeed in developing a new employment arrangement that will safeguard the rights of minority workers. Local-union leaders are under intense political pressure to reject any modification in employment practices that would deprive white workers of their job expectations. In several seniority cases, local-union memberships threatened to strike management if it modified the current seniority arrangement, notwithstanding previous Commission findings that the seniority system discriminated against minorities. Nor is a contempt proceeding an adequate guarantee that the union and employer will bargain in good faith for contract modifications. Contempt is a time-consuming process, and one which is difficult to invoke. In a contempt action, the NLRB has the burden of proving a violation of an enforcement order by a "preponderance of the evidence,"[10] "clear and convincing proof,"[11] or "more than a preponderance of the evidence."[12] These heavy evidentiary standards severely limit the frequency and applicability of contempt citations in bargaining cases.

The scope of NLRB intervention is also restricted by the language of the statute. Under the Labor-Management Relations Act, unions are empowered to "prescribe its own rules with respect to the acquisition or retention of membership."[13] This provision would seem to immunize unions which established admission criteria based on race from the stricture of the act and may explain why so few charges against construction unions were filed before the NLRB between 1964-69.

Intervention by State Commissions on Civil Rights

If the NLRB has not proved to be in practice — or perhaps even in theory — an adequate alternative for the EEOC's remedial process, what other forums of relief are open to the charging party, and to what extent do complainants utilize them? One option is a state Fair Employment Practice Commission (FEPC). Under the Civil Rights Act, the EEOC must defer jurisdiction for a period of up to sixty days to those states which established agencies for administering and enforcing statutes prohibiting discriminatory employment practices. For the deferral to occur, the Commission must be satisfied that the state law provides the state FEPC with sufficient powers to provide relief.[14] After the sixty-day period has expired, the complainant can file the same charge with the EEOC and have it process the complaint, if he feels that his rights are not being adequately protected by the state authority.[15]

As of March 1969, the EEOC deferred to agencies in thirty states on complaints alleging discrimination based on race, religion, or national origin and to fourteen states on complaints claiming discrimination based on sex.[16] Nevertheless, the extent to which discriminatees can seek aid from a state FEPC is limited by the critical fact that in the area of the nation which is the source of approximately 50 percent of all discrimination complaints, such agencies have not been established. During fiscal 1969, the southern non-FEP states accounted for more than 50 percent of all charges.[17] Of the seventy-five cases examined in this study, only fifteen arose in an FEP state. Thus it is clear that the existence of Fair Employment Practice Commissions in over thirty states does not replace the need for vigorous federal civil-rights action.

It should be noted that even the existence of state Fair Employment Practice Commissions in all fifty states may still not operate as an effective alternative to national intervention. There are presently serious questions regarding the efficacy of state FEPC operations. The view of one commentator is that Title VII's mandatory deferral policy has been a serious obstacle to enforcement, because the state agency is typically reluctant or ill-equipped to utilize its powers.[18] The EEOC shares this negative evaluation. In the beginning of fiscal 1970 more than 85 percent of the complaints that had been deferred to state agencies ultimately came back to the EEOC for handling. The Commission feels that this situation is largely due to the failure of state commissions to identify or eliminate discrimination.[19]

Such an assessment may be too critical. Under Title VII, a charging party can immediately request the Commission to assert jurisdiction after the sixty-day period has expired; this is too short a time interval within which to expect a state commission to complete an investigation, adopt a ruling, and develop appropriate relief. In practice, the Commission may be asserting jurisdiction over cases that ultimately could be resolved at the state level.

The data in the fifteen cases that were initially deferred to state commissions, however, lend some support to the EEOC's view. Of these fifteen cases, the state commissions dismissed the complaints in nine cases, declined jurisdiction in two instances, had no complete record of the case in two others, and found a violation in the remaining two cases. The high rate of dismissal is cause for concern. Not only did the Commission find cause in each, but in four of the nine dismissal cases, the attorney general subsequently filed civil suits. In one such case, the state commission investigation revealed that there was probable cause to believe the charge meritorious. The next stage under the state commission regulations would have been the holding of a public hearing and the issuance of a cease and desist order upon a finding of discrimination. No hearing was ever held and the case was "administratively closed" without prejudice. According to a former attorney with the state commission, the chairman felt that the "case was too big for them to handle". Several other "dismissal" cases revealed similar dubious practices. One state commission dismissed a complaint in part on the grounds that the charging party had not exhausted his intraunion appeals process. It also appears that some state commissions in the mid-1960s were taking an overly restrictive view of the kinds of employment practices outlawed by Title VII. Practices which in effect operated to discriminate against minorities were held lawful if they were neutral on their face. Thus one state commission wrote the EEOC that the union's practice of giving preference in union referrals to those who had experience under union contractors was "no violation of the letter of the law [although] same could not be said of the spirit of the law."[20]

The four cases in which state commissions declined jurisdiction or in which their records were incomplete merit further discussion. In one case, the state declined jurisdiction on the grounds that the union which was acting in an employer capacity when charged as a respondent did not employ the minimum number of employees necessary to bring it within the state's jurisdiction.[21] In another, the state refused to accept jurisdiction because the charge was brought by a commissioner. The state FEPC had established the procedure of only processing the complaints of individual charging parties. The two "no record" cases defy simple explanations. In one, the state commission informed the author that while it had a record of the charge and investigation, the file contained no information as to the determination of cause or no cause, the settlement efforts (if any) undertaken, or of its relationship with the EEOC. From the state commission's files, a charge had been filed but never fully processed. In the second case, the state commission indicated it had no record of any kind on this case.[22]

In both cases in which the state commission found cause, evidence indicates that the state acted to curtail and remedy the discriminatory employment practice. In one, the state commission successfully sued in court to enforce its remedial order that a black craftsman be hired as a business agent. In the second case, the state commission proceeded to hold a public hearing and issue a cease and desist order against a printing union for excluding blacks from apprenticeship programs. Thus, in only two of the fifteen cases did the state commissions respond vigorously to the problem. When we couple this record with the absence of state commissions in those areas generating approximately 50 percent of the charges, the need for a federal civil-rights agency pursuing a vigorous compliance program is clearly demonstrated.

Relief through Public and Private Litigation

A final potential source of relief for complainants was the federal courts. Under the 1964 act, a charging party could bring suit if the Commission had been unable to execute a settlement.[23] The attorney general could independently initiate a civil suit when he had "reasonable cause to believe . . . [there is] a pattern or practice of resistance to the rights secured by [Title VII] . . . ."[24] The critical question is whether recourse to the federal courts was a viable option to charging parties. Did complainants in unsuccessful conciliation cases file private suits to protect their employment rights? Secondly, to what extent did the attorney general intervene to file "pattern or practice" suits?

Table 6-2 examines for the several categories of union discrimination the rate at which public and private suits were filed where the Commission had failed to execute a settlement agreement.

Overall, law suits were filed in less than one-half of the unsuccessful settlement cases; eleven of the suits were brought by the attorney general; one was brought by a state attorney general. The remaining thirteen were initiated by the complainants. The singular fact associated with the private suits is that they were nearly all filed in behalf of the charging parties by private civil-rights organizations, such as the NAACP Legal Defense Fund. This was the pattern in

Table 6-2
Public or Private Suit Action in Nonagreement Cases (56)

Type of Case	Number	No Suit Action	Suit Filed	Private Suit	Attorney General Suit
Discriminatory union action against an individual	10	8	2	1	1[a]
Craft union exclusion	13	7	6	2	4
Segregated locals	11	8	3	1	2
Seniority	19	6	13	8	5
Grievance cases	4	3	1	1	—
Totals	57	32	25	13	12

[a]Filed by state attorney general.

twelve of the thirteen private suits. It appears that unless provided with outside assistance, an individual or group of complainants is not likely to file suit. The factors underlying this situation are revealed in Table 6-3, which records the reasons why the complainants in nineteen cases decided not to proceed any further with their charges.[25]

Table 6-3
Factors Responsible for Complainants' Decisions not to Seek Legal Assistance (Responses in Nineteen Cases)[a]

Factor	Number of Cases in which Factor was Mentioned
Concern over costs	14
Danger of retaliation	6
Lack of knowledge as to attorney willing to handle case	4
Partial settlement	3

[a]Some cases indicated more than one factor, hence, the difference in number.

As the table indicates, the concern over the costs of hiring an attorney was the major deterrent to the complainants' filing suit. Lead charging parties mentioned this factor in nearly all the cases. Typically, the charging parties were blue-collar workers with families to support. For them, the costs involved in litigation are prohibitive. Additionally, for charging parties who have been forced to find new jobs, and who therefore may no longer desire reinstatement, the incentive to sue is diminished. In general, one should note that civil-rights cases can be very costly because of the large number of man hours that will be devoted to the case. The complexity involved in determining and proving discrimination and the many procedural issues that may have to be resolved even before a case gets to trial create a heavy manpower burden upon counsel for all parties.[26] The problem is that while corporation and union can undertake the costs of supporting their attorneys, the individual or group of charging parties in a Title VII case are limited in the funds they can provide their counsel. As a result, the case presentation in support of the charging party may be deficient.

A second inhibiting element to the filing of suits is the fear of retaliation. Charging parties in six of the nineteen cases felt that by filing suit they would be labeling themselves "trouble-makers" and perhaps subjecting themselves to further discrimination. Reinforcing their concern was the conviction that in the event of a retaliatory act the Commission would not be any more successful in affording them relief than it was in correcting their oringinal complaints. As one charging party indicated: "I put my head on the cutting block when I filed my charge and the government did nothing for me. I can't take any further risk."

Some charging parties were dissuaded from seeking legal assitance in part because they lacked any knowledge regarding the identity of lawyers who would be willing to handle their cases. In three cases, charging parties who resided in small southern communities were reluctant to utilize the services of the local bar, since the latter might well be antagonistic to their objectives. They expressed a reluctance to seek and pay for legal assistance unless they could have advance assurance of the sympathies of the attorney who would be handling their cases. The fact remains that a large percentage of the private Section 706 suits filed arc handled by a small group of attorneys who are associated with the NAACP or the NAACP Legal Defense Fund. This development has occurred partly because few local attorneys have the expertise to try such cases, and because some local attorneys, after weighing monetary and political considerations, are reluctant to participate in such cases. From the attorney's perspective the civil-rights case will produce little monetary return since the financial capacity of the client is minimal.

At times, the charging parties did not seek legal assistance because the Commission's settlements were partially successful. In three final cases charging parties were denied admission into the union; following issuance of the reasonable cause decision, the respondent unions admitted them into membership. While rejecting the Commission's effort to adopt class remedies, the unions had at least taken the steps to correct the immediate charge, and thereby had satisfied the remedial demands of the charging parties. In so doing, they immunized themselves against the possibility of a civil suit.

As a result of the charging party's disinclination to file suit on his own, the brunt of enforcement activity fell by default upon the Department of Justice and private civil-rights agencies. The evidence suggests, however, that neither, independently or jointly managed this task successfully. As Table 6-2 revealed, approximately half of the union cases in which agreements were not executed were not brought to trial. Additionally, the rate of private and public suits indicated in the table overstated the general frequency of court action for all employment discrimination cases. The Commission has reported that private suit action was initiated in less than 10 percent of the cases where it had found reasonable cause but was unable to achieve a settlement.[27] Nor was the Department of Justice a center of vigorous enforcement activity. Between September 1967 and September 1969, Justice filed Title VII complaints in only thirty-eight cases.[28] This number must be balanced against the hundreds of reasonable-cause decisions in which no settlements were executed.[29]

The relative infrequency of court initiated suits is not surprising. Both the Department of Justice and private civil-rights agencies, such as the NAACP Legal Defense Fund, have broad responsibilities, only one of which is the elimination of employment discrimination. Thus the Civil Rights Division is just one of seven divisions in the Justice Department. Even within that division, financial and manpower resources must be spread over several areas: (1) voting, (2) school desegregation, (3) desegregation of public facilities, (4) enforcement of the fair-housing provision. Clearly, the priority afforded employment cases under Title VII must be weighed against the need for intervention to resolve other critical problems. Private civil-rights agencies share this same burden of having to cover the entire spectrum of civil-rights problems with only limited resources.

What perhaps is surprising is the frequency of court action in the labor-union cases. The 45 percent rate of intervention far exceeded the 10 percent rate that was found for all employment discrimination cases. An examination of Table 6-2 may provide some insight into this development. Two categories of union or union-employer discrimination generated two-thirds of all suit actions — construction and seniority. These cases presented problems of class discrimination as opposed to discrimination against individual workers. Given limited resources, the only rational policy of intervention would be one aimed at bringing relief to the largest number of persons possible. For the Justice Department, such a policy was in fact required by the act, since it was authorized to institue law suits only when a "pattern or practice of discrimination exists." The flagrant nature of discriminatory practices in the construction industry, which often resulted in the complete exclusion of minorities, undoubtedly formed a basis for the decision to attack these violations first.[30]

A factor responsible for the large number of suits in seniority (job advancement) cases was the establishment of a landmark precedent in *Quarles v. Phillip Morris.*[31] This decision destroyed the validity of any seniority arrangement that operated to inhibit the movement of minorities out of inferior job classifications to which they had been restricted. The successful suit in *Quarles* encouraged the filing of similar suits, as Justice Department and private attorneys hoped that other courts would adopt the *Quarles* precedent. Additionally, once the precedent had been adopted, it was expected that other employers and unions which were sued might settle without going to trial.[32]

Intervention by public or private civil-rights agencies only in major cases of discrimination meant that the genral burden of litigation fell upon the individual complainant. In practice, few complainants filed suit because of the financial costs and risks involved in such a venture. Furthermore, those who were willing to bear such costs may have been precluded from doing so by the dearth of attorneys qualified and willing to handle Title VII complaints. Commission personnel have noted that "there [was] almost no experience bar available for charing parties."[33]

This study suggests that the rate of court suits is perhaps higher in labor-union cases than the 10 percent rate noted in all cases. Yet, even if the overall rate was 50 percent, that would be an effective enforcement program. It would mean that charging parties in 50 percent of all cases were unable to obtain further relief. Such a record is inconsistent with the national objective of eradicating discriminatory employment practices. In summary, there is strong reason to believe that niether public nor private litigation has operated as an effective alternative means of enforcing the 1964 act. The failure of the Commission's conciliation efforts more likely than not meant the termination of all efforts under Title VII to eliminate discriminatory practices(s) and to provide relief to the discriminatee. The social consequences of such a deficient enforcement policy are revealed in the following letter written by one charging party following the Commission's unsuccessful conciliation effort:

This is an open letter to whom it may concern. Even though the decision in my case was in my favor and the investigation showed that the company I charged with discrimination to be wrong and the union failed to act in my behalf, . . . I was discharged. Since my case has been dismissed by the Commission, I now feel the injustice of fellow-Negro Americans who take to violence that exists in the United States today. The people who I once condemned for acting the way they do, by destroying and burning and looting have known the injustice that I have just now to know really does exist.

I do not know why you dismissed my case, . . . but I do know that the Commission can and do have the power to deal with this company if it wanted to. Instead, you dumpt the case in my lap and tell me I can file suit in the circuit court, which you know I will lose and become a case for relief.

I will forward my letter from the Commission to the Negro History Library and hope that the people who read them will wonder as I do why this case ended as it did.[34]

This letter summarizes what is most unfortunate about the failure of the Commission's remedial efforts. First, discriminatory practices that deprive minority workers of economic benefits remain in effect. In the above-cited case, the discriminatee was unfairly discharged. This situation was paralleled by hundreds of similar instances where the Commission was unable to execute a conciliation agreement.

A second effect is the generation of feelings of despair, bitterness, and frustration. At times, the charging party cannot comprehend the Commission's inability to provide relief, and, as a result, may even view the Commission's settlement failure as a reflection of the Commission's unwillingness to act. As the charging party noted, he did "know that the Commission do have the power to deal with the Company if it wanted to." It is such feelings of powerlessness and frustrated hopes that create the necessary climate for urban disorders and violence.[35] This, then, is the ultimate consequence of the Commission's inability to fully eradicate discriminatory employment practices.

7

Concluding Observations and Recommendations

Need for Enforcement Powers

In a recent article, Professor Herbert Northrup of the Wharton School argued against granting the EEOC enforcement powers.[1] His position was based upon several factors: (1) notwithstanding the EEOC's lack of enforcement authority, significant progress has been made in eliminating employment discrimination, (2) that much of the job inequality that remains is not due to discrimination per se, but to a variety of socioeconomic factors that cannot be resolved through litigation, and (3) enforcement authority would not enable the Commission to conciliate cases more expeditiously or successfully because of serious deficiencies in the conciliation process.

This study presents data which lead the author to far different conclusions. It is useful, therefore, to critically examine Professor Northrup's observations against the background of the study's finding. In this manner, some of the basic findings of this study will be summarized and placed in proper perspective.

Northrup's first observation is that through voluntary compliance, attorney general suits, and cases litigated by private parties signficant changes have been made in employment patterns. He specifically mentions the government's success in invalidating the discriminatory seniority systems and referral arrangements of the building-craft unions. He concludes that "the case can be far more easily made that the EEOC, as now constituted, has had significant enforcement success rather than the other way around."[2] This assessment seriously overstates the efficacy of the Commission's enforcement efforts. In this study, less than 25 percent of all cases (eighteen of seventy-five) resulted in the execution of a settlement agreement. Moreover, most of the settlement agreements did not contain the remedial elements necessary to both provide relief to the discriminatees and eliminate the practices underlying the complaints. Regarding seniority cases, not one of the twenty-seven such cases resulted in a settlement agreement that implemented the judicially accepted remedy first established in *Quarles v. Philip Morris.*[3] Similarly ineffective results occurred in building-craft union cases and even in those cases where the discrimination affected individuals as opposed to a class of minority workers. It would seem that for every successfully conciliated case, there are scores in which no minimum relief is provided.

There was always the possibility that the charging party or the Justice Department would file suit, and thereby obtain appropriate relief for complainants. Yet these avenues have been shown to be poor substitutes for the administrative enforcement of the 1964 act. Overall, less than 10 percent of all nonagreement cases were litigated. This figure may be higher in labor-union cases, but it is not sufficiently high to guarantee each discriminatee that his rights under the act will be safeguarded.

These findings should not be viewed as evidence that no progress has been made under the act of 1964. Litigation brought by the Justice Department and individual charging parties has produced significant decisions requiring the elimination of employment patterns that restricted minorities into inferior job classifications. The Commission has achieved some success in conciliation. Additionally, the average citizen's desire to voluntarily comply with the act may, as Northrup suggests, generate improvements in minority employment patterns. This study made no attempt to examine what can be considered the spillover effects of EEOC compliance efforts. At the same time, the basic determinant of the need for an administrative enforcement mechanism is whether or not the commission has been able to secure compliance and provide relief to the charging parties through the use of voluntary means. Thus it is the Commission which must respond to the thousands of charges of discrimination filed, and it is the Commission and not the courts which has proven to be the final governmental forum which will make the effort to resolve the complaint in the overwhelming majority of cases. Significantly, this study strongly suggests that powers of moral suasion, mediation, and conciliation are insufficient; therefore, if the rights of charging parties are to be vindicated and discriminatory employment patterns eliminated, the Commission must be armed with enforcement powers. A procedure which provides the Commission with the powers of moral suasion alone violates the basic principle underlying our system of government — that rights created by law are protected rights.

Northrup's second observation is that granting the Commission enforcement powers would be insufficient to eliminate job inequality in the United States. This is certainly true. The advancement of minority workers into better-paying positions is not only dependent on the elimination of discriminatory practices but is also contingent upon the eradication of barriers to equal educational, housing, and training opportunities. Nevertheless, the existence of other problem areas cannot be utilized as evidence of the futility involved in eliminating discrimination through the administrative use of enforcement powers. Northrup himself recognizes the progress that has been made through litigation. Moreover, this study indicates that the lack of enforcement authority has rendered the Commission powerless in the face of persistent union and employer acts of discrimination.

A third observation of Northrup concerns the operations of the conciliation process. He dismisses the notion that enforcement authority would enable the Commission to conciliate cases more efficiently and expeditiously. Here, Northrup is probably correct. As this study has shown, the EEOC decision-conciliation process is plagued by inordinate time delays. It takes on the average eighteen to twenty-four months to handle a case from the investigation through the conciliation stage. This problem is not one which will evaporate by granting the EEOC enforcement powers. Its resolution necessitates the hiring of more and better trained staff and the upgrading of incumbent personnel.

Northrup also feels that enforcement powers would not significantly enhance the Commission's ability to execute settlement agreements. He argues that:

It is possible that if EEOC had enforcement powers more litigants would agree to the proposed conciliation terms. *Many do not now, however, because the basis proposed for settlement by EEOC conciliations is unreasonable.* Cease and desist orders might increase litigation in such instances, but would not necessarily effectuate the purposes of the Civil Rights Act.[4] (Emphasis added.)

Nowhere does Northrup document the charge that the Commission's settlement proposals are unreasonable. Indeed, the general criticism that can be made of EEOC settlement agreements is that they are too soft, failing to contain minimum relief necessary to eliminate the discriminatory employment practice and make whole the discriminatees. Of the eighteen settlement agreements which were examined in this study, only seven achieved the Commission's remedial objectives. Additionally, there was no evidence that the Commission's remedial demands in the nonagreement cases were excessive.

The basic question remains: Will enforcement authority increase the Commission's chances of executing effective settlement agreements? This study suggests an affirmative answer. While it is difficult to determine the magnitude of the positive relationship between enforcement authority and the ability to conciliate, we have a firm basis for concluding that more respondents will settle rather than face the filing of a suit. As noted earlier, many respondents had little incentive to settle, realizing the limited likelihood of a court suit. Thus, in conciliation some respondents openly admitted their skepticism as to the possibility of a court suit. In effect, respondents were negotiating with Commission representatives from the position of maximum bargaining power — high costs involved in settling, minimum costs associated with the rejection of the Commission's settlement proposals. The power to ultimately compel compliance will raise the costs associated with nonagreement. Respondents will be faced at the very least with automatic expenses of litigation, unfavorable publicity, and the possibility of back-pay liability. Exposed to such certain costs, respondents would be more inclined to settle.

Significantly, the experience of the NLRB supports the view that administrative agencies armed with enforcement powers will have greater success in executing settlement agreements. On the average, the NLRB informally settles annually approximately two-thirds of all unfair labor-practice charges that it has found meritorious.[5] The unwillingness of respondents to undergo the expense of litigation and their recognition that there is little chance of winning the case have been shown to be primary factors motivating the settlement of unfair labor-practice cases.[6] These same factors should operate in racial discrimination cases to promote settlement.

There is a final consideration which justifies and, indeed, makes it essential that the EEOC possess enforcement authority. Typically, when a statute grants an administrative agency enforcement powers, it also established a procedure whereby the decisions and orders of the agency are reviewable by an independent body. In the cases of the NLRB and other independent administrative agencies, the courts serve as the reviewing body. They are empowered to reverse administrative decisions that are arbitrary or contrary to established legal or public policy. Aside from ensuring due process, the existence of a reviewing body serves a concomitant purpose. Its mere presence operates as a catalyst for the agency's careful and judicious handling of cases. Under the act of 1964 there was no independent monitoring of the EEOC's activities; consequently, there did not exist the powerful incentive to perform at the highest level provided by the realization that decisions made are subject to scrutiny and reversal. Northrup indicates that the quality of EEOC investigations must be improved.[7] There is no better method of compelling an agency to streamline and improve its operations than by subjecting its work product to independent review and modification.

Equal Employment Opportunity Act of 1972

In 1972 Congress amended the Civil Rights Act of 1964 to grant the EEOC enforcement powers. As a result of these amendments, the Commission can institute civil suits in U.S. district courts against those respondents who have rejected the Commission's conciliation proposals.[8] This provision corrects a major deficiency in the Commission's compliance process. The Commission's power to back up its conciliation efforts with the threat of suit action should significantly enhance its ability to execute effective conciliation agreements.

Passage of the 1972 act was marked by legislative controversy and conflict. Many organizations such as the NAACP, AFL-CIO, and the Leadership Conference on Civil Rights felt that a more effective method of enforcing equal employment opportunities was available. This would involve enabling the Commission to hold formal hearings and to issue cease and desist orders upon a finding that discrimination had occurred.[9] Utilizing some of the observations made in this study, we will examine some of the issues involved in determining which enforcement mechanism — cease and desist or direct court enforcement — can best promote compliance with the act of 1964.

Since its inception, the EEOC has been developing a growing and uniform body of administrative law concerning employment discrimination. For example, EEOC decisions have established guidelines identifying legitimate from illegitimate seniority systems, testing procedures, and recruitment and hiring policies. Given cease and desist authority, the EEOC, as the agency authorized to conduct hearings and to determine the merits of all complaints, would be able to develop and apply a coherent body of principles and guidelines in the area of employment discrimination. With one single administrative agency interpreting the act, charging parties and respondents would be better aware of their rights and obligations. As a result, the number of violations might fall as potential respondents would seek to shape their policies in conformity with Commission rulings. It is also possible that fewer nonmerit charges would be filed, as the law of Title VII would be more understandable to employees.

To some degree these results would be sacrificed by an enforcement mechanism relying on direct court enforcement of civil actions brought by the Commission. Under this approach, the district courts and not the Commission would be trying employment discrimination cases. Instead of a single administrative agency making policy, there would be 100 district courts ruling on complaints. It is likely that serious conflicts among the lower courts would develop as they sought to define and remedy employment discrimination. Consequently, the development of a uniform approach to the problem of employment discrimination that would guide the conduct of those covered by the act would be precluded to some extent and long-delayed in many instances. Thus utlimate reconciliation of conflicting court positions at the district and appellate levels would have to await Supreme Court intervention — a long, slow, and uncertain process.

The cease and desist approach also places a premium on the remedial expertise of the Commission. As this study has shown, the Commission has developed a considerable amount of expertise in remedying employment discrimination. In labor-union cases, for example, the EEOC has fashioned remedies which, if implemented, would have eliminated the practice underlying the complaint and compensated charging parties for their losses. Significantly, the courts have generally acknowledged and deferred to the remedial expertise of administrative agencies, which are authorized to issue cease and desist orders and take appropriate remedial measures.[10] Consequently, a compliance mechanism based on the Commission's exercise of cease and desist powers would enable it to continue to develop and apply a remedial policy capable of resolving complex systems of discrimination.

On the other hand, in a system of direct court enforcement, it is the district courts and not the Commission that are authorized to try and remedy employment-discrimination complaints. In contrast to the administrative cease and desist framework wherein the function of the courts is largely to serve as a check on arbitrary and erroneous rulings, the direct court enforcement process requires the lower (district) courts to try cases on a *de novo* basis. Consequently, the district courts would be fashioning their own remedies, without any requirement that they adhere to the remedial policies formulated by the Commission. In effect, a system of direct court enforcement jeopardizes the considerable reservoir of expertise that the Commission had developed through seven years of involvement in thousands of Title VII cases.

There is also the problem that direct court enforcement of Title VII complaints may generate serious delays before relief is provided. To the already overburdened dockets of the district courts, thousands of new civil rights cases would be added, thereby creating serious court backlogs. In fiscal year 1969, the median time interval from issue to trial in U.S. district courts was thirteen months.[11] In contrast, in fiscal year 1970, the median time interval from the filing of an unfair labor practice charge before the NLRB to a trial examiner's decision was approximately seven months.[12]

Another time element should be weighed in evaluating which compliance mechanism is preferable. Proponents of the direct court-enforcement approach emphasize that although a district court proceeding may take longer to conclude than an NLRB trial examiner's hearing, the decision and remedial order of the district court can immediately be implemented. On the other hand, challenges to the Commission's decision and order would be appealable to the circuit courts. During the appeal, relief to disciminatees would be held in abeyance until the circuit court affirmed the EEOC decision and order. This appeals process consumes lengthy time periods. For example, the average time delay between the issuance of an NLRB order and a decision of the circuit court is two and one-half years.[13] Consequently, it is argued that the implementation of relief in a Title VII case will be delayed inordinately if the discriminatee must first have his case argued before an administrative tribunal.[14]

On the surface, this point is telling. Yet it fails to consider that under a cease and desist approach most charges will be resolved informally even before a trial examiner's decision has been rendered. In the case of the NLRB, approximately 95 percent of all unfair labor practices are disposed without proceeding beyond the trial examiner's stage.[15] In short, in only a limited number of instances would a cease and desist approach generate serious delays before relief could be provided. Against this cost must be weighed the unique benefits that this approach produces. These include the development of a coherent and uniform body of administrative law and remedy which should facilitate compliance with Title VII, induce fewer charges, and promote the implementation of a more effective remedial policy.

While this author believes that the cease and desist approach is the preferable enforcement mechanism, he nevertheless feels that the direct court enforcement process will also enhance the Commission's ability to execute conciliation agreements. By instituting civil suits, the Commission can impose serious costs upon respondents if they fail to accept the Commission's remedial demands. These costs include a continuing and mounting back-pay liability, litigation expenses, and unfavorable publicity. To immunize themselves from such costs, respondents will undoubtedly be more inclined to settle than they were during the period under the act of 1964 when the Commission lacked enforcement authority.

Recommendations for Improving the Conciliation Process

Aside from granting the Commission enforcement powers, several other steps could be taken to improve the conciliation process. They are: (1) the selection of better trained personnel for employment as conciliators; (2) development of a compliance-review program; (3) greater cooperation between international unions, the AFL-CIO Civil Rights Department, and the Commission; (4) joint EEOC-OFCC compliance efforts.

The first requirement should be self-evident. The conciliation of cases requires personnel who are familiar with the employment practices of industry and labor unions. For example, conciliation of a referral case will demand a basic knowledge of the structure and operation of the hiring hall, the union-contractor relationship, prerequisites for referral, the jurisdiction of the union, and other critical elements. Failure to understand the significance of these elements can either abort the settlement effort or at best lead to an agreement which fails to provide adequate or appropriate relief. In three seniority cases, unions with no control over the disputed jobs were charged with discrimination and became the target of the settlement effort. This occurred because the investigator, the decision-writer, and subsequently the conciliator were ignorant of the jurisdictional structure of jobs in the railroad industry. Predictably, the settlement effort failed. Clearly, the Commission must be selective in its hiring or personnel for conciliator positions; it should restrict employment to those with the proper academic or industrial experience allowing them to focus upon the full range of employer or union practices which relate to the charge(s).

The conciliator should also be able to understand and apply the decisions of the courts in employment discrimination cases. Such an understanding is critical since the conciliator's chances of executing an agreement in part depend on his ability to demonstrate to a respondent that the Commission's proposals are sanctioned by the courts and, indeed, are what the courts would order if a settlement agreement is not signed. In effect, the remedial orders of the courts operate as guidelines concerning the type of relief the conciliator must seek to eradicate the discriminatory practice(s) and compensate charging parties. This is not to suggest that conciliators must be lawyers. Experiences of the NLRB strongly demonstrate the ability of individuals with nonlegal academic backgrounds to occupy quasi-legal positions. Thus nonattorneys are hired as investigators and compliance personnel and have served with distinction as regional directors and members of the NLRB. At the same time, while a law degree should not be a prerequisite for employment as a conciliator, the conciliator should have the capacity to understand, explain, and apply the legal requirements of respondents under Title VII as determined by the Commission and the courts.

A second recommendation concerns the development of a compliance review program. The objective of conciliation is the execution of a settlement agreement. Yet the settlement agreement alone is an insufficient indicator of compliance. The agreement normally provides for prospective relief, and thus there remains the possibility that the respondent will violate the agreement or commit new acts of discrimination. Consequently, compliance with the settlement agreement should be systematically reviewed. Each field office should designate a compliance officer whose primary responsibility will be to implement and monitor settlement agreements. To facilitate review, settlement agreements should include a reporting requirement in which the respondent would periodically report to the field office on the steps he has taken to implement the agreement. For example, in a seniority case, the respondent would be obligated to report on the movement of minorities into formerly all-white departments. The report should include data on the number of minorities seeking transfers, the number who transferred, reasons why others were denied transfer, the positions to which minority employees moved, and the wages they receive on the new jobs. This type of reporting requirement would not only facilitate the compliance officer's review duties, but also provide the respondent with the needed incentive to respect the agreement. Thus, aware that their postagreement actions are subject to reporting and review, they would be under more pressure to implement faithfully the agreement. Naturally, a system of compliance reviews is most viable when the administrative agency initiating them posses enforcement powers. Ultimately, the desire to avoid litigation operates as the most effective compliance agent.

Within the headquarters office of the Conciliations Division, the position of chief compliance officer should also be established. This individual would review the adequacy of all remedial programs and would develop new remedies to combat previously unexamined discriminatory practices. The chief compliance officer would also standardize throughout the field offices changes and additions to the Commission's remedial policies. This standardization is essential since the Commission conciliates cases with employers and labor unions throughout the nation. A uniform remedial approach is thus necessary to ensure equitable treatment of both respondents and charging parties.

Another recommendation concerns the EEOC's relationship with labor unions. As was indicated earlier, the Commission did not profit significantly from its efforts to have the AFL-CIO Civil Rights Division (CRD) and the international unions participate in the resolution of charges. Regarding the former, the CRD intervened in the conciliation of only a negligible number of cases, and its presence had no apparent impact on the conciliation process. Thus the Commission was no more successful in executing agreements where the CRD intervene than where it did not. Similarly, the international unions frequently supported their affiliated locals' rejection of the Commission's settlement proposals. One conclusion, therefore, might be that the Commission should terminate its efforts at coordinating its settlement efforts with the CRD and the international unions.

Such a step would be premature. If the CRD directly intervenes in only a limited number of cases, the Commission is partly responsible. Typically, the CRD is notified only after a charge or decision has been issued. It is not notified when settlement conferences are scheduled and, consequently, is often unaware of them. This is unfortunate because the CRD serves the important function as an intermediary between the Commission and the international. While the internationals may often oppose the Commission's settlement proposals, they are often nonetheless indispensable parties to the settlement conference. Consequently, the internationals should be routinely informed concerning the scheduling of a settlement conference, either directly by the Commission or indirectly through the CRD. Such prompt notification could facilitate meaningful negotiations and would enable the conciliator to determine at an early stage whether an agreement is possible. Prompt notification and participation of the internationals would eliminate the present two-tier structure of conciliations which is charcterized by the conciliator's initial meeting with the locals followed by additional meetings and correspondence with the internationals. This procedure occurs where the internationals belatedly learn of the conciliation effort, and it contributes to the excessive time delays in conciliation. A final recommendation involves the EEOC's relationship with the Office of Federal Contract Compliance, the government's principle mechanism for supervising and coordinating federal agency efforts to bring about compliance with Executive Order 11246. This order obligates federal contractors not to discriminate on the basis of race, sex, creed, or national origin and to take affirmative action to eliminate the effects of past discrimination. A contractor's failure to comply with the executive orders can lead to the cancellation of his contract and ultimately to debarment. The latter sanction prevents employers from entering into future contracts with the federal government. While a majority of labor-union cases examined in this study bear only upon internal union practices that are not subject to federal regulation through government procurement policies, a substantial number also involve employers as co-respondents. Twenty-seven of the seventy-five cases grew out of the existence of racially discriminatory seniority systems. If the employer in a seniority case is a federal contractor, then both the EEOC and the OFCC have concurrent jurisdiction to provide relief. In such cases, joint EEOC-OFCC compliance efforts should be initiated; coordination would enhance the Commission's ability to execute effective settlement agreements. Faced with the prospect of contract cancellations and the possibility of mass layoffs, employers and unions would be forced to accept the Commission's remedial demands.

Unfortunately, little effort was made in coordinating EEOC and OFCC compliance efforts during the period 1964-1972 when the Commission's sole remedial powers were "informal methods of conference, conciliation, and persuasion." As a result, conciliators could not augment the limited potency of the conciliation process by incorporating within that mechanism the threat of a contract cancellation or debarment. A move toward greater cooperation occurred in May 1970 when the EEOC and OFCC agreed to use the OFCC enforcement machinery against contractors who rejected EEOC settlement efforts. Under the Memorandum of Understanding signed by the two agencies, it was contemplated that the OFCC would commence proceedings to suspend or cancel the contracts of employers who refused to conciliate.[16]

Between May 1970 and May 1972, when the 1964 act was amended, there were few cases where coordinated compliance efforts occurred. Yet, where joint pressures have been applied against recalcitrant respondents, more effective results have been obtained. One of the most effective conciliation agreements executed by the Commission in 1971 can in part be attributed to the compliance pressure imposed upon the parties by the OFCC. This agreement required major changes in a major defense contractor's transfer and promotion policies. In January 1973 the EEOC and OFCC coordinated their efforts to obtain a settlement agreement from American Telephone & Telegraph Co. This landmark settlement required AT&T to modify its promotion, layoff, recall, and transfer policies, and to provide millions of dollars in back pay to women and other minority workers.[17] This kind of coordinated compliance effort should be continued and applied in cases where unions are parties with employers to discriminatory contractual policies.

In summary, the Commission's settlement process is in need of major reforms. The settlement process can become a viable vehicle for compliance only if the EEOC possesses enforcement powers. That is the key to its ability to eliminate discrimination and compensate discriminatees for their losses. In addition, other measures can be taken that will promote the Commission's ability to effectively resolve complaints. They include: (1) the hiring of better-trained personnel; (2) the development of a compliance review program; (3) prompt notification and participation of the CRD and international unions; (4) coordinated EEOC-OFCC compliance efforts. The implementation of all these measures should help make the conciliation process an effective compliance mechanism. Until now, the impact of the Commission's remedial efforts, at least in labor-union cases, has been negligible. Thus the ultimate conclusion from this study is that the effect of the Commission's conciliation process has been one of illusion rather than promise.

Notes

Chapter 1

The Conciliation Process of the Equal Employment Opportunity Commission

1. Civil Rights Act of 1964 sec. 703(c), 42 U.S.C. sec. 2000e-2(c) (1970).

2. For an excellent account of the scope and nature of racially discriminatory union practices in the decades prior to passage of the 1964 act, see Herbert R. Northrup, *Organized Labor and the Negro,* 1944, and F. Ray Marshall, *The Negro and Organized Labor,* 1964.

3. Civil Rights Act of 1964 sec. 705(a), 42 U.S.C. sec. 2000e-4(a) (1970).

4. Civil Rights Act of 1964 sec. 705(a), 42 U.S.C. sec. 2000e-5(a) (1970).

5. U.S. Commission on Civil Rights, *Federal Civil Rights Enforcement Effort,* 1971, p. 101.

6. Ibid., p. 92.

7. Civil Rights Act of 1964 sec. 710(b), 42 U.S.C. sec 2000e-9(b) (1970).

8. Civil Rights Act of 1964 sec. 706(a), 42 U.S.C. sec. 2000e-5(a) (1970).

9. Richard Nathan, *Jobs and Civil Rights,* 1969, p. 25.

10. U.S. Commission on Civil Rights, *Federal Civil Rights Enforcement Effort,* p. 102. It is the author's estimate that 10 percent of these "cause" decisions concern unions which persued racially discriminatory employment practices.

11. Ibid., p. 105.

12. Civil Rights Act of 1964 sec. 706(a), 42 U.S.C. sec. 2000e-5(a) (1970).

13. U.S. Equal Employment Opportunity Commission, *Field Operations Handbook,* November 1966, sec. 300.3, p. 95. Many of the EEOC guidelines on procedures and tactics in conciliations were first developed by Professor Alfred Blumrosen of Rutgers University, the EEOC's first chief of conciliations. The guidelines he developed (EEOC Memorandum, "Guidelines for Conciliation," November 11, 1965) were subsequently incorporated into the agency's internal rules and regulations.

14. Ibid., sec. 300.61, p. 118.

15. Ibid., sec. 300.81, p. 127.

16. Civil Rights Act of 1964 sec. 706(e), 42 U.S.C. sec.2000e-5(e) (1970).

17. Civil Rights Act of 1964 sec. 707(a), 42 U.S.C. sec.2000e-6(a) (1970).

18. An exception to this occurred where the Commission filed an amicus curia brief in support of the suit which the charging party independently had instituted.

19. EEOC, *Field Operation Handbook,* sec. 300.60(c), p. 117.

20. Equal Employment Opportunity Act of 1972 (Public Law 92-261 approved March 24, 1972) sec.706 (f) (1).

21. See, for example, Burton I. Meyer, "Racial Discrimination on the Jobsite: Competing Theories and Competing Forums," *University of California Law Review,* 12, no. 4 (May 1965): 1203-1204; Michael Sovern, *Legal Restrictions on Racial Discrimination in Employment,* 1966, p. 80.

22. Sovern, *Legal Restrictions,* p. 80

23. Ibid.

24. Alfred W. Blumrosen, "The Individual Right to Eliminate Employment Discrimination by-Litigation," *Proceedings of the Nineteenth Annual Winter Meeting of the Industrial Relations Research Association,* 1967, p. 95.

25. This last category is subsequently divided into two types, one including a local union's failure to process grievances, a second concerning a deliberate effort precipitated by the union itself to adversely affect the minority worker's employment status.

26. No explanation was found in the case records which would explain why the regular Commission procedure of conciliating only following a reasonable cause decision was not pursued in this case.

27. The number comes to eighty-one because in six cases both segregated locals and discriminatory seniority arrangements existed.

Chapter 2
Patterns of Union Discrimination

1. Ray Marshall, *The Negro and Organized Labor,* 1964, p. 89.

2. At the time of the merger between the American Federation of Labor (AFL) and Congress of Industrial Organizations (CIO), there were five labor organizations whose constitutions provided for the exclusion of blacks from admission. These unions and the constitutional provisions barring racial minorities were: the Brotherhood of Locomotive Engineers (BLE): "No person shall become a member of the BLE unless he is a white man."; the Brotherhood of Locomotive Firemen and Enginemen (BLFE): An applicant for membership must be "white born, of good moral character, sober, and industrious. Mexicans, or those of Spanish-Mexican extraction are not eligible."; the Postal Transport Association, AFL: An applicant must be "of the Caucasian race, or a native American Indian,"; the Brotherhood of Railway Trainmen (BRT): An applicant must be "a white male, sober and industrious."; Order of Railway Conductors (ORC): "any white man shall be eligible to membership." National Industrial Conference Board, *Handbook of Union Government, Structure, and Procedures,* 1955, pp. 63-64. The BLE removed its race bar in 1966, the BLF in 1964, the Postal Transport Association upon merger of the AFL and CIO, the BRT in 1960, and the ORC by 1963.

3. Thirteen building-craft union constitutions provide that a candidate for admission as a journeyman must be approved by a vote of the local membership: Asbestos Workers, Bricklayers, Electrical Workers, Operating Engineers, Granite Cutters, Iron Workers, Marble Polishers, Painters, Plasterers, Plumbers, Sheet Metal Workers, and Stone Cutters. Nine international union constitutions require the endorsement or sponsorship of candidates by current union members: Boilermakers, Bricklayers, Carpenters, Granite Workers, Iron Workers, Marble Polishers, Painters, Sheet Metal Workers, and Stone Cutters. Frequently, where an international constitution is silent on the subject of sponsorship or majority approval, the bylaws of the local will nevertheless specify them as prerequisites for admission. U.S. Department of Labor, *Admission and Apprenticeship in the Building Trades Unions,* 1971, pp. 12, 14.

4. Six building-trades union constitutions specify passage of an examination as a prerequisite for admission: Asbestos Workers, Iron Workers, Lathers, Painters, Plasterers, and Plumbers; additionally, six unions authorize local unions at their option to institute a testing requirement. These unions are: Carpenters, Electrical Workers, Operating Engineers, Roofers, and Sheet Metal Workers.

As with the sponsorship requirement for admission, the silence of the national union constitution on a subject such as testing does not mean that a local will not establish such a requirement. Some locals of the Boilermaker, Elevator Constructor, and Metal Polisher unions test applicants, notwithstanding the absence of such a requirement in their national union constitutions. U.S. Department of Labor, *Building Trades Unions,* pp. 12, 14.

5. International Association of Bridge, Structural, Ornamental Iron Workers, AFL-CIO, *Constitution,* 1968, Art. XXI, sec. 2, p. 58.

6. The City of New York Commission on Human Rights, *Bias in the Building Industry, 1963-1967,* 1967, p. 23; State Advisory Committees to the United States Commission on Civil Rights, *Report on Apprenticeship,* 1964, p. 117.

7. U.S. v. Local 86, Ironworkers, 315 F. Supp. 1202, 1205-1206 (D.C. Wash. 1970).

8. Locals seemingly exercise a greater amount of constitutional autonomy in establishing qualifications for entrance into apprenticeship training programs than they do in determining the qualifications for admission into journeyman status. Fourteen of seventeen national constitutions of building-trades unions contain the general statement that apprenticeship qualifications were subject to local union regulation. At the same time, some internationals will specify minimum standards for admission. For example, six unions (Asbestos Workers, Iron Workers, Carpenters, Painters, Stone Cutters, and Lathers) establish age requirements. A smaller number of unions establish constitutional prerequisites based on one's citizenship and passage of an examination. While constitutional regulation of apprenticeship admission criteria is limited, the national unions in

the construction industry have joined employer associations to form joint labor-management committees for the development and improvement of apprenticeship programs. These committees have established standards which, while not mandatory, are frequently adopted by their affiliated locals. The selection criteria generally recommended by these committees involve standards based upon an applicant's age, physical health, educational background, and citizenship. U.S. Department of Labor, *Building Trades Unions,* pp. 23-28, 37-45.

9. Sidney and Beatrice Webb, *Industrial Democracy,* 1920, p. 564.

10. Letter to the Editor, *New York Times,* August 8, 1963, p. 26, col. 5, © 1963 by The New York Times Company. Reprinted by permission.

11. In excess of $77.15 billion was spent for construction during 1968 and public works accounted for approximately one-third of that amount ($26 billion). Pat Romero, *In Black America,* 1969, p. 193.

12. According to a 1963 Labor Department survey, there were 2,708,000 persons training as construction craftsmen of whom 43.9 percent were in apprenticeship programs. While apprenticeship programs are not the exclusive means to gain entry into the unions and the construction industry, they are an important source of entry into some skilled crafts. Thus the Electricians, Bricklayers, and Sheetmetal Workers Unions are expected to meet 20-40 percent of their projected employee needs through apprenticeships. F. Ray Marshall and Vernon M. Briggs, *Negro Participation in Apprenticeship Programs: Report to the Office of Manpower Policy,* 1966, pp. 39-41.

13. In some unions, the reciprocal arrangement between locals is mandatory. Thus the carpenters' constitution requires that each local admit members who transfer from the jurisdiction of one Local Union or District Council to work in another jurisdiction if the members present valid clearance cards from their former locals. United Brotherhood of Carpenters and Joiners of American, AFL-CIO, *Constitution and Laws,* 1971, sec. 46G, pp. 46-47.

14. See, for example, United Association of Journeymen Apprentices of the Plumbing and Pipe-fitting Industry, *Explanation of Hiring Practices,* 1959, p. 7.

15. *Master Labor Agreement Between Southern California General Contractors and United Brotherhood of Carpenters and Joiners of America,* May 1, 1965-May 1, 1968, sec. 204.4.3, p. 209.

16. See U.S. v. Local 86, Ironworkers, 315 F. Supp. 1202 (D.C. Wash. 1970).

17. Robert K. Burns, "Daily Newspapers," *How Collective Bargaining Works,* Harry A. Millis, ed., 1942, p. 66.

18. See Sumner H. Slichter, James J. Healy, E. Robert Livernash, *The Impact of Collective Bargaining on Management,* 1960, pp. 104-210.

19. Dan H. Mater and Garth L. Magnum, "Integration of Seniority Lists in Transportation Mergers," *Industrial and Labor Relations Review* 16, no. 3, (April 1969): 344.

20. See "Title VII, Seniority Discrimination and the Incumbent Negro," *Harvard Law Review* 80, no. 6 (April 1967): 1260-1283, and Peter B. Doeringer, "Promotion Systems and Equal Employment Opportunity," *Proceedings of Industrial Relations Research Association,* 1966, pp. 278-289, upon which this categorization is based.

21. This situation ended in 1967 when the railroad laid off its last black porter upon the termination of passenger service. U.S. Department of Justice, *U.S. v. St. Louis-San Francisco Railway Co. and Brotherhood of Railway Trainmen: Plaintiff's Proposed Findings of Fact and Conclusions of Law,* Civil Action No. 67-C-243(1), 1970, p. 1.

22. Four of the five principal operating crafts subsequently merged into the United Transportation Union in 1969. They included: Brotherhood of Railway Trainmen, Order of Railway Conductors, Brotherhood of Locomotive Engineers, and Brotherhood of Locomotive Firemen. A fifth craft, the Brotherhood of Locomotive Firemen and Enginemen, has remained independent.

23. The railroad line was a wholly-owned subsidiary of a large steel corporation. Failing to gain admission into the white operating craft, they sought representation by the steelworkers' union which chartered a separate local for them.

24. These three cases could properly be designated as "exclusion" cases, similar in kind to the construction union cases previously discussed. They are presented here in the context of a discussion of unlawful seniority arrangements, primarily because it is the placement of black trainmen in a separate seniority unit that precludes their advancement. They are unable to exercise seniority they accrue in their own unit as a basis for determining their job rights vis-à-vis white workers performing the same work.

25. The jobs of hydropulper and blend tank operators were quite similar. The basic difference apparently centered on the different types of waste products the blend tank operators and hydropulpers blended for eventful feeding into the paper machines. At times, hydropulpers were assigned on a temporary basis to blend tank positions.

26. Marshall, *The Negro and Organized Labor* pp. 96-97.

27. 148 NLRB 54 (1962).

28. Hughes Tool Company, 147 NLRB 1573 (1964).

29. Richard J. Boyce, "Racial Discrimination and the National Labor Relations Act," *Northwestern University Law Review* 65, no. 2 (May-June 1970): 234-35.

30. *Statement of Equal Employment Opportunity Commission on Segregated Union Locals and Collective Bargaining Arrangements,* Commissioners' Meeting No. 32, October 5, 1965.

31. Herbert R. Northrup, *Negro and the Paper Industry,* 1969, p. 115.

32. Marshall, *The Negro and Organized Labor,* p. 102.

33. "If we should find evidence in any of our locals of separation, segregation or exclusion on the basis of race, creed, color or national origin; we would make every possible effort to effect a program for ending such segregations, separation or exclusion with all possible speed." American Federation of Labor-Congress of Industrial Organizations, *Joint Statement on Union Program for Fair Practice,* August 8, 1962, p. 1 (mimeo).

34. Ibid., p. 2.

35. As of May 1970, the AFL-CIO reported that of the 60,000 local unions in the AFL-CIO, fewer than 100 were all black in membership. American Federation of Labor and Congress of Industrial Organizations, *AFL-CIO Program for Equal Rights,* May 1970, p. 12.

36. U.S. Department of Justice, *U.S. v. International Longshoremen's Association: Post Trial Brief for the United States,* Civil Action No. 69-B-3, 1970, pp. 3-4.

37. U.S. Equal Employment Opportunity Commission, Decision no. No7-2-106-11 (1967), p. 2.

38. In two cases, the presidents of the black locals indicated their opposition to merger, although a vote had not been taken. In the final two cases, no evidence was available on the locals' positions toward merger.

39. *U.S. v. International Longshoremen's Association: Transcript of Trial,* Civil Action No. 69-B-3, 1970, pp. 863-66, 868-69.

40. Ibid., pp. 1240-1241, 1269.

41. The same concern is felt by white union members when they stand to become the minority in the new local. In one of the seven cases where merger was achieved, the whites were in the minority; in this case the merger agreement provided for the allocation of various positions to former members of both locals. Thus the white members were effectively guaranteed representation which otherwise may have been denied them if all positions had been filled through the electoral process in which whites and blacks voted as racial blocks.

42. These cases arose under the Civil Rights Act of 1964. Concurrently, the National Labor Relations Act imposes the duty of fair representation upon all bargaining representatives. See, for example, Vaca v. Sipes, 386 U.S. 171 (1967).

43. Alfred Blumrosen, "Labor Arbitration, EEOC Conciliation, and Discrimination in Employment," *The Arbitration Journal* 24, no. 2 (1969): 91-92.

44. These construction cases did not involve patterns of exclusion against black workers as a class. In all three, the local unions had admitted and referred minority workers.

Chapter 3
Remedies for Discriminatory Union Practices

1. U.S. Civil Rights Commission, *Federal Civil Rights Enforcement Effort,* 1971, p. 103.

2. No separate discussion on EEOC remedial policy in the fifth category of cases — union discrimination against individuals — will be provided because the remedial policy the EEOC formulated in grievance cases was applied to cases involving union discrimination against individuals. In both, the emphasis is on making whole the individual grievant or discriminatee and insuring that the union will represent fairly all members of the bargaining unit.

3. EEOC Case no. 6-3-1714 (1967), "Conciliation Proposals," p. 5.

4. EEOC Case no. 6-7-6012 (1967), "Conciliation Proposals," p. 4.

5. EEOC Case no. 6-3-1814 (1967), "Conciliation Proposals," p. 5.

6. EEOC Case no. CL7-1-96U (1967), "Conciliation Proposals," p. 4.

7. EEOC Case no. 6-3-1714 (1967), "Conciliation Proposals," p. 3; Charles F. Wilson, *The Conciliator's Handbook,* 1969, p. 20A.

8. A case in point is that of Local 212, IBEW. Before 1965, when it openly gave preference in its apprenticeship programs to relatives of union members, there were few black applicants. After the local introduced in 1965 objective apprenticeship eligibility standards which, if implemented, would have made possible black entry, there was for the first time a significant number of blacks applying for the program. In 1965, 9 of the 108 applicants were black. U.S. Department of Justice, *U.S. v. Local 212, IBEW: Memorandum in Support of Plantiff's Proposed Findings of Fact and Conclusions of Law Relative to the Defendent JATC,* Civil Action No. 6473, 1968, pp. 3-5.

9. EEOC Case no. 6-4-4030 (1967), "Conciliation Proposals," p. 6.

10. EEOC Case no. 6-4-4030 (1967), "Conciliation Proposals," p. 5.

11. EEOC Memorandum, "New Standards for Compliance in the Building Trades Industry," September 28, 1970, p. 4.

12. 292 F. Suppl. 413 (S.D. Ohio 1968).

13. Ibid., at 453.

14. *U.S. v. IBEW, Local 212: Memorandum of Defendent JATC Regarding Pending Motions to Modify Decree,* Civil No. 6473, 1970, pp. 1-4.

15. *U.S. v. IBEW, Local 212: Memorandum Opinion,* Civil Action No. 6473, (S.D. Ohio 1970), pp. 7-8.

16. EEOC Case no. 6-4-4030 (1967), "Conciliation Proposals," p. 70.

17. Neither have the courts provided for back pay relief to discriminatees in referral cases litigated under Title VII. The courts have generally limited the scope of their remedial orders to restructuring hiring hall arrangements so as to eliminate all discriminatory referral criteria. See, for example, U.S. v. Local 86,

Ironworkers, 315 F. Suppl. 1202 (W.D. Wash. 1970) and Dobbins v. Local 212, IBEW, 292 F. Supp. (S.D. Ohio 1968). At the same time one can question the legitimacy of the Commission's policy of not seeking a back-pay remedy. The NLRB has been faced with an identical remedial problem in cases involving a local union's failure to refer nonunion workers. It has nonetheless adopted a back-pay remedy. It has developed several formulas for determining back-pay loss. In one, the NLRB computes one's financial loss in terms of the amount of money earned on the job by the worker who was referred in place of the discriminatee. If the discriminatee is continually bypassed, the NLRB can continue this process of determining the earnings of workers who gained referral at the expense of the charging party. Where the period is lengthy, the NLRB has shortened its computation process by averaging the earnings of a union worker and utilizing this average as the standard for determining a nonunion worker's back-pay loss. The EEOC and the courts could follow a similar approach.

18. Contractors Association v. Schultz, 311 F. Supp. 1002 (E.D. Pa. 1970), *aff'd.,* 442 F.2d 159 (3rd Cir. 1971), *cert. denied,* 404 U.S. 854 (1971); Weiner v. Cuyahoga Community College District, 238 N.E. 2d 839 (Ohio Ct. of Common Pleas 1968), *aff'd.,* 249 N.E. 2d 907 (Ohio Sup. Ct. 1969), *cert. denied,* 396 U.S. 1004 (1970).

19. EEOC Case no. 5-11-2648 (1967), "Conciliation Proposals," p. 4.

20. EEOC Case no. CC 6-11-8867U (1968), "Conciliation Agreement," pp. 3-4; EEOC Case no. CL7-1-9616 (1967), "Conciliation Proposal," p. 3.

21. EEOC Case no. 5-11-2648 (1967), "Conciliation Proposals," p. 5; EEOC Case no. CL 7-1-96U (1967), "Conciliation Proposals," pp. 9-10.

22. EEOC Case no. 5-11-2648 (1967), "Conciliation Proposals," p. 5; EEOC Case no. CL 7-1-96U (1967), "Conciliation Proposals," p. 10.

23. EEOC Case no. CH6-11-182 (1968), "Conciliation Proposals," p. 3.

24. Ibid.

25. Bowe v. Colgate-Palmolive Co., 272 F. Supp. 332 (S.D. Ind. 1967) *mod.,* 416 F. 2d 711 (7th Cir. 1969); Robinson v. Lorillard Co. 319 F. Supp. 835 (M.D.N.C. 1970), *mod.,* 444 F. 2d 791 (4th Cir. 1971).

26. The Commission's use of the "wage rate" as a means for determining one's job rank within the progression line does create problems where there is evidence that the plant's wage structure was itself discriminatory, i.e., that black workers were paid less while performing work of equal or greater difficulty and responsibility. Later on, however, the Commission did strike a note of caution in utilizing the wage rate as a basis for merging jobs when it recognized that "pay rate for the job may be used as an indication of job responsibility and difficulty provided that job rates were not established on the basis that was not [sic] discriminatory because of race." EEOC Case no. 5-12-3129 (1966), "Addendum to Commissioner Decision," p. 1.

27. Whitfield v. United States 263 F. 2d 546 (5th Cir. 1959), dealt with the integration of segregated progression lines. In this pre-Civil Rights Act case, the court held that the company and the union were not obligated to credit black workers in the white progression line for the time spent in the previously all black line of progression.

28. EEOC Memorandum, "Stock House Cases," June 1, 1966, pp. 2-3.

29. U.S. Equal Employment Opportunity Commission, Commissioners' Meeting No. 104, June 7, 1966.

30. Letter from Herman Edelsberg, Executive Director, EEOC, June 8, 1966.

31. EEOC Case no. 5-7-246 (1966); EEOC Case no. 5-7-5R (1965).

32. EEOC Memorandum, "Guidelines on Seniority," November 15, 1965, p. 13.

33. Quarles v. Philip Morris, Inc. 279 F. Supp. 505 (E.D. Va. 1968).

34. U.S. v. Local 89, Papermakers, 282 F. Supp. 39 (E.D. La. 1968), *affirmed,* 416 F. 2d 980 (5th Cir., 1969), *cert. denied,* 397 U.S. 919 (1970).

35. EEOC Case no. 5-12-3129 (1966), "Conciliation Proposals," p. 5; EEOC Case no. 5-9-939 (1967), "Conciliation Proposals," p. 10.

36. The following proposals are illustrative of the Commission's efforts: "All employees reassigned as above provided will be afforded an opportunity for two weeks of on-the-job training before final assignment to the job is effective. In the event of disqualification, the employer may return to his former job or its equivalent. . . ." Wilson, p. 15.

"In selecting between bidders or applications for a permanent vacancy in a traditionally "white" job, or where Negro employees have not had realistic opportunities to obtain experience and develop abilities on such job, the company will not prefer a white employee with less continuous service over a Negro employee with more continuous service on the ground that the white employee has more experience or ability until the senior employee bidding or applying for such job has had a reasonable opportunity to demonstrate that he can perform such job at the minimum acceptable level, or that he can be trained to perform such job with a reasonable amount of training." EEOC Case no. 5-9-939 (1967), "Conciliation Proposals," p. 9.

37. U.S. v. Local 189, Papermakers, 301 F. Supp. 906, 914-915 (E.D. La. 1969), *aff'd.,* 416 F. 2d 980 (5th Cir. 1969), *cert. denied* 397 U.S. 919 (1970).

38. As previously indicated, not all employees locked in inferior jobs would have the ability to handle jobs in other units, nor would all employees with such ability necessarily desire transfer to other units. At the same time, while serious computational problems are present, they are not irresoluble, and measures could be developed to determine appropriate back pay-amounts and identify those warranting such relief.

39. The exceptions are the following cases: Bowe v. Colgate-Palmolive Co., 272 F. Supp. 332 (S.D. Ind. 1967), *mod.,* 416 F. 2d 711 (7th Cir. 1969); Robinson v. P. Lorillard Co., 319 F. Supp. 835 (M.D. N.C. 1970), *mod.,* 442 F. 2d 791 (4th Cir. 1971).

40. EEOC Decision no. 6-9-8144 (1967), p. 3.

41. EEOC Case no. At7-1-49 (1967), "Conciliation Proposals," p. 3; EEOC Case no. 6-7-6158 (1967), "Conciliation Proposals," p. 3.

42. EEOC Memorandum, "Recent Trip to New Orleans Regarding Crown-Zellerbach," February 24, 1966, p. 9.

43. EEOC Memorandum, "Protection of Minority Rights Incident to a Merger of a Previously Segregated Local," p. 1.

44. EEOC Case no. 6-4-4125 (1967), "Conciliation Proposals," pp. 2-4.

45. *U.S. v. Local 189, United Papermakers and Paperworkers,* Civil Action No. 68-205, Section B (E.D. La. 1968).

46. Chicago Federation of Musicians, Local 10 v. American Federation of Musicians, 57 LRRM 2227 (N.D. Ill. 1964).

47. This provision specifies, . . . Every member of a labor organization shall have equal rights and privileges within such orgainzation to nominate candidates, to vote in elections or referendums of the labor organization, to attend membership meetings, and to participate in the deliberations and voting upon the business of such meetings, subject to reasonable rules and regulations in such organization's constitution and bylaws. 29 U.S.C. Sec 411 (A)(1)(1964).

48. EEOC Case no. 6-3-2253 (1967), "Conciliation Proposals," p. 3; EEOC Case no. 5-9-935 (1966), "Conciliation Agreement," p. 3; EEOC Case no. 5-10-1738 (1966), "Conciliation Agreement," pp. 2-3.

49. EEOC Case no. NO-6-10-191 (1968), "Conciliation Agreement," p. 3.

50. EEOC Case no. 5-11-2571 (1967), "Conciliation Agreement," p. 5.

51. Black Clawson v. I.A.M., 313 F. 2d 179 (2d Cir. 1962).

52. Vaca v. Sipes 386 U.S. 171 (1967), at 191-192.

53. Such a modification in the union's exclusive bargaining status finds parallels in NLRB decisions involving unions which discriminated on the basis of race. For example, the Board has revoked the exclusive bargaining certification of local unions which failed to represent black workers fairly [Independent Metal Workers, Locals 1 and 2, 147 NLRB 1573 (1964)] , and has withheld from unions which are signatories to a discriminatory contract the benefits of the Board's contract bar rules [Pioneer Bus Co., 140 NLRB 54 (1962)] .

Chapter 4
Efficacy of the Conciliation Process

1. The total number of unions involved in these twelve cases is fourteen while the total number of violations they committed equals twenty-three. Thus

some locals engaged in multiple violations and one case involved three separate craft unions. The statistical breakdown of the violations is as follows: in four cases, unions excluded blacks from admission, apprenticeships, and referral. In one case, the local union denied blacks apprenticeship and referral opportunities. In four cases, unions blocked the admission of blacks into membership, while in the remaining three — one of which involved three separate craft unions — the unions excluded blacks from apprenticeship training programs. In the following discussion, we will examine separately the Commission's efforts to remedy each type of craft union violation.

2. The cause decision was against the company and the local craft union, both of whom engaged in a classic "pass the buck" strategy of discrimination. The company claimed that it could not promote the black packers until they had been admitted into the craft union which exercised jurisdiction over the apprentice positions. The local craft union contended that it could not admit the black packers into membership before they had been placed in jobs within their jurisdiction. Each claimed the other was responsible for the exclusion of black packers from apprentice positions.

3. For example, in a case involving an iron foundry, one all black unit was the milling department. There, wage scales ranged from $2.47 to $2.55 per hour. In the nearly all-white maintenance department, the wage range was $2.27 to $3.33 per hour. Black workers seeking transfers risked a significant wage reduction. Interviews with several black workers revealed that they did not seek transfers because they would have entered at the beginning rate in the maintenance department.

4. Part of the examination consisted of arithmetic work problems sections. Since the inception of the test, 74.5 percent of all whites who were examined passed, while only 17.5 percent of all black employees who took the test passed. No in-plant validation studies were conducted to determine whether the tests or cutoff points were positively related to satisfactory performance in the apprenticeship program.

5. A clear illustration of the break in the company's past discriminatory policy is revealed in the company agreement (6-4-2641) to "immediately integrate the machine shop and attempt to integrate all other departments, through future transfers and hires." In a second case (AT 6-11-861), the company and union acknowledged "that prior State law imposed certain disabilities upon Respondent Company and its Negro employees, which, now being superceded by the Civil Rights Act of 1964, leaves a continuing deficit of Negro manpower in many areas, classifications and departments; therefore, Respondent Company agrees to utilize the full discretion remaining to it after exact compliance with existing Labor Agreements to move Negro employees to or toward the places they would or might have occupied if racial segregation had never existed."

6. In executing these agreements, the conciliators themselves were aware

that the settlements were in many ways deficient. Yet acceptance was still called for. The following comments by conciliators in these cases are illustrative: (1) "It is a bare bones responsiveness negotiated with extreme care, with nothing for nothing. The conciliation should be called 'successful' for having accomplished all that could be accomplished with these parties, at this time, with this decision, and a charging party unprepared and unwilling to go to court." (2) "In conciliation, Local 710 behaved somewhat like the company; they refused to sign anything more than bare boilerplate, yet are doing more on mere verbal understanding."

7. The designation "all-white" department should be interpreted to include departments which are nearly all-white, i.e., those that have just a token number of black employees. Similarly, "Negro only" departments may contain a limited number of Caucasians.

8. Of a total of twenty employees interviewed, seven indicated this last factor as the reason for their remaining in their original departments.

9. It is unclear whether or not these blacks had bump-back rights. In any case, the court struck down the company and union seniority system and ordered that blacks employed in the plant at the time blacks were restricted to certain departments be able to transfer on the basis of their company seniority. Regarding the tobacco plant case, insufficient employment data precludes any observation on the effect of the Commission's conciliation efforts.

10. The company did eliminate the use of tests in regulating transfer of workers between production departments. It has continued to use tests in controlling transfers into craft departments. The continued use of these tests in part explains why a total of seven craft departments (electrical, plumbing, carpenter, etc.) have remained all white.

11. Normally, the tests were written and consisted of verbal and mechanical aptitude tests that the Commission found had a disparate effect on minority workers. For example, in one case, 74 percent of the white workers tested passed, while only 17.5 percent of black workers passed. In two of the cases, the company required the possession of a high school diploma, in addition to the passage of written tests, of workers seeking entry into white progression lines. Such a requirement inherently discriminated against blacks since a much larger percentage of blacks than whites had not completed high school. In the South, while 64.7 percent of all white males in the 25-44 year-old age group had graduated, only 35.9 percent of all blacks in the same age bracket had high school diplomas. In the second company cited, 90 percent of all blacks were precluded from advancement because they lacked a high school diploma. The employer had never demonstrated that a high school education was necessary for the job. Recently, the Supreme Court in Griggs v. Duke Power Company, 401 U.S. 424 (1971), held that all tests which have a disparate effect upon minority workers are unlawful if they are not valid indicators of job performance.

12. The statistics are based on information supplied by the former president of the porter's local. That black workers were able to transfer despite the top-bottoming of the rosters is attributed to the economic viability of this particular railroad line. Situated in the railroad's transportation center, the company's freight lines were expanding in employment, and as a result, porters seeking transfer could fill brakeman vacancies without upsetting seniority rights of incumbent white brakemen. Additionally, the settlement provided for the merger of the International Association of Railway Employees (IARE), an all-black union consisting of 450-500 members with the United Transportation Union, itself the product of the merger of the principal operating crafts within the railroad industry. In effect, the IARE ceased to operate and its members were allowed for the first time to join the nearly all-white railroad brotherhood.

13. H. Northrup, *Organized Labor and the Negro*, 1944, p. 80.

14. Neither the charging party nor other minority workers were available for interviewing to determine whether black workers have been represented in the postmerger situation.

15. In 6-2-869, the charging party could not be located.

16. Follow-up interviews were prevented in one case by the inability of the author to locate the charging party or other black employees for their assessment of the union's grievance record.

17. The Commission found the union should have sought arbitration in the first case because the company had unfairly denied the grievant promotion on previous occasions. Hence, the employer's promise to "consider" the charging party for promotion was inadequate. In the latter case, the Commission's decision was based on its findings that white workers with equally poor records were not discharged.

18. The complainant did not seek to exercise his rights under the agreement; soon after execution of the agreement, he left the state without paying initiation fees for membership or seeking any contact with the union. He felt that he could do better in a nonunion capacity.

19. An exception occurred in the segregated local cases, where the Commission remedy of merger was implemented in three nonagreement cases.

Chapter 5
Constraints upon the Conciliation Process

1. EEOC Case no. 5-12-3129 (1965).

2. Several of the seventy-five cases specifically involved the local union's use of the grievance arbitration process to block the advancement of black workers into formerly all-white jobs. In one case, the arbitrator found that the employer had violated the contract by replacing a junior white employee with a black

worker who had greater seniority, although the employer's actions were pursuant to an EEOC settlement agreement. In *Crown-Zellerbach,* the local union filed an 8(a)(5) refusal to bargain charge against the company when it attempted to implement without its consent an OFCC sponsored change in the seniority system. The NLRB dismissed the charge. NLRB Case no. 15 CA-3266 (1968).

3. EEOC Case no. 6-8-7457 (1967).

4. It was not unusual in the author's experience that union representatives in conciliation would openly discount the possibility of a law suit. In part, this was a union tactic designed to impress the conciliator that the union could not be "coerced" into accepting the Commission's settlement agreement. At the same time, it was not difficult for the legal representative of any respondent to realize that the threat of litigation was certainly less than 50 percent. One only has to examine the annual reports of the EEOC and the publications of the Bureau of National Affairs to recognize the great disparity between numerous charges filed and the relatively few cases that are litigated. The author's observations were corroborated by those of other more experienced conciliators.

5. EEOC Case no. 6-4-2724 (1966).

6. As noted earlier, Whitfield v. United Steelworkers, 263 F. 2d. 546 (5th Cir. 1959) lends support to the contention that all that was required of respondents was the elimination of all formal discrimination. The ambiguity in the legislative history of the Civil Rights Act concerning the scope of an employer's obligation to revise a discriminatory seniority system also weakened the EEOC's remedial efforts. In several of the cases first litigated under Title VII, lower courts upheld the employer and union view as to their limited remedial obligations under the act. See, for example, U.S. v. H.K. Porter Co., 296 F. Supp. 40 (N.D. Ala. 1968) and U.S. v. Sheet Metal Workers, Local 36, 280 F. Supp. 719 (E.D. Mo. 1968). These decisions were subsequently reversed. Professor Blumrosen reports how respondents utilized the *Whitfield* doctrine as a defense in some of the first cases he attempted to conciliate. Alfred W. Blumrosen, "Seniority and Equal Employment Opportunity: A Glimmer of Hope," *Rutgers Law Review* 23, no. 2 (Winter 1969): 293.

7. Sovern, *Legal Restraints* p. 205.

8. Statement of Stephen N. Shulman, as quoted in U.S. Commission on Civil Rights, *Federal Civil Rights Enforcement Effort,* p. 109.

9. Lewis L. Lorwin and Arthur Wubnig, *Labor Relations Boards,* 1935, pp. 122, 292-93.

10. Ibid. pp. 1344-35.

11. D.O. Bowman, *Public Control of Labor Relations,* 1942, p. 45.

12. U.S. Commission on Civil Rights, *The Federal Civil Rights Enforcement Effort,* p. 99.

13. Charging parties may face similar difficulties when filing charges with state FEP commissions. Discussing the impact of extensive time delays on the discriminatee, one analysis of the New York state FEPC noted that "three to five months is obviously too long a period of time to be effective for a worker who believes, correctly or not, that he is a victim of discrimination. It is not likely that he can afford to remain unemployed for more than a few weeks while his case is being settled. If many weeks go by without a decision, he probably has to find another job and once he does the chances are he will no longer be much interested in the one he failed to get." Morroe Berger, *Equality by Statute,* 1968, p. 184. Significantly, while Berger was examining the adverse effects of time delays lasting a few months, the Commission is faced with delays averaging 18-24 months.

14. Information obtained from Mr. Everett Ware, Thomas King, and Mr. Richard Grossman, conciliators with long experience in the regional offices and in supervisory conciliation capacities in Washington, D.C., June 15, 1971, personal interview, Washington, D.C.

15. EEOC Case no. KC 6-11-8866 (1970), "Conciliation Proposals," pp. 3-4.

16. EEOC Memorandum, March 4, 1971, pp. 1-3.

17. These two cases are not the only examples of agreements which failed to incorporate standard Commission policies. For example, in nearly all seniority cases, the agreement lacked the range of remedies necessary to provide full relief. At the same time, it would be unfair to attribute this failure to the problem we are discussing — oversight and error on the part of Commission personnel. In the bulk of cases where weak agreements were executed, the substantial deficiencies were due to the rejection by respondents of more stringent remedies — thus the conciliator in an effort to achieve some gains, was forced to compromise on his demand. In the above cases, the concessions made by the conciliators whether out of ignorance of Commission policy or inability to evaluate their scope and significance, were so great as to render meaningless the settlement agreement.

18. U.S. Commission on Civil Rights, *Federal Civil Rights Enforcement Effort,* p. 93.

19. Ibid., p. 94.

20. Letter of Chairman Roosevelt to Donald Slaiman, 9-30-65.

21. EEOC memorandum, March 11, 1966.

22. Alfred Blumrosen, "The Individual Right to Eliminate Employment Discrimination by Litigation," *Proceedings of the Industrial Relations Research Association,* 1967, p. 90.

23. Copies of charges were sent from the field offices to the CRD, while copies of the decisions were transmitted from Headquarters in Washington, D.C. In the first year of this informational interchange, copies of both decisions and charges were sent on a sporadic basis. This was the major complaint of the

AFL-CIO when it reviewed its relationship with the Commission in the ensuing months. In 1967 the flow of information was of a more regular nature. For example, of the 68 cases in this study involving AFL-CIO affiliates, 11 were decided in 1966. Of these 11, AFL-CIO received notification in only 5 cases. On the other hand, AFL-CIO was notified in 51 of the remaining 57 cases decided in 1967 and 1968. The initial failure to provide the CRD with information generally reflected the "new-ness" of the procedures; there was a time lag between their planning and implementation.

24. Following the adoption in August 1962 of the "Joint Statement on Union Program for Fair Practices" by the AFL-CIO and 122 of its international affiliates, President George Meany requested each international to select an officer to handle civil rights matters and to maintain contact with the CRD. Information in a letter from George Meany to the presidents of National and International Unions, October 5, 1964.

25. Nathan, *Jobs and Civil Rights,* p. 63.

26. American Federation of Labor — Congress of Industrial Organizations, *Equal Rights For All,* p. 12.

27. For example, the conciliator would routinely seek the international's participation when the local union respondent indicated that, absent international approval, it could not modify the practice which had given rise to the complaint.

28. A 1955 study of 194 international union constitutions revealed that 103 international unions vest final authority to approve locally authorized strikes in the international union. These internationals have the authority to withhold strike funds in cases of an unauthorized strike. Additionally, 96 of the 194 international unions studied have the power to make all collective-bargaining agreements or to authorize the agreements negotiated by local unions. No statistical data was given on the number of international which have the power to revoke the charters of or place in trusteeship local unions which violate international bylaws or disobey international union directives. The study did indicate that in "many" cases the international has this power. National Industrial Conference Board, *Handbook of Union Government, Structure, and Procedures,* 1955, pp. 42-43, 49, 62.

29. Where two locals are considering merger, international involvement is automatic in the long run, since only the international has the power to sanction merger and supervise the distribution of assets of the lodges losing their charters.

30. Harry D. Wolf, "Railroads," *How Collective Bargaining Works,* Harry A. Millis, ed., 1942, pp. 338-339.

31. These officers can be elected by the lodge chairmen who constitute the general committee or by referendum vote of the members. This is the procedure in the Brotherhood of Railway Trainmen.

32. Howard W. Risher, Jr., *Negro in the Railroad Industry,* 1971, pp. 27-28.

33. For example, one railroad brotherhood vests the Grand Lodge president with the power to suspend from office any Grand Lodge or System Division officer who deviates from "any uniform wages, or rules, and working conditions policy that has been or shall be established." Brotherhood of Maintenance of Way Employees, *Constitution and By-Laws,* Art. V, sec. 8, 1966, p. 24.

34. Risher, *Negro,* p. 139.

35. Ibid., p. 148.

36. The UPP president from 1948 to 1968 was Paul Philips, a former union organizer and paper-mill worker. During his term of office, the international fought to perpetuate existing seniority structures. Northrup, *Negro in the Paper Industry,* p. 114.

37. Of the six other segregated local cases which have been classed within the seniority category, the international was named as a respondent in one instance.

38. It can be added that some internationals have expressed the view that they could not legally withhold strike funds if the local was engaged in a legitimate strike.

39. National Industrial Conference Board, *Handbook on Union Government, Structure, and Procedures,* pp. 49-50.

40. For example, the following international unions are provided under their constitutions with broad powers to impose trusteeships or to suspend local union officers: Iron Workers, Operating Engineers, Asbestos Workers, IBEW, URW, IAM, Teamsters, Painters, Railway Carmen, Laborers. See International Association of Bridge Structural and Ornamental Iron Workers, AFL-CIO, *Constitution,* 1964, pp. 32-33; International Union of Operating Engineers, AFL-CIO, *Constitution,* 1964, pp. 21-22; International Association of Heat and Frost Insulators and Asbestos Workers, AFL-CIO, *Constitution, By-Laws, and Policy,* 1967, p. 24; International Brotherhood of Electrical Workers, AFL-CIO, *Constitution,* 1966, pp. 26-27; United Brotherhood of Rubber, Cork, Linoleum and Plastic Workers of America, AFL-CIO, *Constitution,* 1964, p. 44; International Association of Machinists, AFL-CIO, *Constitution,* 1961, pp. 19-20; International Brotherhood of Teamsters, Chauffeurs, Warehousemen and helpers of America, *Constitution,* 1961, pp. 27-31; Brotherhood of Painters, Decorators, and Paperhangers of America, AFL-CIO, *Constitution,* 1965, p. 26; Brotherhood of Railway Carmen of America, AFL-CIO, *Constitution,* 1963, p. 24; International HOD Carriers' Building and Common Laborers Union of America, AFL-CIO, *Constitution,* 1961, pp. 23-27.

Chapter 6
Sources of Relief to Discriminatees

1. In thirty cases, either the charging party could not be contacted or the

charge had been filed by a commissioner of the EEOC. For purposes of conducting these interviews, the "lead" charging party was contacted, since he was the first to file and often was instrumental in getting others to file.

2. Civil Rights Act of 1964 sec. 711(a), 42 U.S.C. sec. 2000e-10(a) (1970).

3. The Railway Labor Board has similar authority over labor unions in the railroad and airline industries.

4. NLRB v. Hughes Tool Co., 147 NLRB 1573 (1964).

5. Based on NLRB data in the author's possession.

6. U.S. Equal Employment Opportunity Commission, *Second Annual Report,* 1968, p. 53.

7. In two cases not counted among the forty-five (because of inability to locate and interview the complainants), data indicates that the charging parties also filed charges with the Board. The Board found the complaints meritorious and issued remedial orders.

8. H.K. Porter v. NLRB, 397 U.S. 99 (1970).

9. An argument could be made that the Supreme Court's ruling concerning the scope of Section 8(d)'s limitations on the Board's remedial authority applies only in cases where the union and employer are in the process of bargaining for and negotiating an agreement. NLRB intervention of the type in H.K. Porter violently interferes with the bargaining process whose outcome should be based upon the relative bargaining power of the parties. Where, however, the negotiation of an agreement is not at issue, the Board may utilize its remedial authority to compel modification of a contractual provision to provide relief to bargaining unit members.

10. NLRB v. Reed & Prince Mfg. Co., 196 F. 2d 755, 760 (1st Cir. 1952).

11. NLRB v. Local 5881, UMW, 323 F. 2d 853 (6th Cir. 1963).

12. Kansas City Power & Light Co. v. NLRB, 137 F. 2d 77, 79 (8th Cir. 1943).

13. Labor-Management Relations Act (Taft-Hartley Act) sec. 8(b)(1)(A), 29 U.S.C. sec. 158(b)(1)(A) (1970).

14. Civil Rights Act of 1964 sec. 706(b), 42 U.S.C. sec. 2000e-5(b) (1970).

15. U.S. Equal Employment Opportunity Commission, *Fourth Annual Report,* 1970, p. 22.

16. U.S. Equal Employment Opportunity Commission, *Third Annual Report,* 1969, p. 20.

17. In fiscal 1969, 7,283 of the 14,471 charges originated in the ten southern non-FEP states: Alabama, Florida, Georgia, Louisiana, North Carolina, South Carolina, Texas, Tennessee, Virginia, and Arkansas. U.S. Equal Employment Opportunity Commission, *Fourth Annual Report,* 1970, pp. 38-39.

18. Nathan; *Jobs and Civil Rights,* p. 15.

19. U.S. Equal Employment Opportunity Commission, *Fifth Annual Report,* 1971, pp. 43-44.

20. In an effort to explain why the state commission dismissed several construction union cases, an official remarked, "had we been more sophisticated, we would have ruled otherwise."

21. The local union only employed four workers. Under the Indiana Act, an employer must have at least six employees. The EEOC accepted jurisdiction on the theory that the local was affiliated with an international which, acting as an employer, satisfied the jurisdictional requirements of the act.

22. How this occurred is impossible to say. The EEOC could have failed to notify the state agency; or the state commission could have misplaced the file. Either alternative suggests a deplorable state of affairs on either the state or federal level. It should be noted that should the EEOC fail to defer to a properly constituted state agency, it may jeopardize any subsequent proceeding against the respondent. For example, in the event the complainant brought suit, the respondent could plead that the suit be summarily dismissed on the grounds that the state FEPC had not been given the opportunity guaranteed to it under the statute to resolve the problem.

23. Private suits were authorized under sec. 706(e). The charging party technically did not have to wait until the Commission had terminated its settlement effort to bring suit. He could bring suit at any point after the end of a sixty-day period following the date of his original complaint, regardless of the stage of the EEOC proceeding. In practice, most private law suits were not filed at least until the EEOC had found "probable cause." Under the 1972 amendments to the Civil Rights Act charging parties may bring suits if, within 180 days of the charge's filing, the EEOC has neither issued a complaint nor entered into a settlement agreement acceptable to them. Equal Employment Opportunity Act of 1972 (Public Law 92-261) sec. 705(b)(1).

24. Civil Rights Act of 1964 sec. 707(a), 42 U.S.C. sec. 2000e-6(a) (1970). The 1972 amendments to the act provide for the transfer of the "pattern or practice" jurisdiction to the Commission by March 1974. At present, the Commission and the attorney general have concurrent jurisdiction in this area. Equal Employment Opportunity Act of 1972 (Public Law 92-261) sec. 707(c).

25. In the remaining thirteen cases where no suit was brought, either charging parties could not be located or the case involved a Commissioner charge. In these cases the files of the Justice Department, the General Counsel's Office of the EEOC, and published reports of the NAACP reveal the absence of any suits filed.

26. Referring to this problem, Jack Greenberg, former head of the NAACP Legal Defense Fund noted that "many of the large number of corporations and labor unions involved in employment litigation are employing some of the most skillful counsel in the country and that a great deal of protracted and difficult

litigation is in prospect." Statement by Jack Greenberg, as quoted in Richard Nathan, p. 79.

27. Testimony of William H. Brown, III, EEOC Chairman, before the U.S. Congress, Senate, Subcommittee on Labor, of the Committee on Labor and Public Welfare, *Hearings on Equal Employment Opportunities Enforcement Act,* 91st Cong., 1st sess.; p. 40.

28. U.S. Commission on Civil Rights, *Federal Civil Rights Enforcement Effort,* p. 120.

29. In fiscal year 1968 alone, the Conciliations Division reported over 300 cases in which no agreements were obtained. Ibid., p. 105.

30. Of the first ten law suits filed by the Attorney General under Section 707, six involved building-craft unions which were charged with excluding blacks from membership, apprenticeship-training programs and referral. Nathan, *Jobs and Civil Rights,* pp. 77-78.

31. Quarles v. Phillip Morris, Inc., 279 F. Supp. 505 (E. D. Va. 1968).

32. U.S. Commission on Civil Rights, *Federal Civil Rights Enforcement Effort,* p. 120.

33. Interview with Charles Wilson, Chief of Conciliations, as reported in U.S. Commission on Civil Rights, p. 108.

34. The Commission did not "dismiss the case." Following the issuance of a cause decision, it unsuccessfully sought to settle the charge. Upon the determination that the respondent would not settle, it informed the charging party that its efforts were unsuccessful, and that the charging party had the authority to bring civil suit. The charging party evidently interpreted the Commission's notification of its inability to proceed further as a "dismissal" of the case.

35. In examining the causes of the summer riots of 1967, the Kerner Commission noted the following contributing factors: "Frustrated hopes are the residue of the unfulfilled expectations aroused by the great judicial and legislative victories of the civil rights movement. . . . The frustrations of powerlessness have led some Negroes to the conviction that there is no alternative to violence as a means of achieving redress of grievances. . . ." The National Advisory Commission on Civil Disorders, *Report* (Kerner Commission), 1968, p. 5.

Chapter 7
Concluding Observations and Recommendations

1. Herbert R. Northrup, "Will Greater EEOC Powers Expand Minority Employment?" *Proceedings of the 1971 Annual Spring Meeting: Industrial Relations Research Association,* 1972, pp. 513-17.

2. Ibid., p. 515.

3. 279 F. Supp. 505 (E.D. Va. 1968).

4. Northrup, "Will Greater EEOC Powers Expand Minority Employment?" p. 519.

5. U.S. National Labor Relations Board, *Thirtieth Annual Report,* 1966, p. 188.

6. Benjamin Wolkinson, "The Remedial Efficacy of NLRB Remedies in Joy Silk Cases," pp. 23-24.

7. Northrup, "Will Greater EEOC Powers Expand Minority Employment?" p. 519.

8. Equal Employment Opportunity Act of 1972 (Public Law 92-261 approved March 24, 1972) sec. 706(f)(1).

9. U.S. Congress, House, Committee on Education and Labor, *Hearings on H.R. 1746: A Bill to Further Promote Equal Employment Opportunities for American Workers,* 92d Cong., 1st sess., pp. 153-159, 176-185.

10. In the case of the NLRB, the courts have recognized the wide latitude the Board has in remedying unfair labor practices. In vesting the Board with power to order affirmative relief, the Supreme Court acknowledged that "Congress could not catalogue all the devices and stratagems for circumventing the policies of the Act. Nor could it define the whole gamut of remedies to effectuate these policies in an infinite variety of specific situations. Congress met these difficulties by leaving the adaption of means to end to the empiric process of administration." Phelps Dodge Corp. v. NLRB, 313 U.S. 177, 194 (1941). Similarly, in NLRB v. Seven-Up Bottling Co., 344 U.S. 344, 346 (1953), the Supreme Court declared that in "fashioning remedies" to undo the effects of violations of the Act, the board must draw on enlightenment gained from experience." It is likely that the Supreme Court would apply the same standard in reviewing the remedial authority of the EEOC if it possessed cease and desist authority. It is interesting to note that the Congressional bill which would have given the EEOC such authority was patterned after the National Labor Relations Act. Thus the Commission's remedial authority was broadly expressed, with the Commission being empowered to "issue and cause to be served on the respondent . . . an order requiring the respondent to cease and desist from such unlawful employment practice and to take such affirmative action, including reinstatement or hiring of employees, with or without back pay, . . . as will effectuate the policy of this Title. . . ." See U.S. Congress, House, Committee on Education and Labor, *Equal Employment Opportunities Enforcement Act of 1971: Report,* 92nd Congress, 1st session, No. 92-238, p. 44.

11. U.S. Congress, Senate, Committee on Labor and Public Welfare, *Hearings on S. 2515, S. 2617, and H.R. 1746, Bills to Further Promote Equal Employment Opportunities for American Workers,* 92nd Cong., 1st. sess., p. 234.

12. Ibid.

13. U.S. Congress, House, Committee on Education and Labor, *Equal Employment Opportunities Enforcement Act of 1971: Report,* p. 59.

14. This was the argument made in the minority report on the bill reported out of the Committee on Education and Labor, which would have granted the EEOC cease and desist authority. See Ibid., pp. 58-63. The remedial problem created by the delays in the appeals process could be rectified by making EEOC remedial orders self-enforcing. Yet when the Senate and House were recently considering bills granting EEOC cease and desist authority, the bills reported out of committee did not contain this feature. As a result, the EEOC would have been compelled to seek judicial review of its remedial orders to force compliance on the part of recalcitrant respondents.

15. Ibid., p. 11

16. U.S. Commission on Civil Rights, *Federal Civil Rights Enforcement Effort,* p. 130.

17. *Daily Labor Report,* January 19, 1973, no. 14, pp. E1-E6.

Bibliography

Books

Berger, Morroe. *Equality by Statute.* New York: Columbia University Press, 1968.

Bowman, B. O. *Public Control of Labor Relations.* New York: The Macmillan Company, 1942.

Burns, Robert K. "Daily Newspapers" in Harry A. Millis, ed., *How Collective Bargaining Works.* New York: The Twentieth Century Fund, 1942.

Lockard, Duane. *Toward Equal Employment Opportunity: A Study of State and Local Antidiscrimination Laws.* New York: The Macmillan Co., 1968.

Lorwin, Lewis L., and Arthur Wubnig. *Labor Relations Boards.* Washington: The Brookings Institution, 1935.

Marshall, Ray. *The Negro and Organized Labor.* New York: John Wiley and Sons, Inc., 1965.

Marshall, F. Ray, and Vernon M. Briggs. *Negro Participation in Apprenticeship Program: Report to the Office of Manpower Policy.* Austin: University of Texas, Department of Economics, 1966.

Nathan, Richard. *Jobs and Civil Rights.* Washington: Government Printing Office, 1969.

National Industrial Conference Board. *Handbook of Union Government, Structure, and Procedures.* New York: The Conference Board, 1955.

Norgren, Paul H., and Samuel E. Hill. *Toward Fair Employment.* New York: Columbia University Press, 1964.

Northrup, Herbert R. *The Negro in the Paper Industry.* Philadelphia: Industrial Relations Unit, Department of Industry, Wharton School of Finance and Commerce, University of Pennsylvania (Distributed by University of Pennsylvania Press), 1969.

_____. *Organized Labor and the Negro.* New York: Harper and Brothers, 1944.

Risher, Howard W., Jr. *The Negro in the Railroad Industry.* Philadelphia: Industrial Relations Unit, Department of Industry, Wharton School of Finance and Commerce, University of Pennsylvania (Distributed by University of Pennsylvania Press), 1971.

Romero, Patricia. *In Black America.* Washington: United Publication Corp., 1969.

Slichter, Sumner, James J. Healy, and E. Robert Livernash. *The Impact of Collective Bargaining on Management.* Washington: The Brookings Institution, 1960.

Sovern, Michael I. *Legal Restraints on Racial Discrimination in Employment.* New York: The Twentieth Century Fund, 1966.

Webb, Sidney and Beatrice. *Industrial Democracy.* London: Longmans, Green and Co., 1920.

Wolf, Harry D. "Railroads" in Harry A. Millis, ed., *How Collective Bargaining Works.* New York: The Twentieth Century Fund, 1942.

Periodicals and Proceedings

Blumrosen, Alfred W. "Antidiscrimination Laws in Action in New Jersey: A Law Sociology Study." *Rutgers Law Review* 19, no. 2 (Winter 1965): 187-287.

_____. "Individual Right to Eliminate Employment Discrimination by Litigation" in Gerald G. Somers, ed., *Proceedings of the Nineteenth Annual Winter Meeting: December 1966,* pp. 88-98. Madison: Industrial Relations Research Association, 1967.

_____. "Labor Arbitration, EEOC Conciliation, and Discrimination in Employment." *The Arbitration Journal* 24, no. 2 (1969): 88-105.

_____. "Seniority and Equal Employment Opportunity: A Glimmer of Hope." *Rutgers Law Review* 23, no. 2 (Winter-1969): 268-317.

Boyce, Richard J. "Racial Discrimination and the National Labor Relations Act." *Northwestern University Law Review* 65, no. 2 (May-June 1970): 232-58.

Carter, Elmer A. "Practical Considerations of Anti-Discrimination Legislation: Experience under the New York State Law against Discrimination." *Cornell Law Quarterly* 40, no. 1 (Fall 1954): 40-59.

Cooper, George, and Richard B. Sobol. "Seniority and Testing under Fair Employment Laws: A General Approach to Objective Criteria of Hiring and Promotion." *Harvard Law Review* 82, no. 8 (June 1969): 1598-1679.

Doeringer, Peter B. "Promotion Systems and Equal Employment Opportunity" in Gerald G. Somers, ed., *Proceedings of the Nineteenth Annual Winter Meeting: December 1966,* pp. 278-89. Industrial Relations Research Association, 1967.

Mater, Dan H., and Garth L. Magnum. "Integration of Seniority Lists in Transportation Mergers." *Industrial and Labor Relations Review* 16, no. 3 (April 1963): 343-65.

Meyer, Burton I. "Racial Discrimination on the Job Site: Competing Theories and Competing Forums." *UCLA Law Review* 12, no. 4 (May 1965): 1186-1206.

Northrup, Herbert R. "Will Greater EEOC Powers Expand Minority Employment?" in Gerald G. Somers, ed., *Proceedings of the 1971 Annual Spring Meetings,* pp. 513-22. Madison: Industrial Relations Research Association, 1971.

"Title VII, Seniority Discrimination, and the Incumbent Negro." *Harvard Law Review* 80, no. 6 (April 1967): 1260-83.

Witherspoon, Joseph P. "Civil Rights Policy in the Federal System: Proposals for a Better Use of the Administrative Process." *Yale Law Journal* 74, no. 7 (June 1965): 1171-1244.

Wolkinson, Benjamin. "The Remedial Efficacy of NLRB Remedies in Joy Silk Cases." *Cornell Law Review* 55, no. 1 (November 1969): 1-43.

Government Publications

The City of New York Commission on Human Rights. *Bias in the Building Industry: 1963-1967.* New York, 1967.

National Advisory Commission on Civil Disorders. *Report.* Washington: Government Printing Office, 1968.

State Advisory Committee to the United States Commission on Civil Rights. *Reports on Apprenticeship.* Washington: n.p., 1964.

U.S. Commission on Civil Rights. *Federal Civil Rights Enforcement Effort.* Washington: Government Printing Office, 1971.

U.S. Congress. House. Committee on Education and Labor. *Equal Employment Opportunities Enforcement Act of 1971: Report.* No. 92-238. 92nd Cong., 1st sess. Washington: Government Printing Office, 1971.

_____. House. Committee on Education and Labor. *Hearings on H.R. 1746, a Bill to Further Promote Equal Employment Opportunities for American Workers.* 92nd Cong., 1st sess. Washington: Government Printing Office, 1971.

_____. Senate. Committee on Labor and Public Welfare. *Hearings on S. 2515, S. 2617, and H.R. 1746, Bills to Further Promote Equal Employment Opportunities for American Workers.* 92nd Cong., 1st sess. Washington: Government Printing Office, 1971.

U.S. Department of Labor. Labor-Management Services Administration. *Admission and Apprenticeship in the Building Trades Unions.* Washington: Government Printing Office, 1971.

U.S. Equal Employment Opportunity Commission. *Second Annual Report.* Washington: Government Printing Office, 1968.

_____. *Third Annual Report.* Washington: Government Printing Office, 1969.

_____. *Fourth Annual Report.* Washington: Government Printing Office, 1970.

_____. *Fifth Annual Report.* Washington: Government Printing Office, 1971.

U.S. National Labor Relations Board. *Thirtieth Annual Report.* Washington: Government Printing Office, 1966.

Union Documents

Agreement between Construction Contractors' Council and International Union of Operating Engineers, Local 77 of Washington, D.C. May 19, 1959-April 30, 1961.

American Federation of Labor-Congress of Industrial Organizations. *Equal Rights for All.* Washington, 1970.

_____ . *Joint Statement on Union Program for Fair Practice.* Washington, August 8, 1962. (Typewritten.)

Brotherhood of Maintenance of Way Employees, AFL-CIO. *Constitution and By-Laws.* 1966.

Brotherhood of Railway, Airline and Steamship Clerks, Freight Handlers, Express and Station Employees, AFL-CIO. *Constitution.* 1967.

Brotherhood of Railway Carmen of America, AFL-CIO. *Constitution.* 1963.

International Association of Bridge, Structural and Ornamental Iron Workers, AFL-CIO. *Constitution.* 1964.

International Association of Heat and Frost Insulators and Asbestos Workers, AFL-CIO. *Constitution and By-Laws.* 1967.

International Association of Machinists, AFL-CIO. *Constitution.* 1961.

International Brotherhood of Electrical Workers, AFL-CIO. *Constitution.* 1966.

International Brotherhood of Teamsters, Chauffeurs, Warehousemen, and Helpers of America. *Constitution.* 1961.

International Brotherhood of Teamsters, Chauffeurs, Warehousemen, and Helpers of America. *National Master Freight Agreement* (Over-the-Road and Local Cartage Employees). September 1, 1964-March 31, 1967.

International Hod Carriers' Building and Common Laborers' Union of America, AFL-CIO. *Constitution.* 1961.

International Union of Operating Engineers, AFL-CIO. *Constitution.* 1964.

Master Labor Agreement between Southern California General Contractors and United Brotherhood of Carpenters and Joiners of America. May 1, 1965-May 1, 1968.

United Association of Journeymen and Apprentices of the Plumbing and Pipe Fitting Industry of the United States and Canada, AFL-CIO. *Constitution.* 1966.

_____ . *Explanation of Hiring Practices.* Washington, 1959.

United Brotherhood of Carpenters and Joiners of America, AFL-CIO. *Constitution and Laws.* 1971.

United Brotherhood of Rubber, Cork, Linoleum and Plastic Workers of America, AFL-CIO. *Constitution.* 1964.

Unpublished EEOC Reports

U.S. *Equal Employment Opportunity Commission. Field Operations Handbook.* Washington, 1966. (Administratively restricted.)

_____. *Report of the Office of Conciliations: FY 1966.* Washington, 1967. (Administratively restricted.)

_____. *Report of the Office of Conciliations: FY 1967.* Washington, 1967. (Administratively restricted.)

_____. *Report of the Office of Conciliations: FY 1968.* Washington, n.d. (Administratively restricted.)

_____. *Statement on Segregated Union Locals and Collective Bargaining Arrangements.* Commissioners' Meeting No. 32, Washington, October 5, 1965.

Wilson, Charles. *The Conciliator's Handbook.* Washington: Equal Employment Opportunity Commission, c. 1968. (Administratively restricted.)

Index

About the Author

Benjamin W. Wolkinson received the B.A. in Economics from George Washington University in 1966 and pursued graduate studies in Industrial and Labor Relations at the University of Chicago and Cornell University, from which he received respectively the M.A. and Ph.D. degrees. Mr. Wolkinson has been employed as an industrial analyst by the National Bureau of Standards and the National Labor Relations Board in Washington, D.C. From February 1970 through August 1971 he worked as a conciliator and as a research analyst for the Equal Employment Opportunity Commission. In August 1971 he was appointed Assistant Professor of Labor and Industrial Relations at Michigan State University in East Lansing, Michigan. He is the author of articles published in the *Cornell Law Review, Proceedings of the Industrial Relations Research Association* and the *Indian Journal of Industrial Relations.*